Realism in European literature

REALISM IN EUROPEAN LITERATURE

Essays in Honour of J. P. Stern
Edited by
Nicholas Boyle and Martin Swales

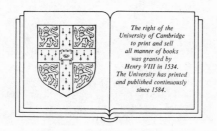

The right of the
University of Cambridge
to print and sell
all manner of books
was granted by
Henry VIII in 1534.
The University has printed
and published continuously
since 1584.

CAMBRIDGE UNIVERSITY PRESS

Cambridge
London   New York   New Rochelle
Melbourne   Sydney

Published by the Press Syndicate of the University of Cambridge
The Pitt Building, Trumpington Street, Cambridge CB2 1RP
32 East 57th Street, New York NY 10022, USA
10 Stamford Road, Oakleigh, Melbourne 3166, Australia

First published 1986

Printed in Great Britain at
the University Press, Cambridge

British Library Cataloguing in Publication Data
Realism in European literature: essays in honour
of J. P. Stern
1. Realism in literature
I. Boyle, Nicholas   II. Swales, Martin
III. Stern, J. P.
809′.912   PN601

Library of Congress Cataloguing-in-Publication Data
Main entry under title:
Realism in European literature.
Includes index.
1. Realism in literature—Addresses, essays,
lectures. 2. European literature—History and
criticism—Addresses, essays, lectures. 3. Stern,
J. P. (Joseph Peter)   I. Boyle, Nicholas.
II. Swales, Martin. III. Stern, J. P. (Joseph Peter)
PN601.R4   1986   809′.912   85–17109

ISBN 0 521 25487 6

GG

Contents

Foreword

The essays in this volume are all attempts to think further about problems touched on by J. P. Stern in *On Realism*, and in related studies and papers. *On Realism*, which first appeared in 1973, is noteworthy for the generosity of both its conception and its execution. Stern delights in the historicity (or, to use one of his favourite words, the 'dateability') of literary texts, while at the same time insisting that literary realism, is 'a perennial mode' – and works a perennial magic. Works of literature are not timeless icons, but equally they are not so completely the creatures of their time that we cannot feel that some of them, whenever they were written, are more true to life – our life – than others. Yet Stern is also clear that not all art is realistic, that realism is not the *sine qua non* of literary greatness. He is sceptical of theoretical tidiness and prefers the manner of a Wittgensteinian 'investigation'. He avows a debt to Erich Auerbach's *Mimesis*, welcomes (rather than regrets) that the term 'realism' operates both in 'literature' and in 'life', and hints implicitly at a link between realistic literature and the language of the gospels. These – and other – features of *On Realism* have worn remarkably well in the years since its first publication. Equally, neither time nor literary criticism has stood still. In 1973 the *nouveau roman* was still new, structuralism promised at once a modern aesthetics and a modern anthropology for urban and increasingly post-literate man, and only the most forward positions of the English-speaking avant-garde had heard the distant rumble of deconstruction and a new wave of psychoanalytically based literary criticism. The contributors to this volume have welcomed the chance to take further the thoughts and formulations of Stern's study with the benefit of hindsight afforded by the intervening ten years or so of critical discourse.

As editors, we have tried to compile a group of essays that reflects the range of Stern's arguments on realism. There are both theoretical pieces and individual studies of writers or periods with which Stern is particularly associated, or for which he has shown a particular

Foreword

affection, several of these taking account of the possible social determinants of literary representations. The names of Auerbach and Wittgenstein can be glimpsed in the background of more than one contribution; and Stern's own pointers to the Nietzschean origin – or implications – of much contemporary debate about language are acknowledged. We are particularly grateful to Richard Brinkmann for rounding off the volume with an informal survey of the present state of the discussion, including his own comments on as many of the essays in the volume as the editors' and contributors' somewhat eccentric timetable made available to him. For his patience and good humour we owe him an especial debt of gratitude.

On 30 September 1986, J. P. Stern, having completed his sixty-fifth year, retires from the Chair of German at University College London. It is hoped that this collection may be both a tribute to the distinction with which he has served in that office, as in the entire *res publica litterarum*, and a mark of the affection which he universally inspires. For the editors it has been an agreeable and instructive privilege to bring together essays from philosophers and critics, with interests in English, French and German literature, and working on both sides of the Atlantic, in a volume in which the informing presence is the scholarship of Peter Stern. It is the unanimous wish of the contributors to this symposium that it should be dedicated to him.

NICHOLAS BOYLE
MARTIN SWALES

Note on the text

Except for a few recalcitrant passages, where it seemed that a translation might be helpful, quotations in French have not been translated. Passages in German, however, in so far as they are not adequately glossed in the main text, have been translated.

The papers by Richard Brinkmann and Wolfgang Harms were written in German and have been translated by the editors.

Notes on language, its deconstruction and on translating

ERICH HELLER

I

Only a fool would deny that no hunger has ever been fed by the word 'food'. He would even know that the word 'food', fed to a hungry man, would rather increase his hunger; and that not even the smallest nail has ever been hammered into a wall by one's exclaiming 'hammer'. This is as obvious as are only the most trivial assertions. How is it, then, that a mind as searching as that of Heraclitus did, as far as we can judge from his *Fragments*, spend much thought on concluding that there are 'right' names attaching to things, almost to the point of being identical with them, right by some dispensation higher than the 'naming' habit of men; right names, and thus also demonstrably false names? The right names were, one supposes, of the kind that Adam, no doubt with the Lord's approval, gave to the things around him. Of course, he could not possibly have invented the word 'brother' because there was no one to whom he might have given it. Yet, had he not fallen from grace, his descendant Cain surely would not have acted against the god-willed meaning of 'brother' by killing Abel. This is how Adam's original sin was horribly compounded, and the Lord said to Cain : 'The voice of thy brother's blood crieth unto me from the ground' (Gen. 4.10). With this, the word 'brother' assumed a moral meaning. Henceforth naming has a moral aspect to it.

Socrates was once asked to arbitrate in the debate between Cratylus (one of the *Dialogues* bears his name) and Hermogenes, the first being a Heraclitean and the other a precursor of Saussure, insisting that names are nothing but 'signifiers' and have no 'natural' relationship to what they signify. But the arbitrator hardly arbitrates. He is at his most elusive and ironically undecisive and often plain facetious, just as if he wished to defend himself against the upsetting seriousness of the problem. 'After much study', he says, 'I am more puzzled than I was before I began to learn.' And in the end he encourages Cratylus

1

to retire to the solitude of the country and think; and Hermogenes 'shall set you on your way', and 'when you have found the truth, come and tell me'.

Words, certainly, are signs that 'signify'; but in signifying what they themselves are not, our consciousness tends to run them into one so that they become more than simple 'signifiers'. They become symbols (or even, in times long passed, magical conjurations that survive to this day as superstitions), acquiring a meaning beyond the function of mere signification. Aristotle's thought moves into this direction. We use the names (*onomata*) as symbols (*symbola*). In 'naming' (*onomazein*) we transcend both the 'pure' naming as well as the thing thus named. Heidegger, in interpreting Aristotle's thought on language, is almost as self-willed as he is with many other interpretations of Greek sayings, but his own thought, in this instance, moves in closer proximity to its source. Indeed, anyone asking himself whether he is able to *experience* his own name, called out or written, mispronounced or misspelled, as a haphazard 'signifier', has already entered the antechamber of the unsettling mystery that St Thomas, taking his cue from Aristotle, persistently pursues and St Augustine, with disarming simplicity, points to by saying that 'word' both *is and means* a word. How is it that a problem which at first glance seems to be as uninteresting as calling a spade a spade and not an orchid, becomes ever more complex, fascinating, and philosophically as absorbing as the problem of language? How is it that thinkers, secure in their reputation of possessing intelligence or even profundity, hardly ever are content with a simplistic interpretation of language? Surely, it is not only because we cannot avoid speaking about language through language, in itself a dizzying enterprise. No; thinking about language creates a disquiet that is all its own. And soon we are lost in the endless problems arising as soon as we touch, as we do with the admirable Wilhelm von Humboldt, on the connection between thought and word, until gradually we become quite sure that consciousness is unimaginable without the articulations of language. 'I know what I mean, but I can't say it.' Wittgenstein used to pounce upon this with excessive derision : 'No, you don't *know* what you mean before you can say it.'

It is characteristic of our epoch that, with a mixture of bravery and masochism, it falls in love with 'explanations' that lower the status of the human being. For it is neither the love of truth nor the convincingness of arguments that explains why, after some initial resistance, most men positively *like* to be persuaded that the human race has been sent on its way not by the creative will of God, but has come into being through an accidental biological mutation; or that economic circumstances (greed) and not autonomous mind is the moving agent of history; or that the dark forces of the unconscious rather than conscious determinations are behind the events of human existence. Whether or not such theories are correct, they tend to reduce the demands an individual is encouraged to make upon the spiritual or moral conduct of his life. The same may well apply to the theories of language and literature that, in a rather uncommunicative idiom, nowadays expound the unspeakable hazards besetting linguistic communication. And how not? As these theorists hold that only the naively uninitiated still believe in a firm link between words and meanings, all attempts at communication through language and literature must issue in a kind of 'nihil', an ultimate meaninglessness.

2

Ever since Nietzsche diagnosed the malady of speech in a nihilistically dissolving society (for this is what he did by saying, for instance, that 'every word is a prejudice', while his Zarathustra was sure he had overcome this menace when, in the illumination of his solitude, he proclaimed that everything that exists, 'desires to become word') – ever since, that is, the self-revelations of his age made Nietzsche rehearse the varieties of nihilism in order to overcome them, there would seem to be a grain of truth in those 'deconstructive' speculations : 'Only disconnect', the reversal of E. M. Forster's famous adage, appears to rule their deliberations. Yet that grain is so small that it eludes the coarse machineries of the harvesters. I have heard it said and seen it printed that 'there are no texts, but only interpretations' – interpretations in a void, interpretations voiding themselves. For in the virtual absence of a text, what is there to interpret? May I ask permission to be so literal-minded? Of course, there is again that grain, this time not of truth but of salt. For even where madness is the order of the day, nobody is *so* mad not at least to *see* the text, whatever he makes of it. Whatever he makes of it : thus every reader becomes the co-author of what he reads and ultimately perhaps even its only author. Heaven forbid ! And if this is not meant to sum up *the* theory of deconstruction, then this is largely because it hardly exists in a teachable shape. Indeed, given the inexhaustible vagaries of language, how could it? But it is the adumbration of a modish trend.

3

When Macbeth's three witches conclude their brief opening appearance by chanting in unison that 'fair is foul, and foul is fair', it is not their intention to denounce the unreliability of language; they merely exhibit, in the 'filthy air', their supernatural perversity. And when they ask 'When shall we three meet again?', the answer could surely be more precise than 'When the hurlyburly's done.' They could, for instance, agree to come together again in the same spot at midnight tomorrow, and know for certain that the same spot is this one in the Highlands of Scotland, and midnight not noonday. But with this we have left Shakespeare's dramatic poetry and entered the domain of common prose where meetings and class schedules are arranged by dependable linguistic communication.

Is it, then, only through literature that the confounding multivalence of language shows? If so, where is the line dividing the literary uses of language from the language of a textbook that, say, sums up for its readers (its 'interpreters'?) Darwin's theory of evolution? Kafka's *Letters to Felice*, to cite only one example, are literature, and never mind the postage stamps that he affixed to them as if they were 'mere' letters. Indeed, they could not be anything but literature, written as they were by one who *in them* said that he himself was hardly a real person but 'nothing but literature'. A manner of speaking? No, a truth truthfully felt and suffered, and borne out by the observation of an intelligent reader that these letters are Kafka's only completed novel. Where, then, is the point at which a letter ends and literature takes over? It cannot possibly be ascertained because it does not exist.

Only in recent chapters of literary history have literature and poetry ventured into regions of apparently unheard-of experiences, inexpressible within the syntax and vocabulary afforded by our shared language. The concomitant of such poetic enterprises is those speculative musings that purport to lead to a novel perception of language. For the poetry itself has become difficult, often to the point of incomprehensibility. When T. S. Eliot, still the most intelligent if not the most modern of modern critics (second only to Friedrich Schlegel) said that 'poets in our civilization . . . must be *difficult*', he meant the kind of poetry that has to employ every manner of conceit, indirection and evasion to avoid, vulnerable as it is, the aggressiveness of the 'age of prose' : only the most secluded shelter of obscurity and incoherence seems to offer the poetic a chance of remaining untainted by prosaic contaminations. Eliot meant, in fact, his own poetry and the poetry to which it was indebted : French Symbolism. In retrospect there can be little doubt that the utopian strategy of that poetic movement – namely, ultimately to liberate words in poetry from their prosaic labour to 'mean', mean a prosaically polluted object – required a 'New Criticism', one that would allow pure words in poetry to fend for themselves without the reader's understanding being assisted by history or biography.

The next phase of such 'modernism', stupidly called 'post-modernism', required even more radical theories : 'the systematic undoing . . . of understanding' itself, any understanding, its categorical abolition, a destructive act consistent with the discovery of 'the absolute randomness of language', as one of the doctrinaires of deconstructionism would have it. Amazing that he does not notice that his sentences fly in the face of his doctrine. For his sentences 'mean' something even if this something is, implicitly, only the inauguration of gibberish as a mode of speaking. That he remains unaware of this is, I think, due to the fatal over-emphasis that this linguistic theory and all its kin place on the meaning of words rather than sentences. For while it may well be a random option to call a rose a rose (an 'option', if it is one, that yet has so long a history that the first choosers have receded into the impenetrable mists enveloping most beginnings), the tribal and national acceptance of syntax and grammar would be unthinkable if these ordering principles were merely the arbitrary inventions of an ingenious individual or a group of them, mysteriously endowed with the power to impose them on whole multitudinous communities. These orders could not possibly have become so 'popular' had they not been met by a deep-rooted disposition of the human mind and its spontaneous perceptions of a 'meaningful' world. Is this an unfounded metaphysical assumption? So be it. How else would we be able to understand even the strange proclamation of 'the systematic undoing of understanding'? 'I understand', we may say upon listening to this absurdity, and turn away from a nihilism that finally would undo even the ethical connotations of such words as lie, fraud or murder, not to remark upon the ungainly attire of these thinkers' thoughts. It is seven sizes too big and can only be worn with disfiguring strain.

Before these tenets of nihilism were as much as thought of, poetry, foremost lyrical poetry, did aim at bringing together word and meaning into the closest possible unity. In some perfect poems word and sense have become inseparable, the word affecting us as if it were the incarnation of its meaning. Of course, this is not literally so; yet it is poetically true, true within and through the poem. The 'Ruh'

in Goethe's poem 'Wandrers Nachtlied' *is* the evening stillness above
the mountain peaks, just as the sick rose or the 'tyger burning bright'
in Blake's poems *is* the 'realisation' ('la réalisation', as Cézanne used
the term), unrealisable in any other way. But this gives nobody the
right to say that the meaning has taken leave of the word. On
the contrary, it has merged with the word without losing its
'meaningness'.

Might Goethe just as well have had in mind a blizzard, and Blake
a dandelion or a glowworm? Had we not known from our own
experience what 'Ruh' is, or never been moved by the sight of
roses just opening their buds or wilting, we would not recognise
what the poems are about. And yet they are not 'about' 'Ruh' and
rose but have become what they mean, awakening us to the *true*
meaning of 'Ruh' and rose, a meaning we would not have discovered
without the poem. Absurd? Only to those who are ready to dismiss
as absurd the notion that there can be a profounder understanding
of 'Ruh' or rose than is acquired by consulting a dictionary, or by *any*
absence of noise or *any* glimpse into a garden. It is this profounder
understanding of 'Ruh' or rose which justifies the 'absurd' pronounce-
ment that in a great lyrical poem the word merges with its meaning.
This, indeed, is something different from what, for instance, radical
deconstructionists mean (yes, *mean*) when they come close to saying
that words in a poem have no meaning, being mere elements in a
'linguistic structure'. (Deconstruction – what a word! It sounds as if
the operation were to be carried out not on poetry but on products
of mechanical engineering, bombs, perhaps, including their detona-
tion. Regrettably, legal codes know of no penalty for the murder of
language. Yet there is an obvious link between such disabling
linguistic theories and the technological feats that enable us to
atomise ourselves and our world.)

3

Whether or not there is a dependably objective text in the classroom
of the learned pedagogue who asks the question in the very title of a
book about literary criticism, the implied theory makes literature
into something that is all but arbitrarily interpretable – and if not
arbitrarily, by which standards is the quality, or even the interpretation to be judged? Still, the theory comes a cropper in the face of
translations; the relative adequacy, and the immense importance
of translations within our cultural context remains too often un-

remarked. However labyrinthine and endlessly intricate the problems are that arise from the translations of the Hebrew–Aramaic–Greek Scriptures into Latin and modern languages, into Luther's German, for instance, or the King James' English version (quite apart from the thousand doubts that beset the original texts themselves), these cannot diminish the meaning and effect they had on our religious and cultural inheritance. It is unimaginable what course the history of the Western world would have taken if the rabbis of ancient Jerusalem had asserted for ever their puristically respectable will that the Bible should never be translated into any secular language from the divinely authentic Hebrew, and thus prevented Ptolemy II of Alexandria from appointing his seventy-two erudite men to produce the Septuagint. Might it not strike some nostalgic purists as a belated justification of those rabbis' obstinacy that, after centuries of Latin unalterably dominating the Roman Catholic liturgy, Mass was recently celebrated by the Pope in pidgin English, a rather drastic conclusion of the journey begun by the Septuagint, a journey that could never have been undertaken if the original words had had no meaning common to both languages?

When we turn from the sacred record of Creation itself to our philosophical and literary tradition, it would be blatantly impossible to account for them without the numberless translations from Greek and Latin, and finally the unceasing efforts to settle French, English, Russian, German literature and thought in linguistic regions not their own. Of course, we know that not every translation of what is a masterpiece in its own native language keeps faith with the original. Regrettably, more often than not it lacks even common or garden accuracy (accuracy! – if this were impossible to achieve, teachers of languages and judges of translations would have no work), and this is to leave aside the dangerous question whether it ever reaches the aesthetic level of the original, or gives us as much as a hint of the sensibility embodied in it, its style, that is; and the style is, after all, the very life of descriptions, of the portrayal of conflicts, and of moral perceptions. And yet, in what an impoverished state of mind would we live if, alarmed by the unavoidable shortcomings of all transla-tions, we had ever asked whether there really was such a text as the *Divina Commedia* in the class that undertook to acquaint us with the changing perspectives of the human mind. Yet whatever the perspective, it is the same mountain range that is viewed.

In any case, those translators of Alexandria assuredly did not feel as free in dealing with the original as does Goethe's Faust when he sets out to render Saint John's *logos* in his 'beloved German'. 'In the beginning was the word' – no, this will not do for Faust. Is a word not too feeble a thing, may it not be even a meaningless word? Whereupon he replaces it by 'Sinn', the sense and meaning that was in the divine head as He created the world. This does not satisfy Faust either; and becoming ever more Faustian, he chooses 'Kraft', power, force, energy, and finally 'Tat', deed, action. In the beginning, then, was the deed that translated the Creator's imaginative design into actuality. This may well be how the distrust of the word made its first poetic appearance, the distrust that finally conceived or mis-conceived the modern theories of language, those little insurgents against *logos*, disquieting symptoms of *dementia philologica* that are likely to stay with us until 'the hurlyburly's done'. (Which, thinking of the speed with which fashions come and go, may be next week.) In any case, Faust's blatant mistranslation of *logos* makes his companion, the famous poodle, reveal its 'right name' : Mephistopheles.

The Grecians of Winckelmann and Goethe, the Orientals of Victor Hugo, Wagner's Edda personages, Walter Scott's Britons of the thirteenth century – it was all 'immeasurably wrong', and 'one day the whole farce' of our historical fantasies will stand revealed. Nietzsche wrote this and, in the case of Goethe's flawed conception of Greek antiquity, he added : But never mind : 'How fruitful these errors were !' – although, to be sure, not all misrepresentations of the past produced such radiantly noble dramas as *Iphigenie auf Tauris* or as surpassingly beautiful poetic allegories as the Helena act of *Faust* II, nor would they have come into being, had the poet been conscious of his 'error'. If Goethe had a mistaken idea of ancient Greece, this was undoubtedly due to faulty translations. But the recognition of their faultiness depends on our comparing two *mean-ings* : the original's and the translation's. This is the indispensable premise of the notion 'mistranslation'. With regard to the near-impossibility of perfect translations, an attitude of good-natured indulgence and generous tolerance commends itself in the case of such mundane enterprises as long as the results do not offend our sense of literary virtue. For the rest, we may, perhaps, be confident that 'natural selection' would lead to the emergence of a culturally serviceable knowledge of foreign works in translation.[1]

Of course, no theories whatever are needed to convince us that translations of *poetry* can ever be a perfect substitute for the originals, not even those translations that have acquired a durable position in the canons of their own natural literatures, such as Schlegel and

Tieck's Shakespeare, the greatest and most amiable German conquest of foreign territory; or perhaps Dryden's *Aeneid*, despite the discomfort Virgil suffers from having rhymed couplets imposed upon him; or, perhaps, Pope's Homer. (I have never been sure about Hölderlin's Sophocles, that moving, majestic and possibly quixotic attempt to stretch German poetic diction far enough to accommodate in it his profoundly idiosyncratic perception of Greek, even if some readers believe that he has thereby much enriched modern German, making it, for the first time, capable of sounding the depths of Attic tragedy. Heidegger notwithstanding, Hölderlin's *Antigone* has remained an isolated event in the history of translations. All in all, it might be easier to learn Greek than fully to appreciate Hölderlin's version.) Goethe has never had the good fortune of finding the perfectly congenial translator. If only Thomas Mann had been an English writer! The author of *Faust* was not only himself an admirable and admirably patient translator (of, for instance, the long autobiography of Benvenuto Cellini) but also the most thoughtful and devoted counsellor of people engaged in the business of translation. He regarded translations as one of the most important means for educating a people and knew that a good translator must not only have the courage to struggle with the foreign language but penetrate it to the point where he will see and respect what is untranslatable. For 'there lies the value and character of every language'. His belief in the cultural significance of good translations caused him even to say that the Germans have so many of them that they can save themselves the labour of learning to read the originals. Frederick the Great, for example, did not know Latin, but read Cicero in French and knew him as well as 'we who read him in the language in which he wrote'. Deconstructionists ought to nod assent. For why should a translator, having mastered the foreign language, not be an equally reliable 'interpreter' of Cicero as Latin readers?

Apart from the few 'canonical' translations there will always be the need for new ones. For all translations, with the exception of those that are in themselves convincing works of literature, unavoidably become victims of history and linguistic fashions. Like old family photographs, they fade and yellow without acquiring the ennobling patina that graces the copper coverings of ancient buildings. No, their fate is rather like that of old films, rendered embarrassingly comic by their outmoded photographic techniques, costumes and gestures, unless they are rescued by timeless geniuses of the grotesque like Chaplin's or classical faces like Garbo's from either the museums of cinematography or the ephemeral enthusiasm of 'camp'. Yet the passage of time and fashion is almost innocent of the difficulty, indeed the near-unfeasibility, of transferring purely lyrical poems from one language to another. Here it is the music that determinedly resists the operation – music, not of course in the literal sense, but rhythm and metre and often rhyme, the rise and fall of words, the tone of voice, its lilt or tragic solemnity, and above all the elusive and nameless reverberations set off by words in the mind and memory of their own language. It is this aura that ever so many words have acquired in one language that cannot possibly be reproduced in another, not even such dictionary simplicities as the German 'Wald' or 'Wiese' or 'Gottesacker' (forest, meadow, churchyard), for the words and the things they denote have become inseparably one ever since they entered together a child's imagination. Is this, then, a matter of psychology? No, it is a matter of the certainties of the soul.

The oneness of word and thing constitutes the Imaginative Realism of every successful lyrical poem. Imaginative realism is a close relation of the ancient philosophical realism that endowed 'universals' with the status of reality – with a real, not merely imaginary reality, in fact, with the reality of Plato's Ideas; and every pure noun in our language that is not a 'proper name', as for instance 'rock' in contrast to 'Brighton Rock', denotes a universal, a 'concept', as it is called in un-Platonic parlance. Literary *art*, even outside lyrical poetry, strives for such 'realism', indeed *is* the incarnate desire to establish the grandly absurd equation word-thing. It may well be the only justification for allowing literary realism to introduce itself by the name of that old philosophy, a philosophy not only Platonic but also faintly illuminated by a reflection of St John's visionary message. For with the Word having become all but inaudible, it has fallen to the lot of countless words to chase after reality. How could they even hope to express any of it in the infinite variety of their assemblages if, in their entirety as language, they had no idea, no intuition, what it is that they are after? And they *have* this intuition because they partake of the nature of reality. This involvement in what really is they cannot help, even where the very makers of words vacuously and destructively proclaim the belief that their words express nothing but themselves.

NOTE

1. 'Such mundane enterprises.' I had hardly written this when I gathered from the first page of the *New York Times* of 9 June 1984 that the world has been shaken by the discovery of wrong words in a text that is not by God but by James Joyce. A computerised and handsomely subsidised team of scholars has found out that the usual editions of James Joyce's *Ulysses* contain 5,000 errors. I thought the time had passed when the words of modern secular writers were regarded with the awe that was once reserved for the voice from on high, but lo and behold, it has taken already $300,000 and seven years (seven: a sacred number) to detect these misdeeds. 'It amounts to a new book', said an expert, obviously not a deconstructionist. If he were, he might not greatly mind that part of the deconstruction was done by the typesetters. In any case, the industry is saved and there is great rejoicing at the prospect of new tenured positions in English departments all over the world.

Significant objects: a possibility of realism in early narratives

WOLFGANG HARMS

In talking of the world-pictures available to the Middle Ages it is scarcely possible to avoid quoting the lines of Alan of Lille that speak of 'reading' Nature :

> omnis mundi creatura
> quasi liber et pictura
> nobis est et speculum[1]

and precisely these lines are quoted by the semiotician and medievalist Umberto Eco as he introduces us by his own narrative arts into the world of medieval signs. In his novel *The Name of the Rose* he makes the learned friar William of Baskerville recite these lines, in which the things of this world are understood as speaking to us as book, as picture or as mirror, when reminding his pupil Adso of Melk of the wholly indisputable fact that the world is a great book, the letters in which are creatures, by means of which God the Creator is able to speak to the human reader.[2] Of this only a preliminary reminder is needed and William's actual instruction begins with the next step in which he makes the signs in the world speak also for anyone who embarks on the search for clues like a detective. No sooner have William and the attentive Adso begun to pursue and decipher this palpably real rhetoric of natural signs than Eco's descriptive evocation of the merely actual is transformed into a representation of doubly meaningful signs that point beyond themselves: at the crossroads the trackers find in the freshly fallen snow the hoofprints of a horse pointing down a side-road to the left. What contemporary reader of a medieval romance, or what reader nowadays of a modern medievalising novel – whether himself a medievalist or simply a modern reader – could overlook the hidden meaning in these *vestigia*? What author of a medieval romance or of a modern semiology of narrative would not know what content, given in advance,[3] not needing to be constructed by the author, the reader could associate with and decode from the signs 'crossroad', 'right and left', 'broad and narrow'? Even Jean Paul Richter, in the late eighteenth century, was still a master in the art of decoding the book of Nature, though he could no longer treat the authentically medieval ascription of reliability to the message of creation (Alan of Lille speaks of a *fidele signaculum*) as so self-evident a presupposition as it is for Eco's clerical sleuths. Jean Paul had an immensely extensive knowledge of everything that has ever been recognised in literature as a possible significance for a created thing (thanks to various encyclopaedias, polymath predecessors and his own card-indexes); but his understanding of the metaphor of the book of Nature had lost the ground that gave it authority, the theological dimension to its meaning.[4] But from the Middle Ages until, roughly, Jean Paul, the 'Book of Nature' could stand beside the Bible as a second means of access to divine revelation.[5] Created things (*res*) from either book, inserted as 'real' into his own work by a narrator, could be associated with possible or probable meanings that went beyond a literal reading. In such cases the originator of these significations is not the author of the narrative himself : rather, by means of his narrative signals, the probability can be increased or reduced that a particular meaning or meanings are to be associated with the thing in the narration. These possibilities have more to do with the narrator's exploitation of established procedures of interpretation and their products, and less with the creative introduction of a double meaning by the narrating author, but they involve us to some extent in the discussion of realism, in so far as it is concerned, *inter alia*, with 'the riches of the represented world; its weightiness and resistance to ideals' and sees itself as 'variations on the kinds of undertaking we find in Auerbach's *Mimesis*'.[6] This is not in any way to undermine the much larger consideration that the nature or existence of any 'realism' cannot be determined in the first instance on the basis of the reality of its objects.[7] By contrast with modern 'realistic' literature,[8] it is possible in earlier literature, which can refer to a world-view dependent on a divine creator, for certain qualities of the real material, or 'things', to which it alludes, to affect some of the narrative procedures.

In his chapter 'The Knight Sets Forth' Auerbach shows convincingly how far medieval courtly romance – in this case that of Chrétien de Troyes – did not 'apprehend' the chivalric or courtly 'reality in its full breadth and depth'. Moreover, it is from precisely those elements which are remote from the reality of courtly life that the realistic structure of the story is derived, in which a moral meaning is recognisable and specifically the ideal knightly existence projected by the narration is made meaningful and credible.[9] But in the medieval courtly romances not all the material things referred to are either magical or courtly and real. There also exist quotational references to more complex forms of a pre-structured significant reality.

In the ninth book of Wolfram von Eschenbach's *Parzival* the natural substances[10] are listed that have been used without success to treat the sickness of Anfortas, the Grail King (ed. Leitzmann 481, 5–483,18). Admittedly it is emphasised that the medical literature (*arztbuoche* 481,6) has been consulted in the search for these remedies, but the inefficacious substances listed have a more than technical significance : thus the waters mentioned from the four rivers of Paradise point beyond mere geographical fact to inter-pretations that would have to derive from the soteriological impor-tance of the rivers' place of origin; the Sibyl's branch refers back to Christian interpretations of the 'golden bough' in the *Aeneid*; the mention of the pelican allows us to glimpse the themes of love (*minne*) and compassion associated with Anfortas and the family of the Grail; the unicorn (*monizirus* 482,24) and the carbuncle growing on its head point to the commandment of purity (*kiusche*) breached by Anfortas but which will need to be obeyed if there is to be any act of redemption. This is not the place to attempt an explication of all the details drawn from nature, and from nature transformed and interpreted by poetry, technical literature and exegesis : that would involve taking account of complex relations not only with earlier technical literature but also with preceding and subsequent medieval interpretations and elaborations. Ziolkowski furnishes a model of such a venture in his discussion of the carbuncle in the light of didactic fiction and of non-fiction in the Middle Ages, and uses the example of a medieval student of Wolfram, the author of *Titurel the Younger*, to show how far the carbuncle as natural object can be a sign of 'the sacred light of divine inspiration which entices erring man on to the right path'.[11] The list of fruitless remedies is full of meaningful objects which are given a double sense not by the narrative work itself but by a tradition which had already com-pounded real thing and meaning before Wolfram wrote. So dense an accumulation of these things is unusual in Wolfram as in most other writers of his time and for this very reason tends to give this section a particular weight. In the context of the narrative this emphasis is necessary in order that the manifest fruitlessness of all the medicaments that the world can offer should lead directly to the expectation of a redemption by Parzival (483,20ff.). Only this narrative situation[12] enables these objects to realise the full weight of their potential meanings. So if one particular area in the story is here strikingly dense with allusions to significant objects, this means not that it is part of a structure of allegorical imagery distributed equally across the whole work and capable of systematic interpretation at various levels, but rather that it is an insertion by the narrator of a certain reality whose very concreteness here includes certain dimensions of meaning.[13] This reality of significant objects in the narrative literature of the age does not seem to be affected by the argument about universals in theology and philosophy; there is no indication that any universal is accorded a more elevated rank, as *ens realissimum*, in a hierarchy of real objects.[14]

Wolfram sees the beautiful pagan Belakane, weeping for the loss of her beloved Gahmuret, the father of Parzival, as a dove on a withered bough (ed. Leitzmann, 57,10f.). Although in the late fifteenth century the widely-read Ulrich Füetrer refers to this motif of Wolfram's in a short allusion confined to the image of the dove (*Buch der Abenteuer*, ed. Nyholm, 457), the substitution for the weeping lover of the natural object that is the dove was not an idea original to Wolfram.[15] Here too an older scientific and literary tradition, continuously growing by means of theological exegesis, the description and interpretation of the natural world and the transformative work of poetry, assumes the role of a thesaurus, of a well-authorised range of sources such as was provided and passed on in the Europe of those days by oral transmission and above all by the great encyclopaedic works of an Isidore of Seville, a Rhabanus Maurus, Vincent of Beauvais or Bartholomaeus Anglicus.[16] In this way a reference to what has become conventional wisdom about the actual constitution or the concretely utilitarian or allegorical value of a natural object can always be linked to an original descriptive or interpretative act on the part of the individual author. The dove, like any object in nature, can only ever be given, by such an act of interpretation, those meanings which are grounded in reference to specific qualities; because it lacks means of defence and is reputed to have no gall, the dove can serve as a sign of peace. Its white colouring justifies seeing it as a sign of chastity. If it is contrasted with a hawk it expresses the opposition of the contemplative and the active lives.[17] If it sits on a withered bough uttering mournful cries it is to be taken as a sign of the marital fidelity that remains devoted to the spouse even beyond death. In his imagery of Belakane as a mourning dove on a withered bough Wolfram, therefore, is taking up only some of the prescribed qualities and the potential meanings attached to them. By means of this sign (*signum*) the narrator helps to make it possible, even in a Christian context, to put a high value on the love of this pagan woman; the meaning of an episode or situation in the story may be made plain not only by its structural position – e.g. in the schema of the journey and the stations by the way[18] – but also by the material elements in the metaphors and similes used. At the same time the material element in this sign-language can be seen as contributing to the visualising impetus of literature, which enables verbally formulated and pictorially formulated iconographies to interact with each other.[19]

When at the end of the thirteenth century the anonymous author of *Reinfried von Braunschweig*, who was plainly well-read both in poetry and in works of learning, makes of a dove (*tûbe*, also *turtel-tûbe*) a leitmotif in the opening part of a narrative which is courtly and very rich in worldly detail, close at times to romance and at times to history, he is *inter alia* aware of a relation to the motif in Wolfram that we have just discussed. However his references to the dove draw sustenance also from other traditions of meaning than those passed on by Wolfram. In *Reinfried* a dove is offered by the royal Danish court as the prize for victory in a tournament which draws to Denmark the finest princes and knights of central and northern Europe. When however the motif of the dove is introduced for the first time in the report of a messenger (*ein junge turteltûben*, ed. Bartsch, 209), there is no simple assumption that this dove is directing us to a meaning contained within it. The messenger, giving his report from Denmark to the Brunswick court, is careful to add immediately that it is to be taken as a sign from which the purity of the Danish princess Yrkane can be deduced, who will be presenting the prize (*bezeichenlîche klûben sol man ir kiuschekeit dar an*, 210f.); and the meaning is extended in the next sentence, so that the simplicity (*einvalt*) of the princess, as well as her chaste purity, has to be understood as the content of the sign of the dove. There is here therefore no presumption that the reader will of his own accord be able to connect the material dove named in the story with particular significances made recognisable by the general context or by special signals (something which the author of *Reinfried* is otherwise quite willing to ask of his reader in analogous cases). Rather, a particular content is laid down, from within the poem, to be the meaning intended here.

When it then becomes apparent in the later mentions of the dove and of Princess Yrkane that the actions of Reinfried, the principal character, centre on the values embodied by the Danish princess and made significant by the dove, it is clear why the author constructs the exposition of the entire Reinfried–Yrkane plot on the basis of a meaning for the symbolic leitmotif of the dove which is not simply suggested but is unambiguously explained. Several times the narration sets about representing the simple action of Yrkane's handing over the dove to the victorious Reinfried (780, 1224, 1327), but each occasion produces only a richly developed narrative description of the external and internal commotion caused by this approach of Reinfried and Yrkane to each other. Here we find a sparing use of the possibility of furnishing a relatively large field of action with notions of meaning and purpose by referring to the significance of a real object; by contrast with other parts of *Reinfried*, there is in the opening episode, the tournament in Denmark, which runs to some 3,000 lines, remarkably little reference to real things which function as signs pointing beyond themselves (e.g. the diamond and the ruby). The episode of the tournament, together with the appropriately Arthurian natural *topoi* (green branches, the song of unspecified little birds, flowers of the field; 1438ff., 2819ff.) is a kind of reality different from that of the dove; with this courtly action, a *sensus duplex*, to use Auerbach's term, with a moral meaning, is constructed out of the events of the romance itself, whereas with the dove there is a reference back to a given reality, which in a sense the work cites, and in which a meaning was immanent of which we now need only to be reminded.

A different sequence however is possible for the introduction of given, significant, reality into the larger framework of a narrator's intentions. Albrecht, the author of *Titurel the Younger*, who even into the nineteenth century was thought to be identical with Wolfram, in his prologue treats the theme of purity, and purification, with reference to the Biblical *exemplum* of the three children in the fiery furnace; he adds the prayer that God may so guide him that his soul remains pure and he is spared the fires of Purgatory (ed. Wolf, 78ff.). At the same time this part of the prologue is an anticipation of the salamander motif, which Albrecht will repeatedly use to characterise his hero Tschionatulander: the salamander is here taken to be an animal that can live in fire and can survive the associated purification. Now when it comes about that the hero of the story has the salamander concretely present in his coat of arms, he is being measured against the meaning contained in that significant animal; the salamander here may mean the lover, for whom love is the element of life; it may also mean the man strong in faith who cannot be burned by the negative forms of fire – temptation and mere earthly pleasure. It is not the text itself that makes plausible these and other decodings of the sign of the salamander :[20] rather, the narrative invokes a simultaneously descriptive and interpretative natural history of the salamander, which had thus at a pre-poetic stage become a sign which could also be used poetically. By his reference to the salamander Albrecht does not acquire a new motif for the development and interpretation of the events in his romance, rather he elaborates significations that have already been introduced, by means of multiple references to the salamander which function as confirmation, legitimation, and also as variation. Within this significant reality, in which the communication of truth is not dependent on the authority of the narrator, the narrator can weave authoritative elements into the fabric of event and reflection in his story.

The way in which these narrative writers of the thirteenth century treat the particular possibility of a reality replete with meaning is anything but unreflective. The author of *Reinfried* takes the opportunity to extend the simple mention of the natural and at the same time significant *res*, the elephant and the salamander, into a narratively expansive depiction of amazing exotic sights (Reinfried's journey to the East is shot through with descriptions of an unknown world which are reminiscent of the travelogue). But he interrupts his description with the comment that he might be open to the charge of offering lies (26391ff.). He points out that somebody could object to the statement that salamanders live in fire : 'wâ wart ie creâtiure/lebende in dem fiure/ân erden wazzer unde luft?' Here he is alluding to the characteristic of the animal, known since Aristotle, which meant that it frequently became the symbol for fire as an element – to which was added the interpretation that, thanks to its constant purification in fire, the animal came to stand for supreme purity. The narrator's assured – rather than explicatory – reply to the 'tumben' who raise doubts becomes an extensive summary of the doctrine of the four elements and the four temperaments. He reports individual characteristics of the salamander which presuppose that fire is its natural element. And this in its turn accounts for the meaning – at this point in the text it is only hinted at and not made explicit – which links the salamander to the elephant. Both are seen as pure animals : in particular, both are averse to sexuality. Of the reality of those characteristics, which are at the root of the interpretations, there can be no doubt.

It is by no means to be attributed to the peculiarity of the literary genre adopted that, in the untypical courtly romance *Partonopier und Meliur* by Konrad von Würzburg, the salamander, together with the phoenix, is introduced with negative implications. Both animals are here associated with features of a place of love which, through reference to both those animals, is shown to be the setting for untrue love. It follows from the openness of that process of thinking in significances which in the Middle Ages saw the things of the created world as the bearers of hidden, but discoverable, meanings that things can potentially be interpreted either negatively or positively and only the individual context will determine the evaluation. This openness also entails a potential multiplicity of meanings whose wide divergence one from another neither lessens the plausibility of any one individual meaning nor invites the charge that the meaning is posited as an act of mere subjective caprice. Indeed, the context can even allow the polyvalence to continue, can evade the fixed and unambiguous interpretation. The salamander and the phoenix, which are normally invested with a predominantly positive significance, can be employed negatively in context by Konrad von Würzburg without our having to conclude that he has thereby broken with the system or tradition.[21]

I shall just mention briefly[22] that, alongside animals, plants, stones, and numbers, space and time can belong to the most important significant *realia* of medieval narrative. Even such natural *realia* as animals can express interpretatively precise temporal notions. Hence in the prose *Lancelot* (ed. Kluge 1, 508, 15ff.) the leopard and the lion can, by means of interpretative statements that are inherent in the action, be understood as announcing the precursor and the redeemer, in the sense that, by analogy to the 'leopard' John the Baptist and to the 'lion' Christ, Lancelot is here interpreted as the precursor of his son Galaad who, as the successor who is able to redeem the worldly order of knights, can be seen as the *imitator Christi*.[23] It is the conventional interpretations – and not the descriptions of particular characteristics of the leopard or the lion – that form the basis of the prophecies which evaluate characters and mark the narrative off into temporal divisions.

The examples I have given above of the narrative deployment of a predetermined significant reality have necessarily been a simplified summary of lengthy and often disparate acts of description and interpretation and of hermeneutic mediation. If I were to cite the whole range of possible examples then other, more differentiated, interpretative tasks would emerge – such as we are now familiar with in respect of the ambiguous lion in Chrétien's *Yvain* and Hartmann's *Iwein* narratives.[24] We would also need to go into the problem of how far an aesthetic tradition of interpretation (whether literary or pictorial) can achieve the same effect as an interpretation of nature or reality which is not aesthetically mediated, which is anchored in simple observation of nature (or at any rate claims as much).[25] In each individual context it is no easy task to discover the special function – and thereby the present interpretative content – of a particular object in its narrative connections. And that task is not accomplished and justice will not be done to the context if the critic comes with a too narrow expectation of unambiguous rightness. For the purposes of such decoding there is no detailed key to the vocabulary – not in the admittedly useful encyclopaedias of Isidore of Seville and Vincent of Beauvais nor even in the large encyclo-paedia of terms and meanings *Magnum Theatrum vitae humanae* of Laurentius Beyerlink from the seventeenth century. In a study on the cedar and the aloe Reinitzer has shown very thoroughly[26] how works of natural history as a general rule provide the basis for allegorical and related interpretations, and also how a similarity between two physical objects can lead to a kind of transposition and thereby to a transference of meaning from one phenomenon (in this case a plant) to another. Affinities in natural phenomena can there-fore lead to affinities in the meaning ascribed to many things without the reality of the whole, of the phenomenon together with its mean-ing, being in any way called into question. Hence in the 'lignum Aloe' there may be a reference to the mention of the aloe in the book of Proverbs (7. 17f.) and to the interpretative tradition associated with the wood of the cedar tree : moreover if we wish to determine the immediate meaning, we may also have to consider the confusion of the aloe plant and the aloe wood, and may have to give a significant role to the history of medication and to the whole exegetical tradition. All these factors will have to be borne in mind in any attempt to reconstruct the interpretative possibilities open to the contemporary public : and only then can one inquire into the process of precise selection which determines the one or several meanings, taken from the available interpretative arsenal, which are operative in the particular narrative context.

The enrichment by, and the authorial validation of, meanings inherent in objects is a process which can be traced well beyond the thirteenth century right down to the late seventeenth century in romances and other larger narrative forms. In Lohenstein's prose romance *Arminius* where the encyclopaedic knowledge displayed is to be investigated by means of the various appendices and indexes, objects and situations can be linked to interpretative traditions; in Moscherosch's prose satire *Philander von Sittewald* the satire of the journey into Hell can be connected with the whole tradition of allegorical journeys;[27] in the 'Continuatio' to Grimmelshausen's *Simplicius Simplicissimus* we are reminded of the essential metaphor of the book of the world – the world is seen as a great book which can lead to knowledge of God's creation and hence can initiate us into the story of salvation. The hero of Grimmelshausen's *Das wunderbarliche Vogelnest* (Part II, Chapter 2) interprets the bulbs of flowers in this sense : he finds them in a garden and sees in them a sign of hope that he, just like the bulbs, may look forward to the coming of spring, and he accordingly begins to ask himself how he too can become 'recht grün'. Here Grimmelshausen turns an old spiritual interpretation of bulbs into a worldly one, but he still takes his stand on the fundamental assumption that the meaning is immanent in the natural object 'bulb'.[28] And yet in the seventeenth and eighteenth centuries we can increasingly detect signs of a waning belief in the interpretative significance and trustworthiness of the 'book of nature', a tendency which the 'physico-theology' of the eighteenth century seeks to resist in a broad literary – albeit not narrative – counter-offensive. This is known to a Jean Paul but it does not determine his interest in the 'long, unending picture gallery of nature' (in the Preface to the second edition of *Quintus Fixlein*). Yet in view of this tendency one should at least remark[29] that realism is not necessarily incompatible with a religious world-view.

The awareness that the narrative deployment of many *realia* in a medieval or early modern work can bring with it an increase in possible pre-established meanings does not, however, entitle us to reach either systematic or dogmatic conclusions. To show that in particular sections of a narrative work certain dimensions of meaning are operative – whether they derive from theological, pictorial, or literary traditions – is not to prove that in the work as a whole objects are meant to be subject to sustainedly allegorical interpretation. Nor does it follow that because in one work a particular object has a particular meaning that same object will with certainty bear the same meaning in another work.[30] A change in context, or in historical situation, will significantly call into question any such attempts at definitive interpretation. Any concern with the interpretative dimension of things and images in early central European literatures will, in principle, work more successfully with an open semiotic[31] rather than within any ideal of unambiguous precision. For it is common to medieval theories of the recognition and exegesis of the multiple senses inhering in words and things that the starting point is the ambiguity of individual interpretative components.[32] Polyvalence of words and things is regarded not as proving that any meaning communicated lacks objective validity : rather, the individual author must, by means of contextual signals, hold that polyvalence in check without forfeiting the possibility of ambiguity. Against this background it becomes clear that the interpretative employment of *realia* in older narrative literature amounts to a realism – whether one defines it aesthetically as the incorporation of reality or stylistically as a quantitative concentration on elements of external reality – which does not need to be defined as an opposition to the 'ideality' of certain narrative contents, and certainly not as a realistic withdrawal from the courtly, an approximation to bourgeois narrative forms. It remains methodologically difficult to define with any precision which sections of the public were able to appreciate the full range of the interpretative background, and whether a varying degree of textual understanding on the part of differently informed kinds of readership was intended. In respect of the public for Middle High German literature we lack the kind of clear evidence which is available, for example, in respect of possible contemporary interpretative responses to Dante's *Divine Comedy*. His son Jacopo Alighieri wrote a commentary which addressed only the literal sense of his father's work; but his son Pietro, on the other hand, uncovered step by step those fourfold interpretative layers operative in the treatment of things, characters, and events which were clearly comprehensible to another sector of the readership at the same time in the same place.

The understanding of the real which includes the interpretative dimension as an essential component is by no means confined to theological or narrative texts in the Middle Ages and in the subsequent period of transition to the modern age. Literature of this time which is devoted to the description of nature – whether it be the all-embracing encyclopaedic compilations or the shorter tract literature – tends generally to give its users practical hints and other ways of making use of literature. This applies as much to medical prescriptions for horses as to tips which include within the uses of precious stones allusions to their colour and allegorical meaning. The notion of practical value (*usus*) extends to include instruction, by means of picture and text, in the ways of deriving moral and spiritual benefit from the contemplation of natural objects. Hence the great polymath of the sixteenth century, the Zürich doctor Konrad Gesner, is only offering a summary of what was conventionally accepted when, in his *Historia Animalium*, a scholarly standard work of the sixteenth and seventeenth centuries, he not only deliberately enlarges the scope of empirical description but also summarises all the results of ancient, medieval, and contemporary thinking in respect of the interpretative significance of animals. This animal encyclopaedia of humanistic scholarship, like so many monographs of the early modern age,[33] takes as its starting point an unquestioned unity of word, thing, and meaning (*vox, res, significatio*)[34] and in the process reflects yet again a view of *realia* which could be taken for granted and used by both earlier and later narrative writers. As long as narratives followed works of natural history in seeing the *significatio* as a component of the real object, the realistic and the allegorical narrative mode could be identical : to incorporate reality and to build up interpretative backgrounds could coincide in one single act in which one can still feel the full tension of the 'coexistence of allegorical and empirical perceptions'.[35] Yet it depended on the individual narrator and on the intentions of his particular work – or, indeed, of specific parts of that work – whether the reader's attention was drawn to the opportunity of perceiving pre-existent meanings in the given context. The narrator's standpoint and intention alone can give the individual particle of reality a direction which distinguishes it from mere documentation of the real : a fragment of already existing interpretation of the world is incorporated into a specifically narrative model of reality, and so a new possibility is gained to apprehend both world and meaning.

The references which I have been discussing to dimensions of meaning which were recognised and fixed in pre-existent interpretations of nature must be distinguished from those internally constituted interpretations of things which characterise realistic novels of the nineteenth century. When Theodor Fontane, in the first chapter of *Der Stechlin*, presents two aloe plants of contrasting shape as the paradoxical image for possible evaluations of the events,[36] he does so without a securely established scheme of reference to a conventionally interpreted universe. When Theodor Storm in *Der*

Wolfgang Harms

Schimmelreiter casually introduces the motif of the kingfisher, this moment acquires its interpretative value from the narrative sequence itself – perhaps also from literary allusions – but certainly not from any predetermination in the sense of a medievally derived *mundus symbolicus*.[37] When Wilhelm Raabe, with the help of biblical quotation and allusion invests the things and settings of his novel *Unruhige Gäste* with particular meanings, this is a process of quotation which does not depend on a pre-existing unity of palpable reality and significance.[38] In Fontane's novels there is an abundant world of things, which as 'props' can function as 'signs within the narrative coherence' and can thereby acquire 'something akin to symbolic meaning'.[39] But among these concrete references thanks to which the author goes beyond and modifies the conventional expectations which at that time were associated with such everyday objects there is not one example where the thing as it were automatically brings its meaning with it. This does occur, exceptionally, with the 'unavoidable pelican' in Chapter 26 of Fontane's *Unwiederbringlich* which pre-supposes a knowledge of its allegorical meaning : but in the very same breath the traditional claims of this sign of compassion and sacrificial death are brushed aside with a verbal gesture of sheer weariness. With the loss of that binding status which the metaphor of the 'book of nature', written by God for man, had for earlier ages, the modern age forfeits that perceptual certainty which could see in natural things a meaning that was binding because it did not depend on man. In so far as literary realism is an engagement with real things, this comment could prove useful for research into the realism of a number of periods.

NOTES

1. Alanus ab Insulis, *Rhythmus quo graphice natura hominis flux et caduca depingitur* in *Patrologia Latina* ed. J. P. Migne, 210, column 579 A. For a discussion of this possibility of a language of things which derives not from a human author but from creation itself, see Friedrich Ohly, 'Vom geistigen Sinn des Wortes im Mittelalter' in Ohly, *Schriften zur mittelalterlichen Bedeutungsforschung* (Darmstadt, 1977) pp. 1–31, especially pp. 3–5 and 17 and Max Wehrli, *Literatur im deutschen Mittelalter: Eine poetologische Einführung* (Stuttgart, 1984) pp. 249–53.
2. Umberto Eco, *The Name of the Rose* tr. William Weaver (London, 1983) p. 23.
3. On the biblical, ancient, and early medieval versions of the determinable contents of such path symbolism see Wolfgang Harms, *Homo viator in bivio* (Munich, 1970).

4. See Friedrich Ohly, 'Das Buch der Natur bei Jean Paul' in *Studien zur Goethezeit: Erich Trunz zum 75. Geburtstag* ed. Hans-Joachim Mähl and Eberhard Mannack (Heidelberg, 1981) pp. 177–232 and Peter Frenz, *Studien zu traditionellen Elementen des Geschichtsdenkens und der Bildlichkeit im Werk Johann Gottfried Herders* (Frankfurt am Main and Berne, 1983) pp. 241–55 ('Buch der Natur').

5. See 'All Geschöpf ist Zung' und Mund' in *Vestigia Bibliae* 6 (1984) and the introduction to *Natura Loquax* (cf. n. 21) pp. 7–16.

6. See J. P. Stern, *On Realism* (London, 1973) §§ 17–18, Erich Auerbach, *Mimesis: Dargestellte Wirklichkeit in der abendländischen Literatur* (Berne, ⁴1967) especially chapters 5 and 6, Richard Brinkmann, *Wirklichkeit und Illusion* (Stuttgart, ²1966)) especially p. 317.

7. See Brinkmann, *Wirklichkeit und Illusion*, pp. 76 and 310.

8. See Stern, *Realism*, §26 and n. 14.

9. Auerbach, *Mimesis*, pp. 138, 125, 131.

10. See Herbert Kolb, 'Isidorische "Etymologien" im *Parzival*' in *Wolfram-Studien* (Berlin, 1970) pp. 117–35.

11. See Theodore Ziolkowski, 'Der Karfunkelstein' in *Euphorion* 55 (1961) pp. 297–326, p. 307 and 312–13.

12. See Stern, *Realism*, §114.

13. Stern, *Realism*, §84, discusses the coexistence of different styles.

14. See the general comments of Harry Levin, 'What is Realism?' in *Comparative Literature* 3 (1951) pp. 193–9, p. 194.

15. See Hans Messelken, 'Die Signifikanz von Rabe und Taube in der mittelalterlichen deutschen Literatur', PhD dissertation (Cologne, 1965), p.. 77ff. and 95ff., Arthur B. Groos, ' "Sigune auf der Linde" and the Turtledove in *Parzival*', in *JEGP* 67 (1968) pp. 631–46.

16. Christel Meier, 'Grundzüge der mittelalterlichen Enzyklopädie', in *Literatur und Laienbildung im Spätmittelalter und in der Reformationszeit*, ed. Ludger Grenzmann and Karl Stackmann (Stuttgart, 1984) pp. 467–500.

17. Friedrich Ohly, 'Probleme der mittelalterlichen Bedeutungsforschung und das Taubenbild des Hugo de Folieto,' in Ohly, *Schriften*, pp. 32–92, especially pp. 49ff.

18. See Walter Haug, 'Die Symbolstruktur des höfischen Epos und ihre Auflösung bei Wolfram von Eschenbach' in *DVLG* 45 (1971) pp. 668–705, p. 668.

19. See V. A. Kolve, *Chaucer and the Imagery of Narrative* (London, 1984) and Wolfgang Harms, *Homo viator*.

20. For a detailed discussion see Hans-Henning Rausch, *Methoden und Bedeutung naturkundlicher Rezeption und Kompilation im "Jüngeren Titurel"* (Frankfurt am Main, Berne, Las Vegas, 1977) pp. 93ff.

21. See the exemplary differentiations made by Heimo Reinitzer, 'Vom Vogel Phoenix: Über Naturbetrachtung und Naturdeutung' in *Natura Loquax: Naturkunde und allegorische Naturdeutung vom Mittelalter bis zur frühen Neuzeit* ed. Wolfgang Harms and Heimo Reinitzer (Frankfurt am Main, Berne, Cirencester, 1981) pp. 17–72.

22. For a discussion of spatial significance see Ingrid Hahn, *Raum und Landschaft in Gottfrieds Tristan* (Munich, 1964); space and time are discussed by Uwe Ruberg, *Raum und Zeit im Prosa-Lancelot* (Munich, 1965). The typological bracketing of historical periods before and after Christ is treated by Friedrich Ohly, 'Typologie als Denkform der Geschichts-

betrachtung' in *Natur, Religion, Sprache, Universität: Universitäts-vorträge 1982/83* (Münster, 1983) pp. 68–102 and Theodore Ziolkowski, 'Some Features of religious Figuralism in twentieth-century Literature', in *Literary Uses of Typology from the Late Middle Ages to the Present,* ed. Earl Miner (Princeton, 1977) pp. 345–69.

23. See Uwe Ruberg, *Raum und Zeit,* pp. 127f., and Klaus Speckenbach, 'Handlungs- und Traumallegorese in der "Gral-Queste" ', in *Formen und Funktionen der Allegorie: Symposion Wolfenbüttel 1978* ed. Walter Haug (Stuttgart, 1979) pp. 219–42, especially p. 219.

24. See Max Wehrli, *Formen mittelalterlicher Erzählung* (Zürich and Freiburg, 1969) p. 179, and Max Wehrli, *Literatur im deutschen Mittelalter,* p. 252.

25. See the detailed discussion in *Formen und Funktionen der Allegorie,* pp. 561, 737.

26. Heimo Reinitzer, 'Zeder und Aloe: Zur Herkunft des Bettes Salomos im *Moriz von Craûn*', in *Archiv für Kulturgeschichte* 58 (1976) pp. 1–34.

27. For a discussion of similar implications in Grimmelshausen see Klaus Haberkamm, ' "Fusspfad" oder "Fahrweg"? Zur Allegorese der Wegewahl bei Grimmelshausen', in *Rezeption und Produktion zwischen 1570 und 1730: Festschrift für Günther Weydt* (Berne and Munich, 1972) pp. 285–317.

28. See Dietrich Jöns, 'Emblematisches bei Grimmelshausen', in *Euphorion* 62 (1968) pp. 385–91 and Erich Trunz, 'Weltbild und Dichtung im deutschen Barock', in *Aus der Welt des Barock* ed. Richard Alewyn (Stuttgart, 1957) pp. 1–35.

29. Stern, *Realism,* §33, and with reference to the relationship of realism and religious transcendence in medieval literature, §35.

30. Somewhat risky attempts have been made in this direction: see Wiebke and Hartmut Freytag, 'Zum Natureingang von Wolframs von Eschenbach Blutstropfenszene', in *Studi Medievali* 14 (1973) pp. 301–34.

31. See Umberto Eco, 'Latratus canis', in *L'uomo di fronte al mondo animale nell'alto medioevo* ed. Raoul Manselli, Spoleto 1985, Umberto Eco, *Semiotics and the Philosophy of Language* (London, 1984), especially the chapters 'Symbols' and 'Dictionary vs Encyclopaedia'.

32. See F. Ohly 'Vom geistigen Sinn des Wortes', Hartmut Freytag, *Die Theorie der allegorischen Schriftdeutung und die Allegorie in deutschen Texten besonders des 11. und 12. Jahrhunderts* (Berne, 1982). On the medieval view of the reality behind the words see Walter Blank, *Die deutsche Minneallegorie* (Stuttgart, 1970) pp. 21f.

33. As – in themselves heterogeneous – examples of many such treatises: Christian Ludwig Schlichter, *Observationes philologicae de turture eiusque qualitatibus, usu antiquo, et emblemate* (Dissertation Halle, 1739); Johann Paul Wurffbain, *Salamandrologia, h.e. descriptio Historico-Philologico-Philosophico-Medica Salamandrae quae vulgo in igne vivere creditur* (Nürnberg, 1683); Georg Christoph Petri, *Elephantographia curiosa* (Erfurt, 1715); Georg Caspar Kirchmaier, *Disputationes zoologi-cae de basilisco, vnicornv, phoenice, Behemoth et Leviathan, dracone ac aranea* (Jena, 1736); Christian Hänel, *Disputatio historico-philogica de phoenice* (Leipzig, 1665); Georg Wolfgang Wedel, *De ligno Aloes* (Jena, 1693).

34. See Wolfgang Harms, 'On Natural History and Emblematics in the

sixteenth century' in *The Natural Sciences and the Arts*, ed. Allan Ellenius (Stockholm, 1985) pp. 67–83.

35. See Hans Geulen, 'Wirklichkeitsbegriff und Realismus in Grimmelshausens *Simplicissimus Teutsch*', in *Argenis* 1 (1977) pp. 31–40; Rolf Tarot, 'Grimmelshausens Realismus', in *Rezeption und Produktion*, pp. 233–65, p. 259.

36. See Heimo Reinitzer, 'Zeder und Aloe', pp. 15f.

37. See Wolfgang Harms, 'Der Eisvogel und die halkyonischen Tage: Zum Verhältnis von naturkundlicher Beschreibung und allegorischer Naturdeutung', in *Verbum et signum: Festschrift für Friedrich Ohly* 1 (Munich, 1975), pp. 477–515.

38. See Rainer Gruenter, 'Ein "Schritt vom Wege": Geistliche Lokalsymbolik in Wilhelm Raabes *Unruhige Gäste*', in *Euphorion* 60 (1966) pp. 209–21.

39. See Richard Brinkmann, 'Der angehaltene Moment: Requisiten – Genre – Tableau bei Fontane', in *DVLG* 53 (1979) pp. 429–62.

'Enter Mariners, wet': realism in Shakespeare's last plays

ANNE BARTON

On the twenty-ninth of June 1613, realism – that most elusive and shifting of aesthetic concepts – contrived to burn the Globe theatre to the ground. The play involved was almost certainly Shakespeare's *Henry VIII*, presented under its alternative title, *All Is True*. According to Sir Henry Wotton, who described the catastrophe a few days later in a letter to his nephew, unusual efforts had been made by the King's Men to reproduce the ceremonial, dress, orders and insignia of Henry's court, 'even to the matting of the stage'.[1] Wotton had his doubts about such fidelity to fact. The effect, he grumbled, was 'within a while to make greatness very familiar, if not ridiculous'. Indeed, there is a distinctly judgmental note in Wotton's account of how the theatre cannon, shot off here not as the usual Elizabethan and Jacobean shorthand for a battle (something always difficult to stage) but simply to dignify Henry's arrival as a masquer at York House, accidentally set fire to the playhouse thatch, a calamity which went unnoticed until too late by 'eyes more attentive to the show'.

Thirteen years earlier, the Chorus of *Henry V*, Shakespeare's penultimate English history, had admitted humbly that only an impossible set of conditions – 'a kingdom for a stage, princes to act, / And monarchs to behold the swelling scene' – could possibly bring forth 'the warlike Harry, like himself' (Chorus. I.3–5).[2] In effect, the only satisfactory way of telling this story would be for it actually to happen again, on 'the vasty fields of France' (12). The *Henry VIII* Prologue, by contrast, makes not the slightest apology for the inadequacies of the theatre this play was destined to destroy. The spectators, it predicts calmly, will 'think ye see / The very persons of our noble story / As they were living' (25–7). Nor do they have to make any special imaginative efforts to 'piece out our imperfections with your thoughts' (*Henry V* Chorus. I.25), 'play with your fancies', or 'eke out our performance with your mind' (Chorus. III. 7, 35). They need only admire the stage pictures, weep for the characters and, above all, recognise that what they are about to see is 'true' (21).

But in what sense 'true'? Ignoring Philip Sidney's dictum in the *Apologie for Poetrie* – that the poet 'never maketh any Circles about your Imagination, to conjure you to beleeve for true, what he writeth', that he gives names to men 'but to make their picture the more lively, and not to build anie Historie'[3] – dramatists in the period frequently laid claim in their titles to factual truth. This is the case, above all, with history plays, a relatively new form lacking classical sanction and driven, as a result, to seek it elsewhere, and also (for similar reasons) with domestic tragedy. Hence *The True Tragedy of Richard III* (1591), *The True Chronicle History of the Whole Life and Death of Thomas Lord Cromwell* (1602), *The True and Honorable History of Sir John Oldcastle* (1599) – the last a riposte to what the four joint authors dismissed as the 'forg'de invention' of Shakespeare's *Henry IV* plays[4] – or *A Yorkshire Tragedy: Not So New, as Lamentable and True* (1606). Even Heywood's *The Four Prentices of London With the Conquest of Jerusalem* (1600), an egregiously wild invention, billed itself as *True and Strange*.

The majority of such claims are scarcely more serious than those of Autolycus in *The Winter's Tale*, when he assures the shepherdesses Mopsa and Dorcas that the ballads he has for sale – about usurers' wives who give birth to money-bags, or hard-hearted maids turned into fish, who repent tunefully 'forty thousand fadom above water' (IV.4.277) – are all 'very true'. Heywood, indeed, made a joke out of his alternative title in the Prologue to *The Four Prentices of London*:

1 Touching the name why is it called True and Strange. or The Foure Prentises of London? A Gentleman that heard the subject discourst, sayd it was not possible to be true; and none here are bound to believe it.

2. 'Tis true that Alexander at thirty-two yeares of age conquered the whole world; but strange he should do so. If we should not beleeve things recorded in former ages, wee were not worthy that succeeding times should believe things were done in these our ages.

1. But what authority have you for your History? I am one of these that wil believe nothing that is not in the Chronicle.

2. Our Authority is a Manuscript, a Booke writ in Parchment; which not being Publick, nor generall in the World, we rather thought fit to exemplifie unto the publicke censure things concealed and obscur'd, such as are not common with every one, than such Historical Tales as every one can tell by the fire in Winter . . .

1. You have satisfied me: and, I hope, all that heare it.[5]

That supposed manuscript authority, the 'Booke writ in Parchment', is oddly premonitory of those fake documents upon which the early English novel, from Defoe and Richardson to Scott, so often pretended to rely. Long before the word itself came into common usage, new and heterodox types of fiction were already seeking support from what we should now find it natural to designate as the 'real'.

Henry VIII takes a number of liberties with the historical facts of Elizabeth's father's reign. Yet, on the whole, it honours the contract its Prologue makes with 'such as give / Their money out of hope they may believe' (7–8). Certainly, by comparison with Samuel Rowley's earlier dramatisation of Henry's life, *When You See Me, You Know Me* (1605) – a cheerfully preposterous piece in which bluff King Hal, disguised, had exchanged fisticuffs with a rogue called 'Black Will', endured a night in one of his own prisons on a disorderly conduct charge, and jettisoned Anne of Cleves for Katherine Parr in the space of four lines – the relatively sober and accurate account which the King's Men were offering might well claim to represent 'truth' (9, 18). The trouble with this truth is that it is so naked and unmediated, so cunningly full but contradictory and unshaped, as to create serious problems of interpretation. As is so often the case in Shakespeare's late plays, characters and their motivations, viewed from outside rather than from within, remain riddling and opaque. No soliloquies resolve the question of Buckingham's innocence or guilt, divulge Henry's genuine reason for divorcing Katherine, the extent of Wolsey's fidelity to the crown, or make it plain in what spirit Anne makes her way to Henry's bed. Judgment, as a result, or even understanding of these events which (in one sense) are being so accurately presented, becomes almost impossible. As one critic has observed, 'It is not the presence of fact or chronicle-matter in *Henry VIII* but the restraint of the imagination's transforming power that is distinctive.'[6]

Consistently, where analysis or personal revelation might be expected, the play offers spectacle instead : Buckingham formally escorted to his execution, the masque and banquet at York House, Queen Katherine's state trial, the great procession at the coronation of Anne, and then at Elizabeth's christening, the vision which appears to the sleeping Katherine shortly before her death. With the significant – and deliberately puzzling – exception of the last, all of these ceremonies and pageants are versions of things which the members of Shakespeare's audience might reasonably be expected to encounter outside the theatre. They were also events which a company with the resources of the King's Men could represent plausibly on the stage. (Although there is much talk, for instance, about the Field of the Cloth of Gold, with its horses and knightly combats, no attempt is made to include it in the action.) The tableaux of *Henry VIII*, moreover, appear to be there purely for their own sake : they serve no essential plot or thematic purpose. When Heywood, in *If You Know Not Me, You Know Nobody* (1604), had shown Elizabeth on the way to her coronation receiving a Bible and a purse from the Lord Mayor of London, and scrupulously named the lords she confirmed in their offices, while receiving from them the insignia of rule, he was making a powerful statement about support for a Protestant queen among the nobility and in the City. Shakespeare, by contrast, in stage directions so elaborate that they might almost belong to a film script, specifies that Anne returned from Westminster Abbey preceded by trumpets, two judges, the Lord Chancellor 'with purse and mace before him', choristers, the Lord Mayor of London, Garter, then 'Marquess Dorset, bearing a scepter of gold, on his head a demi-coronal of gold. With him, the Earl of Surrey, bearing the rod of silver with the dove, crowned with an earl's coronet. Collars of Esses', and so on, down to the 'old Duchess of Norfolk' who carried the queen's train, merely (as it seems) because this, with surprisingly few alterations and omissions, was how this procession had looked, according to Holinshed, in 1533.

In objecting to what might be described as the documentary aspect of *Henry VIII*, to its concern to reproduce certain public events of the last century as they might have appeared to people living then, Wotton displayed an uneasy sense that the theatre was over-reaching itself. To claim that, thanks to the indulgence and imaginative efforts of the spectators, a cockpit, a wooden O, might for a little while pretend to 'hold the vasty fields of France' was one thing. The English theatre had played this game, in one form or another, for centuries. What seems to have disturbed him about *Henry VIII* were its trespasses upon the real, a confident annexing of the actual which appeared to threaten the integrity and status of the things imitated. The term itself was not available to him, but in effect Wotton was made uneasy by the *realism* of *Henry VIII* as performed at the Globe.

'The terminology of "the real" ', J. P. Stern has written, 'is no more than the dispensable cultural option of an era.'[7] As he remarks, the word 'reality' does not appear in the whole of Shakespeare. But then, apart from a very few, special instances, it cannot be traced anywhere until the late seventeenth century. 'Real' makes its entrance much earlier, but for long remained an uncommon word, the precise sense of which, as the OED notes, tends in context to be difficult to define. Towards the end of Elizabeth's reign, it could apparently be regarded as affected. In *The Scourge of Villanie* (1598), Marston has a fling at three 'new-minted Epithets' of 'Torquatus', one of which turns out to be 'Reall'.[8] It has been claimed that Torquatus was meant to represent Ben Jonson, in whose work the word does appear seven times: five times in the plays, twice in non-dramatic poems. But, apart from the fact that none of these Jonson texts was available to Marston at the time he was writing his satire, it seems odd that the word as Jonson uses it – invariably in the traditional scholastic sense of idea or essence as opposed to accidental particularity or mere name[9] – should attract derisory attention.

Shakespeare's three uses of 'real' (in *All's Well That Ends Well*, 'A Lover's Complaint' and *Coriolanus*) are more complex and innovative. Moreover, he found its converse 'unreal', a word he may well have invented, necessary to him twice, in *Macbeth* and *The Winter's Tale*. The incidence of 'real' in Shakespeare is, of course, slender when compared with his lifelong reliance upon the word 'true' and its cognate forms. That vocabulary cluster fills nine and a half columns in the Spevack Concordance. 'Real' and its partner 'unreal', however, are very special words as Shakespeare employs them. If, as has recently been suggested, both *All's Well That Ends Well* and 'A Lover's Complaint' are Jacobean works,[10] then these are terms which come into play only during the second half of Shakespeare's writing life. Three out of the five passages are cited in the OED as being the earliest recorded use of the word in this particular sense. All constitute a deliberately chosen alternative to the word 'true', or to its usual Shakespearean antonym.

The prefix 'un-' was a particular favourite of Shakespeare's, a way of negating something within a specific context while continuing to affirm its general existence. A number of these compounds seem to have been original with him : 'unchilded', 'unknowing', 'unfellowed', 'unpolluted', 'unaneled', and many more.[11] Others – 'unhappy', for instance, or 'unworthy' – were already in common use. So was the word 'untrue'. Yet whereas two hundred and fifteen instances of 'happy' in the Concordance are matched by forty-one uses of 'unhappy', and two hundred and thirty-eight of 'worthy' by thirty-nine of 'unworthy', the massive entry for 'true' – eight hundred and forty-nine – is countered by only seven examples of 'untrue'. Normally, Shakespeare locates the obverse of 'true' in the monosyllable 'false', a word he employs three hundred and thirteen times. Lexically independent of 'true', 'false' is autonomous as compounds beginning with an 'un-' prefix are not. Yet the two contrasting words were so closely associated in Shakespeare's mind that the one tended to summon up the other automatically, sometimes within the same line, more often at a little distance. Usually, this partnership serves to activate the moral connotations implicit in both, even in contexts where such a meaning is far from primary.

'Real' and 'unreal', on the other hand, never keep company in Shakespeare. Neither harbours any sense of moral judgment. In 'A Lover's Complaint', the forsaken maid is bitterly accusatory when she describes her beautiful seducer as being able, in his personal conduct, to 'livery falseness in a pride of truth' (105). The young man is a 'false jewel' (154), a deceiver whose smooth tongue makes specious use of words like 'truth' and 'troth'. Only his horsemanship, so uncanny that beholders were led to question its basis, was no illusion. In defending the integrity of this one quality, its foundation in fact, Shakespeare's maid shies away from the slippery and contaminated word 'true'. His 'real habitude', she declares, 'gave life and grace / To appertainings and to ornament' (114–15). Appertainings and ornament, false appearances, guileful shows, lies that look like truth: these are common currency in the courtly world of 'A Lover's Complaint'. That is why the unusual word 'real' has to be invoked in order to characterise the single, wholly amoral activity of the young man which tangibly is what it seems to be.

Again, in *Coriolanus*, the protagonist reaches out for the word 'real' when trying to convince his fellow patricians that to allow the plebeians any sway in the government of the state must be to sacrifice 'real necessities' to 'unstable slightness' (III.1.156–7). 'Real necessities' are not the same as 'true needs'. Nor do they have anything to do with the idealist/nominalist debate. They are part of that world of solid, firm, visible entities, of scars and swords, oak garlands and brazen instruments of war, in which Coriolanus feels at home. Diplomacy and compromise, patrician willingness to adapt to the times, can only (in his eyes) violate 'the fundamental part of state' (150). The 'real', for Coriolanus, is what can be touched and felt and seen. It does not inhabit words or 'voices' – the 'yea and no / Of general ignorance' (144–5) – but, taking the word back to its primal Latin root in *res*, seen actions and changeless, massy things.

The 'real' in Shakespeare is neither good nor bad, and only in a morally neutral sense 'true'. 'Unreal', its converse, is similarly amoral. All the associations of this word are with ambiguous, riddling, intangible things : ghosts and shadows, dreams, nothingness, or names without substance. Macbeth tries to rid himself of Banquo's all too palpable ghost by addressing it as 'horrible shadow, unreal mockery' (III.5.104–5). Leontes, commenting more acutely than he knows upon his predicament, observes that 'affection' communicates with 'dreams' : 'With what's unreal thou co-active art, / And fellow'st nothing' (*The Winter's Tale* I.2.138–42). In the most complicated of the three instances, the supposedly dead Helena, in *All's Well That Ends Well*, forces from the King of France the startled inquiry : 'Is't real that I see?' (V.3.306). Her immediate disclaimer – 'No, my good lord, / 'Tis but the shadow of a wife you see, / The name and not the thing' (306–8) – reinterprets the King's question. France wondered if some 'exorcist / Beguiles the truer office of mine eyes' (306–8), whether he was looking at a living woman or a ghost. Helena understands this. She also plays with the familiar nominalist/idealist distinction. Yet her reply is addressed fundamentally to Bertram, not the King. She wants her husband to concede that she is fully and physically his wife, not merely the possessor of an empty title. Only Bertram's acknowledgement that this is so : 'Both, both, O pardon' (308), can now make Helena 'real'.

For most of Shakespeare's characters, seeing is believing. 'If there be truth in sight', Duke Senior announces confidently, in the moment that 'Ganymede' metamorphoses into the lost Rosalind, 'thou art my daughter' (*As You Like It* V.4.118), and he is echoed by Orlando and Phebe. Horatio would not have credited the ghost in *Hamlet*, for all that Bernardo and Marcellus have to say about it, 'without the sensible and true avouch / Of mine own eyes' (I.1.57–8), and Thersites finds it particularly exasperating that Troilus should refuse to accept what he has not only overheard but – more importantly – seen outside Calchas' tent : 'Will 'a swagger himself out on's own eyes?' (*Troilus and Cressida* V.2.136). Although eyes may, on occasion, play tricks on their owners (Macbeth, confronted with the airy dagger, is unsure whether they 'are made the fools o'th'other senses', or are 'worth all the rest' (II.2.44–5)) normally, they are the highest and most reliable of the five senses. Yet they cannot guarantee, or even significantly control, a correct understanding of what they communicate. Othello did actually see the handkerchief in Cassio's hand, Gloucester the blood flowing from Edmund's self-inflicted wound, and Claudio and Don Pedro a 'ruffian' being outrageous without rebuke outside Hero's bedroom window. Eyes were not to blame for what followed, only the misinterpreting mind ensnared in a carefully constructed deceit which has known how to make false use of the visually true.

In the romances, characters continue to misconstrue or be baffled by the evidence presented to their eyes. Yet it is rare, now, for such uncertainties to result in *moral* confusion. Apart from a few isolated blunderers – Leontes, Posthumus, or King Cymbeline – upon whom moral obtuseness descends suddenly, like a disease, characters in these plays usually find it simple to separate honesty from dissembling, white from black. So, everyone in *Cymbeline*, except the King, recognises effortlessly that Imogen and Posthumus are good, and worthy of each other, the Queen wicked, and her son Cloten a brute. No one but Leontes, in *The Winter's Tale*, makes the mistake of believing Hermione unchaste. The incestuous solution to the riddle game at Antioch is so obvious that King Pericles can scarcely miss it – something which certainly could not have been said of the caskets facing Bassanio in Portia's Belmont. In *The Tempest*, only Caliban, and the equally inexperienced Miranda who naively includes Antonio in her 'brave new world', misjudge the people around them. The very words 'true' and 'false', in these plays, although they continue to summon up one another, are no longer highly charged opposites. Indeed, they often seem to change places, as they do in Pisanio's paradox: 'Wherein I am false I am honest; not true to be true' (*Cymbeline* IV.3. 42). The overall result is to shift attention away from 'what our seemers be' (*Measure for Measure* I.3. 54) towards more specialised, aesthetic concerns : issues which we would find it natural to speak of now in terms of the unreal and the real.[12]

In *Pericles*, 'absolute Marina' (Chorus. IV. 31) is said to be so skilful with her needle, composing

> Nature's own shape of bud, bird, branch or berry,
> That even her art sisters the natural roses,
> Her inkle, silk, twin with the rubied cherry. (V. 5–8)

Like the painted cherries of Zeuxis, at which real birds pecked, Marina's embroidery obliterates a boundary, inviting misinterpretation as substance rather than shadow. Such conceits, of a visual art rivalling life, or even more lifelike than life itself, were of course common in the Renaissance. Usually, however, they concede some degree of failure, as in the poem appended to the Droeshout engraving of Shakespeare in the First Folio, where the artist's 'strife' to delineate his subject's 'wit' as well as his features, and 'out-doo the life', ends in defeat. Because it makes (apparently) no attempt to imitate the human form, let alone mind or personality, Marina's needlework satisfies realistic criteria more easily than the work of artists whose subject matter is more animate and ambitious. Buds and branches, berries, roses or cherries, after all, do not require her to apologise for needlework's inability to incorporate motion and sound. Only the bird might be thought to suffer any diminution in consequence of being, perforce, both voiceless and immobile.

When, on the other hand, Iachimo praises the unknown sculptor responsible for the carved chimney piece in Imogen's bed-chamber ('chaste Dian bathing') as 'another Nature, dumb', a man who 'outwent her, motion and breath left out' (*Cymbeline* II.4. 84–5), the qualifications make significant inroads on the praise. Movement and sound are components too important in this mythological scene not to make their absence felt, for all the artist's skill, even as they are in the 'conceit deceitful' of that 'skilful painting made for Priam's Troy' before which Shakespeare's Lucrece momentarily forgets herself, tearing at the image of Sinon, Tarquin's surrogate, with her nails, only to rebuke herself at once : ' "Fool! fool!", quoth she, "his wounds will not be sore" ' (*The Rape of Lucrece* 1423, 1367, 1578). Lucrece is particularly distressed by Hecuba's speechlessness : the painter 'did her wrong, / To give her so much grief and not a tongue' (1462–3). For all his cunning with foreshortening and perspective, with things which 'seem' real, the Troy artist was no 'god'. All he created, in the end, was the 'liveless life', 'in scorn of nature', of things which can neither speak nor move (1374).

'Seems' and 'seem'd' recur frequently in the account of the Troy painting. Although morally neutral, they carry with them an underlying sense of inadequacy which can slide easily into disparagement. It is rare, in Shakespeare, for the visual arts to escape some kind of contact with the dubious vocabulary of scorn and mockery, counterfeiting and deceit. Only for an instant do the painted eyes of 'fair Portia's counterfeit', which Bassanio discovers in the leaden casket, seem to move. In the next moment, he is recognising how painfully 'this shadow / Doth limp behind the substance' (*The Merchant of Venice* III.2.115, 128–9). Even the vainglorious Painter in *Timon of Athens*, flattered by the Poet that his work is so lifelike that 'to th'dumbness of the gesture / One might interpret', feels it necessary to brush the hyperbole away : 'It is a pretty mocking of the life' (I.1.33–7). He may, as Timon later accuses him, with a deliberate play on words, draw 'a counterfeit / Best in all Athens', and 'most lively' : he cannot escape the limitations of his medium, a medium which perpetually invites description not in the morally neutral terms of the unreal and the real, but in the more pejorative ones associated with falsehood and truth (V.1. 80–3).

When Paulina, in the fifth act of *The Winter's Tale*, unveils the statue of Hermione, she avails herself of just this suspect vocabulary: 'prepare / To see the life as lively mock'd as ever / Still sleep mock'd death' (V.3.18–20). In speaking about the statue earlier, the anony-mous third gentleman had described its supposed creator, Julio Romano, in familiar terms : Nature's 'ape', a man who might indeed put her out of business if only he possessed personal immortality and 'could put breath into his work'. One of the marvels reported about Hermione's statue (the gentleman does not say that he credits it) is that it is so lifelike the beholder might be tempted to address it, 'and stand in hope of an answer' (V.2.94–101)). Perdita, in fact, will do just this, while her father stands torn between his rational knowledge that no 'fine chisel / Could ever yet cut breath', that if the eyes of the image seem to move, that is because 'we are mock'd with art' (V.3.78–9, 68), and a delirious persuasion that he may be right in supposing 'that it breath'd, and that those veins / Did verily bear blood' (64–5).

'Verily' is an interesting choice. In the first act of *The Winter's Tale*, Polixenes' recourse to just this word had let him in for a good deal of affectionate teasing from Hermione. Shakespeare often treats that group of relatively new and still uncommon English words derived from the Latin *veritas* – 'verily', 'verity', 'verify', 'veritable' – as mildly comic and affected. Hamlet makes 'verity' an ingredient in his parody of Osric's inflated rhetoric (V.2.116); Kent in *King Lear* uses it to satirise courtly language (II.2.105). 'Verified' is one of the grandiose words Dogberry flaunts without understanding (*Much Ado About Nothing* V.1.218), while both 'verify' and 'verily' suffer as a result of the attentions, however well meaning, of Fluellen in *Henry V* (III.2.71, V.1.61). In *The Winter's Tale*, Archidamus has already inflicted some damage on 'verily' in the opening scene by relying on it (in vain) to help him finish a particularly stilted and ineffective sentence of compliment (I.1.11). Hermione's subsequent mockery of what she calls Polixenes' 'dread "verily"' (I.2.55) threatens to finish the word off. Yet at the end of the play, Leontes will need 'verily', not as a pretentious term, but for reasons akin to his earlier need for 'unreal' : because, in a scene which carefully avoids 'true' and 'false', the uncommon and arresting adverb 'verily' is better able to suggest what is special and extraordinary about a stone image which, by laying claim to motion and speech, is about to break through the barrier dividing even the most realistic sculpture from life.

Shakespeare never provides an answer to Polixenes' baffled inquiry in the last moments as to just how Hermione 'has stol'n from the dead' (115). Was Paulina, like everyone else, including the theatre audience, deceived in Act III by a semblance of death from which the queen later revived? Or did she lie to Leontes when assuring him that 'she's dead; I'll swear't. If word nor oath / Prevail not, go and see' (III.2.203–4). According to his own admission in Act V, Leontes did 'go and see', and what he found was a corpse (V.3.139–40). How this particular 'dead' queen re-lives is indeed 'to be question'd' (139). All that can be said with any confidence, however, is that the life she regains is specifically that of the theatre, the one art whose prerogative it is to present images which can both move and speak, as those of the painter and sculptor cannot.

For both audiences, the one on and the one off stage, Paulina carefully defines the nature of the miracle :

> that she is living,
> Were it *but* told you, should be hooted at
> Like an old tale; but it *appears* she lives,
> Though yet she *speak* not.
>
> (V.3.115–18, italics mine)

Report, addressed solely to the ear, without visual confirmation, would be as suspect as those ballads peddled by Autolycus, fictions to be credited only by hearers as naive as Mopsa and Dorcas. But Hermione's resurrection is not dependent upon narrative, a tale told at secondhand. She 'appears' to live. In the late sixteenth and early seventeenth centuries, the meaning of the verb 'appears' was almost always straightforward : 'to come forth into sight' (sometimes from a place of concealment), 'to become visible'. When the music wakes her, and she steps forward to embrace her husband, Hermione satisfies that criterion of reality. Leontes' cry, 'O, she's warm !' adds further tangible confirmation and yet, significantly, it is still not enough. 'She hangs about his neck', Camillo exclaims wonderingly, but he goes on to demand : 'If she pertain to life, let her speak too' (112–13). Prompted gently by Paulina, Hermione formally blesses her daughter and, in the moment that she utters these words, her metamorphosis from stone to flesh becomes complete.

Shakespeare set up this *coup de théâtre* with enormous care. Critics, while recognising that the dramatist would naturally have been reluctant to risk either anti-climax or a repetition of the earlier reunion of Pericles and Marina, have often felt dissatisfied nonetheless with the scene which immediately precedes the final one : that conversation between Autolycus and the three Sicilian gentlemen which is as close as Shakespeare allows us to get to the highly charged moment, off-stage, when the farthel was opened and Leontes recovered his lost child. The scene itself is cast entirely in prose, of an ornate and consciously distanced kind, a narrative mode reminiscent, both in sentence structure and in many of its conceits, of that employed by Sidney in *The Countess of Pembroke's Arcadia*. It has not infrequently been attacked as long-winded, undramatic, and excessively contrived. Yet Shakespeare is doing something here of crucial importance to our understanding of the statue scene. Of the three gentlemen, the Second (Rogero) knows about the finding of Perdita only from report. He and, as he suggests, others in the same position are by no means able to believe what they have heard : 'This news, which is call'd true, is so like an old tale, that the verity of it is in strong suspicion' (V.2.27–9). The word 'verity', whatever it may have been for Kent and Hamlet, is in this context no more risible than Leontes' 'verily' will be a few moments later. It too is being asked to extend and complicate the meaning of 'true'. The First Gentleman has been somewhat more fortunate than the Second. He was actually present when the farthel was produced, and 'methought, I heard the shepherd say, he found the child' (6–7). At this point, however, he and all the other courtiers were ordered to leave the room. The last thing he took away with him was the sight of Leontes and Camillo standing staring at one another like a pair of carved or painted images. Like the Poet in *Timon of Athens*, he was struck by the eloquence of these silent figures : 'There was speech in their dumbness, language in their very gesture.' The passion expressed was clearly that of 'wonder', but whether 'they had heard of a world ransom'd, or one destroy'd', the First Gentleman could not say. As he points out, even 'the wisest beholder, that knew no more but seeing, could not say if th'importance were joy or sorrow' (11–19).

Only the Third Gentleman, Paulina's steward, permitted as it seems to stay behind when the others left, can banish the doubts of that courtier who has heard about the finding of the king's daughter without seeing it, and also content the First Gentleman by discovering the meaning of what he has merely seen. His interlocutors accept the combined evidence he offers of eye and ear. Yet the Third Gentleman finds explication extraordinarily difficult. 'That which you hear', he begins confidently, 'you'll swear you see, there is such unity in the proofs' (30–2). But as he proceeds with his account of what happened in the palace, narrative, although pushed to its figural and descriptive limits, reveals itself increasingly as inadequate to its task. The meeting between Polixenes and Leontes, the Third Gentleman is obliged to confess, was 'a sight which was to be seen, cannot be spoken of' (42–3). As for what ensued, it 'lames report to follow it, and undoes description to do it'. These events become, in fact, when related, once more 'like an old tale, which will have matter to rehearse, though credit be asleep' (57–8, 61–2), as even their narrator is aware.

Such a story, the First Gentleman muses prophetically near the end of the steward's account, deserves to be staged before an 'audience of kings and princes, for by such was it acted' (79–81). This is the old, seemingly impossible set of conditions of which the Chorus in *Henry V* had dreamed : 'a kingdom for a stage, princes to act, / And monarchs to behold the swelling scene'. But, as the three gentlemen depart for Paulina's house in order to admire, along with the members of the royal party, a rare work of art whose existence has never before been mentioned in the play, those conditions are about to be realised. Before an on-stage audience of kings and princes, there will be enacted the resurrection of a real, not a player queen. And, when Paulina's show is over, although no one in either the stage or theatre audience can be entirely clear as to the nature of what they have both heard and witnessed, it cannot be easily dismissed, 'hooted at like an old tale'. 'The art itself is Nature' (IV.4.97), not because, as Polixenes claimed earlier in the sheepshearing scene, human meddling with the integrity of the original creation is itself part of that creation, but because of the special relationship which the theatre enjoys with the real.

In a scene from *The Two Noble Kinsmen* which was almost certainly the work of Shakespeare, not of his collaborator Fletcher, Theseus tries to persuade his sister Emilia to be present at the combat between her suitors Palamon and Arcite :

> She shall see deeds of honour in their kind
> Which sometimes show well, pencill'd. Nature now
> Shall make and act the story, the belief
> both seal'd with eye and ear. (V.3.12–15)

These lines carry Sidney's (and Aristotle's) paradox, that 'Oft cruel fights well pictur'd forth do please',[13] one crucial step further. Recognising that Emilia shrinks from what she calls the 'dread sights' (V.3.10) of a tournament which must end with the death of one of her lovers, Theseus complicates Sidney's position by establishing Nature itself as an actor/dramatist whose creations, surpassing those of the painter's pencil because incorporating movement and sound, may nonetheless be viewed with that aesthetic detachment which makes tragedy possible as a form. His argument is unsuccessful. Like Perdita with Polixenes, Emilia refuses either to debate the issue or to abandon her previous resolution. Shakespeare makes her do so, at least in part, because – as with the Field of the Cloth of Gold in *Henry VIII* – the tournament in question could not have been enacted in any but the most perfunctory and unrealistic way. Here, close to the end of his career as a dramatist, the Shakespeare who once (however apologetically) allowed 'four or five most vile and ragged foils / Right ill-dispos'd in brawl ridiculous' to represent the glories of Agincourt (*Henry V* Chorus. IV.50) seems to have felt disinclined to stage anything the King's Men could not invest with some significant degree of visual realism. So Emilia, and the theatre audience, remain behind when Theseus and his train depart for the lists, to learn the fortunes of the day only by report.

That the King's Men, working at the Globe and at their new indoor theatre in Blackfriars, were now capable of much that would have seemed almost miraculous to the audiences of the 1580s and even 1590s is obvious from the texts of *Pericles, Cymbeline, The Winter's Tale, The Tempest, Henry VIII* and *The Two Noble Kinsmen*. Dream visions, elaborate pageantry, or the sudden descent on a golden eagle of a god wielding thunder have all become theatrical opportunities, not moments which provoke lamentation for the inadequacies of the stage. The oft-cited influence of the Jacobean court masque upon such things as Queen Katherine's dream in *Henry VIII*, the disappearing banquet in *The Tempest*, Jupiter's appearance in *Cymbeline* and Diana's in *Pericles*, the dance of satyrs in *The Winter's Tale*, or the initial tableau and later temple scenes of *The Two Noble Kinsmen* certainly cannot be discounted. Yet it is also true that, in a theatre with technical resources comparatively recently developed, the plot material to which Shakespeare now seems to have been drawn encouraged him to re-think the function of the eye in determining 'belief'.

About 1596, when he wrote the 'Pyramus and Thisbe' scenes for *A Midsummer Night's Dream*, Shakespeare had mocked the antiquated plays of the early Elizabethan period,[14] and also the literal-mindedness they encouraged in Bottom and his associates, men unacquainted with the theatre and its ways. The mechanicals are parody realists. Faced with the fact that Thisbe and her lover met by moonlight, their initial reaction was to inquire of the almanac whether there would be a moon on the night of their performance at court. There is one, they discover, and yet Peter Quince remains doubtful that, merely by leaving a casement open in the window of the chamber where they are to play, its beams can be introduced effectively into the action. Hence the second-best but (to their minds) necessary expedient of equipping one of their number with lantern, dog and bush and allowing him to introduce himself as 'Moonshine'. The wall which divided the lovers has to be similarly tangible, and so Snout plasters himself over with loam and rough-cast and comes in carrying a stone. What worries them about their lion – Snug the joiner in a beast's skin – is that it is likely to terrify the ladies in the audience unless it explains its true nature : 'Nay, you must name his name, and half his face must be seen through the lion's neck, and he himself must speak through, saying thus, or to the same defect; "Ladies", – or "Fair ladies" ' (III.1.32–5).

Although Time in *The Winter's Tale* speaks verse far better than any at Moonshine's disposal, he is a personification of the same general kind. As Presenter, effortlessly preparing the audience for what it is about to see as well as hear, old Gower in *Pericles* seems more akin to Peter Quince as Prologue – rambling, unstrenuous, confident that only a slight effort is required to participate imaginatively in the stage events towards which he points – than he does to that anxious Chorus which cajoles and nags its way through *Henry V*. The audience of *Pericles* can 'sail seas in cockles, have an wish but for't' (IV.2.2). For the three dumb-shows he introduces, themselves obvious relics of the Elizabethan past, Gower makes no apology: 'Like motes and shadows see them move a while, / Your ears unto your eyes I'll reconcile' (IV.4.21–2). Like the pageantry at the courts of Antiochus and the good king Simonides, these silent tableaux contribute to the new emphasis upon visual realisation evident throughout *Pericles* and the last plays generally : a readjustment of the claims of eye and ear in which the literalism of the mechanicals, no longer just a case of comic misunderstanding, takes unexpectedly sophisticated and ambiguous forms. Even 'Lion' reappears in the form of that notorious bear which chases Antigonus off stage in Act III of *The Winter's Tale*.

Like 'Lion', this bear may have been played by an actor costumed as an animal. But it is also possible that, for at least the first few performances of the play, it was real. There seems to have been a vogue (as yet unexplained) for stage bears in 1610–11, when *The Winter's Tale* appeared. Two were called for in Jonson's masque *Oberon*. More important is the revival, by the King's Men, of the anonymous play *Mucedorus* (c. 1590), 'Amplified with new additions ... before the king's Maiestie at Whitehall on Shrove-Sunday night'. Prominent among those additions is a scene in which the clown, Mouse, falls over a bear. In the earliest text of *Mucedorus* (1598), the stage directions had called for the heroine Amadine and her cowardly lover Segasto to enter 'runing ... being persued with a beare'.[15] The Jacobean bear has a significantly larger part, and it is tempting to believe that this is so because the King's Men, arrestingly, had found it possible to replace the fake bear of the original *Mucedorus* with a live animal, presumably better trained and more biddable than most, which had become temporarily available. This hypothesis at least goes some way towards explaining why such a creaking, old romance should suddenly receive a court performance before James, and also why it became, after that performance, astonishingly popular, running through four quarto editions over the next five years.

Mucedorus was one of the plays attributed to Shakespeare during the Restoration. No one now accepts that attribution. It may be, however, that his hand in the 1610 additions has been too readily dismissed. As resident dramatist for the King's Men, Shakespeare would have been expected to alter and refurbish old plays for revival by the company.[16] C. F. Tucker Brooke, the most recent editor of *Mucedorus*, concedes that the additions 'are of greater poetic merit than the rest of the comedy, and more in Shakespeare's manner',[17] without arguing for his authorship. All that can be said, perhaps, is that there does seem to be some kind of link between the bear in *The Winter's Tale* and the one featured in *Mucedorus* as performed in the same year by the same company, and that a live animal – far more than an actor in a bearskin – would have upset ordinary audience assumptions about stage illusion in a way that seems consonant with the practice of Shakespeare's late plays. After all, even in the twentieth century, animals tend to elicit a confused response in the theatre. In Peter Hall's RSC production of *Richard II* in 1964, a horse, caparisoned for the lists, trotted across the stage just before the combat between Mowbray and Hereford. 'Is that horse *real*?' one member of the Stratford audience was heard to inquire anxiously on the opening night. Real it was, and it had no business appearing in *Richard II* at all, but the uncertainty it provoked is revealing. For a Jacobean audience, conditioned to expect that wild beasts in plays would all be superior versions of the impersonation contrived by Snug the joiner, the entrance of a live bear must, for a moment at least, have been bewildering. Certainly the clown's joke in the bear scene added to *Mucedorus* in 1610 becomes far more piquant if the animal described here, and just about to make its first appearance on stage, was going to turn out to be real : 'A Beare? nay, sure it cannot be a Beare, but some Divell in a Beares Doublet : for a Beare could never have had that agilitie to have frighted me.'[18]

Although it called for a lion, the story of Pyramus and Thisbe at least did not require the mechanicals to cope with the problem of staging a shipwreck. If, like many plays of the period, it had, Bottom and Peter Quince would surely, in line with their approach generally, have insisted upon drenching the actors involved with water, so that they entered after the event demonstrably wet. And here, for once, according to the canons of the professional theatre in the time, their realism would not have been misplaced. On the Elizabethan and Jacobean stage, wet actors seem to have been almost as mandatory a shorthand for disaster at sea as alarms and excursions were for a battle. It did not matter in the least that most plots of this kind were egregiously far-fetched and fantastic. The condition of the newly shipwrecked was 'real'. So, the anonymous *Thracian Wonder* (1599) contains the direction : *'Enter old Antimon bringing in Ariadne shipwrecked, the Clown turning the child up and down, and wringing the Clouts. They pass over the stage. Exeunt. Enter Radagon all wet, looking about for shelter as shipwrecked.'*[19] In *The Four Prentices of London*, Heywood made not the slightest effort to render the catastrophe itself plausible – all four brothers are cast away simultaneously on Goodwin Sands, yet one is washed ashore near Boulogne, the second several hundred miles down the French coast, the third off Ireland, and the fourth in the region of Venice – but they arrive in these different locales in the approved manner : 'all wet', or 'all wet with his sword'.[20] When Jonson composed his parody shipwreck for the collaborative play *Eastward Ho!* (1606), he mocked this theatrical convention. The usurer Security emerges from the Thames 'wet', according to the stage direction, and it is plain from the dialogue ('I see y'ave bene washt in the Thames here') that the other survivors of the wreck were also depicted as soaked to the skin.[21]

In *Twelfth Night*, interestingly enough, Shakespeare had declined to follow this practice. Although the Folio text was almost certainly set from a theatre prompt-copy, there is not the slightest indication in either stage directions or dialogue that Viola – or her twin brother Sebastian – was meant to be shipwrecked into Illyria 'wet'. In *Pericles*, on the other hand, some seven years later, it is stated explicitly that the king, staggering ashore in 'an open place by the seaside' at the beginning of Act II, enters 'wet'. Because of the problems surrounding the text of *Pericles*, there can be no certainty that Shakespeare himself was responsible for that stipulation. He was, on the other hand, undoubtedly the author of the stage direction in the first scene of *The Tempest* : 'Enter Mariners, wet'. And here, what is ordinarily a somewhat naive piece of realism suddenly becomes complex. That frightened crowd of sea-soaked mariners which stumbles in just before Alonso's ship drives on to the rocks was clearly designed to make the calamity as convincing and tangible as possible, for characters and theatre audience alike. Modern directors rarely retain Shakespeare's wet mariners, preferring to bypass what presumably seems to them the crude literalism of the Jacobean stage in favour of sound and lighting effects not available to the King's Men. But an audience which has not actually seen those drenched garments in the opening scene loses some of the carefully planned contrast with the one that follows. For Shakespeare's contemporaries especially, accustomed as they were to regarding 'wet' actors as straightforward indications of disaster at sea, Prospero's calm revelation that the storm was a triumph of art, and that no one has suffered the slightest harm, must have been completely unexpected. It matters too that although the realistic presentation of the seamen seems to foreshadow the condition in which Ferdinand, Alonso and the other members of the court party must arrive on the island, in fact it does not. Prospero describes Ferdinand as 'somewhat stain'd' to Miranda, but it is with grief for his father's loss, not sea-water (I.2.414). Not only are the courtiers' clothes not wet, it seems to Gonzalo that although 'drench'd in the sea [they] hold, not-withstanding, their freshness and glosses, being rather new-dy'd than stain'd with salt water' (II.1.63–5). This, he admits, 'is almost beyond credit' (60),

45

and indeed neither Antonio nor Sebastian will credit it. Here, as with
the related argument as to whether the island is really the green and
balmy place Gonzalo apprehends, or Antonio and Sebastian's barren
fen, the theatre audience, already disorientated by Shakespeare's
cunningly inconsistent use of the dramatic code of 'playing wet',
could not have been quite sure what it was meant to believe.

Characters in the last plays are continually having to revise their
standards of the 'real'. Even those two pragmatists, Antonio and
Sebastian, confronted with the magical banquet in Act III, find their
grasp on the actual badly shaken : 'Now I will believe / That there
are unicorns; that in Arabia / There is one tree, the phoenix' throne,
one phoenix / At this hour reigning there' (III.3.21–4). Old tales,
attested to by the eye as well as the ear, become true. 'If I should tell
my history', Marina confesses to King Pericles, 'it would seem / Like
lies disdain'd in the reporting' (V.1.118–19). Her admission, anticipating Paulina's statement in *The Winter's Tale* that 'were it but
told you', Hermione's return to life 'should be hooted at like an old
tale', governs much in the last plays. Here, Pericles, who has not seen
what we have seen of Marina's life at Tharsus and in the brothel at
Mytilene, nonetheless consents to listen to her story because of what
his eyes, confusedly but urgently, convey : 'falseness cannot come
from thee, for thou lookest / Modest as Justice. [. . .] I will believe
thee, / And make my senses credit thy relation / To points that
seem impossible, for thou lookest / Like one I lov'd indeed'
(V.1.120–5).

In the romances, an odd kind of credit attaches itself to things
which, in narration, would seem blatantly fictional. Shakespeare, in
his a-typical handling of the frame in *Pericles*, comes close to spelling
this out. A Presenter, speaking to the audience directly, Gower and
his tale ought to seem closer and more real than the stage action he
conjures up. As a story-teller, his attitude is intimate and confiding,
and yet the rhyming octosyllabics employed by this ghostly medieval
poet, full of archaisms, self-consciously literary, are clearly much
further removed from ordinary speech than the iambic pentameters
of the inset play. Those portions of Pericles' story which Gower tells
seem, as a result, far more remote, less immediate and believable than
what we see enacted. By turning the frame inside-out in this way,
planes of reality are made to shift and blur in a fashion characteristic
of the late plays.

Not only Old Gower, but the statue scene in *The Winter's Tale*, the
bear, the wet mariners and deceptive spectacles of *The Tempest*,

the unexpected appearances of gods, all seem designed to perplex a theatre audience, at least momentarily, as to the existential status of what it sees. Even *Henry VIII*, generally so much more straightforward in its realism than the romances, has its moment of mystification. The celestial vision which appears to the sleeping Queen Katherine is unequivocal only for her. Her attendants, Patience and Griffiths, although they sit wide awake in the chamber, are aware of nothing, even as Lysimachus, Helicanus, Marina and the others on board the Tyrian galley cannot hear Pericles' music of the spheres. The theatre audience is more privileged. But how is it to interpret what it has been given? Up to this point in Act IV, all the pageantry with which *Henry VIII* is filled – trial scenes and coronation processions, feasts and masquings – has been entirely earthly and rational. The 'six Personages clad in white robes, wearing on their heads garlands of bays, and golden vizards on their faces' look, as they dance ceremoniously about the queen, very like masque figures. But that cannot, in context, explain what they are. When Shakespeare abruptly introduced the god Hymen at the end of *As You Like It* in 1599, he made it possible to recognise in this figure Corin or Amiens in disguise, an option which the theatre has usually taken up. The garlanded dancers of *Henry VIII*, by contrast, like Jupiter in *Cymbeline*, or Diana at the end of *Pericles*, suddenly disrupt the audience's previous understanding of the 'real', leaving it in its own version of Gonzalo's uncertainty; 'Whether this be / Or be not, I'll not swear' (*The Tempest.* V.1.122–3).

Ultimately, of course, the spectators unlike the characters know that what they are watching is a dramatic spectacle, only a play. Outside the theatre lies a reality superior to anything the stage can contrive. Yet, in the last plays above all, Dr Johnson's eminently sensible view of an audience as always rationally conscious of stage artifice, aware that what it sees is a performance, pure and simple, seems to break down. This is partly because of the special dramatic techniques which they employ, the obfuscations and the sleights of hand. It is also, surely, because they appeal so poignantly to our sense of how we should like the world to be, and know that it is not: ultimately gracious and restorative, a place where losses are not final, and even the most terrible mistakes can be redeemed. Like those 'subtleties o'th' isle' of which Prospero speaks in *The Tempest*, the plays themselves will not quite 'let you / Believe things certain' (V.1. 124–5). That paradox is responsible in large part for their special quality, a quality which can be fully experienced only in the theatre –

the place where the statue visibly moves and, in doing so, forgives our illusions.

NOTES

1. Sir Henry Wotton, quoted in Geoffrey Bullough, *Narrative and Dramatic Sources of Shakespeare* 4 (London, 1962) p. 436.
2. All quotations from Shakespeare refer to The Riverside edition, ed. G. Blakemore Evans *et. al.* (Boston, 1974). Dates given for plays are those suggested in Alfred Harbage, rev. S. Schoenbaum, *Annals of English Drama 975–1700* (London, 1964).
3. Sir Philip Sidney, *An Apology For Poetry*, ed. Geoffrey Shepherd (Manchester, 1973) p. 124.
4. See the Prologue to *Sir John Oldcastle*, in *The Shakespeare Apocrypha*, ed. C. F. Tucker Brooke (Oxford, 1908) p. 129.
5. Thomas Heywood, *The Four Prentices of London*, in *The Complete Dramatic Works of Thomas Heywood* 4 (London, 1874) p. 169.
6. Judith H. Anderson, *Biographical Truth: The Representation of Historical Persons in Tudor-Stuart Writing* (New Haven, Conn., 1984) p. 132.
7. J. P. Stern, ' "Reality" in Early Twentieth Century German Literature' in *Philosophy and Literature*. Royal Institute of Philosophy Lecture Series: 16. Supplement to *Philosophy* 1983 (Cambridge, 1984) p. 47.
8. John Marston, 'To Those that seeme judiciall perusers', *The Scourge of Villanie*, in *The Poems of John Marston*, ed. Arnold Davenport (Liverpool, 1961) p. 100.
9. Jonson's use of this word is discussed, usefully, in Vol. 9 of the Oxford edition of Jonson's *Works*, ed. C. H. Herford and Percy and Evelyn Simpson (Oxford 1925–53) p. 436. Jonson's Oxford editors, while admitting the possibility, in some instances, of other connotations, stress the primacy of the scholastic meaning.
10. In his forthcoming edition of Shakespeare's *Sonnets* (Penguin), with 'The Lover's Complaint', John Kerrigan argues persuasively for a Jacobean date for the latter poem. I am indebted to Gary Taylor, co-editor of The New Oxford Shakespeare, for outlining to me his reasons for believing that *All's Well That Ends Well* must now be placed later than *Measure For Measure*.
11. S. S. Hussey, *The Literary Language of Shakespeare* (London, 1982) p. 55.
12. See my earlier essay, 'Leontes and the Spider: Language and Speaker in Shakespeare's Last Plays', in *Shakespeare's Styles: Essays in Honour of Kenneth Muir*, ed. Edwards, Ewbank and Hunter (Cambridge, 1980). The present essay is in many ways a complement to the previous piece.
13. Sidney, 'Astrophil and Stella', 34, in *The Poems of Sir Philip Sidney*, ed. W. A. Ringler (Oxford, 1962) p. 181.
14. In his book, *Something of Great Constancy: The Art of A Midsummer Night's Dream* (London, 1966), David Young provides a full account of the older dramatic material parodied.
15. *Mucedorus*, in *The Shakespeare Apocrypha*, ed. Brooke, pp. 107–8. See Brooke's discussion of the difference between the two texts in his introduction to the volume, pp. xxiii–xxvi.
16. Gerald Eades Bentley, *The Profession of Dramatist in Shakespeare's Time, 1590–1642* (Princeton, N.J., 1971) pp. 235–63.

17. Brooke, *Sir John Oldcastle*, p. xxv.
18. *Ibid.*, I.2.3–6 (p. 107).
19. *The Thracian Wonder*, in *The Dramatic Works of John Webster* 4, ed. William Hazlitt (London, 1857) p. 135 (I.3).
20. *The Four Prentices of London*, pp. 177, 178.
21. Ben Jonson, *Eastward Ho!*, in *Works*, ed. Herford and Simpson, IV.1. 32.

Language and reality in *Bleak House*

GRAHAM HOUGH

I

In the second chapter of his book *On Realism* Stern brushes away a
few metaphysical cobwebs (Is the world real? How do we know
whether it is real or not? – that sort of thing), and then in passing
makes one of the most pregnant observations in the whole work : that
in realistic fiction the epistemological cracks that appear in the
foundations of reality are not explored but transformed into the
psychology of characters. The main thrust of recent critiques of
realism – Balzacian realism is the usual target – has been that it thinks
of language as entirely self-effacing, a mere instrument of reproduction, the quicksilver on the mirror that reflects an outer reality. And
the enlightened view that was to replace this naive positivism was the
exact converse – that language in realistic literature as elsewhere is
not merely reflective, but is itself constitutive of reality. The torrent
of discussion that has surged around this matter could have been
more easily tamed if attention had not been so much concentrated
on Balzac. It may be true that Balzacian *écriture* disingenuously forgets that it is *écriture* and professes to be reality reading itself to us.
But this is not, as French criticism of fifteen or twenty years ago was
wont to suggest, the paradigm of realistic writing. Realism is not
typically, as has been suggested, 'a monologue of re-presentation'. In
the most vigorous realist writing the signifier is as much the object
of concern as the signified, and the numerous devices by which the
signifier is varied and foregrounded – letters, conversations, inter-
polated narratives, interior monologue – all testify to this; and
testify too to what is implied by Stern's observation : that it is via
the psychology of character, revealed in distinctive utterance, that
both the constitutive role of language and its relation to a non-
linguistic reality are guaranteed.

Balzac's authoritative 'objective' pronouncements on the natural
history of women, financiers, haberdashers or young men in a hurry

have not many parallels in the English novel. The status of its reality is not a problem for the English novel, for its reality is always mediated as the experience of an individual : the world as seen by Emma Woodhouse, the world as seen by Paul Morel; and in the most accomplished examples, in the very language and ordonnance of the personage concerned. Realistic fiction does not typically claim, as its detractors suppose, to be the voice of history or society or the world-soul. It speaks in the language of fallible human beings who have lived too close to the events they describe for the completeness of an inventory or the precision of a diagram. 'Le réalisme, ce ne peut donc être la copie des choses, mais la connaissance du langage', Roland Barthes has remarked. This has a kind of truth, but it rests on a false antithesis; *connaissance du langage* is the avenue to *connaissance des choses*.

2

I wish to examine these modulations of discourse in the writing of Dickens, taking *Bleak House* as the exemplary text. Our recollection of the novel from a distance, as with all Dickens's novels, is not at first of its linguistic quality; it is of 'characters' and scenes. That is to say we tend to pass through the language to the larger structures that the language goes to compose, and to their complex interweaving. But a second thought immediately corrects this. *Bleak House* is a complicated contrivance; but this is not only by reason of the number and variety of the characters, the diversity of social range, the elaborate intrigue; there is also the diversity of rhetoric : highly-wrought evocative descriptions, flashes of indignation, sustained heavy irony, rational evaluative discourse, and in addition, every species of mania, obsession, eccentricity, inarticulacy, in the speech of the supporting characters. A novel by Jane Austen is a lucid, obviously functional piece of apparatus; every part has a purpose and the purpose can be clearly seen. *Bleak House* recalls rather some antiquated factory, from designs by Piranesi. One enters a large sombre building; a massive engine is working, with a good deal of clanking and noise, heavy pistons and a huge fly-wheel turning. From an unseen axle belts run off to drive other wheels, some of them also unseen on the floor above. Valves open and shut; every now and again there is a puff of steam, obscuring the view. Suddenly one becomes aware of another and smaller piece of apparatus, dimly lit up in the distance, moving at a different speed and to quite a different rhythm. Is it connected with the first, a governor or regulator, perhaps? Or is it entirely independent? Before any solution can be reached, a trap-door opens above, and a large object whose shape cannot be properly discerned, is lowered heavily to the ground. A reading of Dickens leads one into this kind of metaphorical excess. As mere analysts however we have to ask by what linguistic means this elaborate structure is brought about.

The most obvious formal peculiarity of the book is that the narrative falls into two parts, one told by an anonymous narrator, with rich and varied dialogue; the other told in the first person by one of the internal characters (Esther Summerson), also with rich and varied dialogue. They divide the book evenly between them, in alternate sections, sometimes of one chapter, more usually of two to four chapters. Esther appears only in her own narrative. Some of the other characters appear only in her narrative – Ada, Richard, and with one insignificant exception, Mr Jarndyce. Some of the characters appear only in the anonymous narrative. (I use this label as it cannot possibly be called 'objective' or 'impersonal'.) Some of the characters appear in both narratives. This is a complicated structural device to start with, and we naturally ask what its purpose is. We should expect the anonymous narrative to be historical, objective, distanced, and the first-person narrative of Esther Summerson to be subjective, immediate, at close range. But a mere inspection of the tense-system employed shows that this is not so. The anonymous narrative is done throughout in the present tense :

He goes to his crossing, and begins to lay it out for the day. The town awakes; the great teetotum is set up for its daily spin and whirl; all that unaccountable reading and writing, which has been suspended for a few hours, recommences. Jo, and the other lower animals, get on in the unintelligible mess as they can. It is market-day.

Esther Summerson's narrative is told normally, in the past tense. It is retrospective. This dichotomy runs through the whole length of the book. To decide whether it is a mere mannerism or whether it is of greater significance we shall have to examine the two parts more closely.

3

The anonymous narrative makes a sustained use of the present tense; apart from that it is hard to make a general statement about it, for all is heterogeneity and variety. An immediately noticeable feature is the prominence of highly wrought descriptive passages. It is immediately noticeable because the longest and most celebrated of all is the description of the fog with which the book opens : but there are many others. The fog at the beginning is followed as early as Chapter II by the description of the waters in Lincolnshire. Later instances are the legal quarter in the long vacation (Chapter XIX), Lincoln's Inn at night (Chapter XXXII); and there are many shorter passages. Some of these are deeply emotional and rhetorical – 'emotional' meaning deeply felt, 'rhetorical' meaning that every endeavour is made to enforce this feeling on the reader, to attack his nerves and sensibilities, openly and directly. It is in such passages that we hear the undisguised authorial voice. We must return to a fuller account of the descriptive technique in a moment.

There is a good deal of rather heavy-handed irony, exercised particularly on the Dedlock world. The free indirect style is employed in such passages, in an aggressive comic-satiric manner, effectual but unsubtle. A good example is the rendering of Lord Boodle's conversation with Sir Leicester Dedlock in Chapter XII :

He perceives with astonishment, that supposing the present Government to be overthrown, the limited choice of the Crown, in the formation of a new Ministry, would lie between Lord Coodle and Sir Thomas Doodle – supposing it to be impossible for the Duke of Foodle to act with Goodle, which may be assumed to be the case in consequence of the breach arising out of that affair with Hoodle. Then, giving the Home Department and the Leadership of the House of Commons to Joodle, the Exchequer to Koodle, the Colonies to Loodle, and the Foreign Office to Moodle, what are you to do with Noodle? You can't offer him the Presidency of the Council; that is reserved for Poodle. You can't put him in the Woods and Forests; that is hardly good enough for Quoodle. What follows? That the country is shipwrecked, lost, gone to pieces (as is made manifest to the Patriotism of Sir Leicester Dedlock), because you can't provide for Noodle !

This manner is not infrequent, but it is peripheral. The free indirect style does not occupy the central and functional place in Dickens that it does in Flaubert or Jane Austen.

In between these extended scenes there is a good deal of rapid narration, in which the characters are bustled briskly around; but even here the narrative tends to proliferate into descriptive glimpses and fragments of dialogue. The narrator can hardly move one of his characters from one place to another without making every detail of the transition visibly and audibly present, however trivial the occasion :

Smallweed dismisses his friends with a cool nod, and remains behind to take a little admiring notice of Polly, as opportunity may serve, and to read the daily papers: which are so very large in proportion to himself, shorn of his hat, that when he holds up the *Times* to run his eye over the columns, he seems to have retired for the night, and to have disappeared under the bedclothes.

Mr Guppy and Mr Jobling repair to the rag-and-bottle shop, where they find Krook still sleeping like one o'clock; that is to say, breathing stertorously with his chin upon his breast, and quite insensible to any external sounds, or even to gentle shaking. On the table beside him, among the usual lumber, stand an empty gin-bottle and a glass. The unwholesome air is so stained with this liquor, that even the green eyes of the cat upon her shelf, as they open and shut and glimmer on the visitors, look drunk. (Chapter XX)

The only necessary function of this fragment of narrative is to get Guppy and Jobling from an eating-house to Krook's shop; but it is as if the merely contingent, the world – accidental, ugly and grotesque – so forces itself upon the narrator's consciousness that it must find expression in description and metaphor, refuses to be passed by. A more austere style of narrative would reject these solicitations : but it is essential to Dickens's vision that all must be accepted – accepted with an enormous appreciation. Smallweed is a quite unimportant and wholly unsympathetic character; but the picture of him, absurdly enveloped in the newspaper, is done with a kind of joy. The evaluative faculty is almost completely in abeyance; the world is there, in all its accidental detail, and whatever its character, better there than not.

This sense of the immediate presence of things finds its rankest and most abundant flowering in the dialogue. Its range is entirely unrestricted, both socially and rhetorically. It includes class and professional dialects, like those of Sir Leicester Dedlock and Mr Tulkinghorn. It includes every variety of personal eccentricity and mania, such as the speech of Miss Flyte and Mr Chadband. It ranges from the solid dignity of Mrs Rouncewell to the barely articulate mutterings of poor Jo. The narrative delights in bringing together an incongruous selection of persons in a single scene, as in Chapter XXVII, where Tulkinghorn, old Smallweed and Trooper George are brought into confrontation, with a grotesque collision between their several modes of utterance. The use of fine variations within an essentially common style is obviously impossible for Dickens. He employs the widest possible range of tone-values, and the sharpest possible contrasts of light-and-shade and texture. But he is far from the classic method of opposition between the high and the low style – as in Shakespeare, for instance, where the serious characters are confined to one rhetorical mode, the comic characters to another. Nor is his procedure like that of Scott, who employs roughly the Shakespearean social dichotomy, with the difference that the 'low' characters may be the vehicle of the most serious values. Dickens's dialogue overturns these time-hallowed distributions and replaces them by an apparently chaotic mixture of styles. But the result is not chaos; it is an ultimately coherent fictional world, though composed of innumerable violently asserted quiddities.

To come back now to the descriptive passages and their relation to the rest of the narrative. It is here that the character of the anonymous narrator is most fully displayed. I have slipped into calling him simply Dickens, excusably, for he is very close to the historical personality of Dickens himself; but erroneously, for Dickens is also the creator of Esther Summerson's quite different narrative, the creator of other fictions, a participator in other activities that have nothing to do with fiction at all. The anonymous narrative of *Bleak House* has a distinct quality of its own, and to that extent its narrator is a fictional personality, created to be the bearer of that quality. Let us call him CD, in recognition both of his nearness to the historical Dickens, and of his distinctness.

The descriptive passages in which he speaks most clearly are very highly worked, and quite self-consciously so. It is not a Flaubertian case of immersion in the imagined situation until it delivers itself of the uniquely appropriate words. The descriptions in *Bleak House* are spoken out to an audience, and a variety of emphatic rhetorical devices is employed to control the audience's response. In the opening pages on the fog we are indeed vividly aware of London, of the river, of the surrounding countryside, and of a varied, crowded population. The impressionist technique of verbless sentences, juxtaposed glimpses, the implacable repetition of the word 'fog' suggests at first simply a powerful piece of scene-painting. By the fourth paragraph, however, we become aware that this is a purposeful, tendentious piece of discourse. We are being led somewhere, and for a reason; and the effect is to be composed and directed, not diffused.

The raw afternoon is rawest, and the dense fog is densest, and the muddy streets are muddiest, near that leaden-headed old obstruction, appropriate ornament for the threshold of a leaden-headed old corporation: Temple Bar.

The signs are unmistakable; the syntax changes from the static present participles, the sentences without principal verbs, to a more active construction; we are approaching a climax, the ultimate concentration of the fog. In 'leaden-headed old obstruction [. . .] leaden-headed old corporation' we are momentarily taken away from the scene to the narrator, who suddenly shows his hand, reveals his temperament and his attitude in a flash of testy imagery. The strong rhythmical manipulation, the balance and reiteration, found in this paragraph are taken up again in the next two :

Never can there come fog too thick, never can there come mud and mire too deep, to assort with the groping and floundering condition which this High Court of Chancery, most pestilent of hoary sinners, holds, this day, in the sight of heaven and earth.

On such an afternoon, if ever, the Lord High Chancellor ought to be sitting here – as here he is. [. . .] On such an afternoon, some score of members of the High Court of Chancery bar ought to be – as here they are. [. . .] On such an afternoon, the various solicitors in the cause, some two or three of whom have inherited it from their fathers, who made a fortune by it, ought to be – as are they not? [. . .]

What begins as evocation of a milieu, in itself singularly vivid and complete, soon turns out to have an ulterior motive, to be founded on the pathetic fallacy. This is regularly so. In the next chapter the passage beginning 'The waters are out in Lincolnshire' is both minutely observed and delicately beautiful – a prose-poem in its own right.

The weather, for many a day and night, has been so wet that the trees seem wet through, and the soft loppings and prunings of the woodman's axe can make no crash or crackle as they fall. The deer, looking soaked, leave quagmires, where they pass. The shot of a rifle loses its sharpness in the moist air, and its smoke moves in a tardy little cloud towards the green rise, coppice-topped, that makes a background for the falling rain.

But it stands there to be a symbolic reinforcement of the dank dreariness of Lady Dedlock's life.

Sometimes a description is arranged and hung up as a piece of scenery – like the tranquil moonlight scene towards the end of XLVIII, which is simply the contrasting back-drop to a pistol-shot. But more usually the scenes are settings for the characters and intimately bound up with them. We feel that the characters move around with their appropriate settings, which constitute an aura that is almost a part of them. I was betrayed a moment ago into using the word 'symbolic' which I had hoped to avoid because 'symbolism' commonly suggests a picking of objective correlatives out of the air, regardless of their status in reality. This does not happen in Dickens. However 'symbolically' appropriate the streets, rooms and landscapes may be, their actual existence, their external reference is always firmly assured. There really were such fogs in London; Tom-all-alone's and Lincoln's Inn really were as they are described. The much besymbolised dust-heaps of *Our Mutual Friend* were actual facts of the London sanitary system. One of the roots of Dickens's popular art is that it takes us back to an extremely primitive way of seeing the world – a way that still authentically survives beneath the surface of a more utilitarian vision : it is as though Dickens moves in an animist universe in which outer objects are endowed with a mysterious life, a life that is partly intrinsic to them, partly the creation of layers of human experience. This is no guarantee against bad writing : Dickens often offends against conventional taste by an uncontrolled exuberance; he sometimes offends really by allowing local effects to expand grossly beyond their contribution to the whole. But writing of his kind can never be merely inert. We are always plunged in the lived to-and-fro between consciousness and the world. The intrusion of *faits divers* and unassimilated information that we often encounter in Balzac is never found in Dickens.

What at first look like descriptive set-pieces turn out to be not merely that. The landscape becomes populated, the scene breaks up into dialogue and modulates into a human situation. This may not involve the central characters, but rather the innumerable subsidiary figures who flit in and out of the byways of CD's London. Chapter XXXII begins with a night scene in Lincoln's Inn. Then Mrs Piper and Mrs Perkins appear, Krook is talked about. Then Weevle enters, and finally Mr Snagsby. Whatever the state of affairs it is always soaked in affectivity and emotion.

It is a close night, though the damp cold air is searching too; and there is a laggard mist a little way up in the air. It is a fine steaming night to turn the slaughter houses, the unwholesome trades, the sewage, bad water, and burial grounds to account, and give the Registrar of Deaths some extra business. It may be something in the air – there is plenty in it – or it may be something in himself, that is in fault; but Mr Weevle, otherwise Joblin, is very ill at ease. He comes and goes, between his own room and the open street door, twenty times an hour. He has been doing so ever since it fell dark. Since the Chancellor shut up his shop, which he did very early to-night, Mr Weevle has been up and down, and down and up (with a cheap tight velvet skull-cap on his head, making his whiskers look out of all proportion), oftener than before.

It is no phenomenon that Mr Snagsby should be ill at ease too: for he always is so, more or less, under the oppressive influence of the secret that is upon him.

Partly this affectivity is that of the characters, however individually insignificant they may be. It is surprising, for example, how much of the inner processes of Mr Snagsby and Mr Guppy we are allowed to share. But more than that it is the feeling and the experience of the narrator, or the author, that impregnates the situations. We have considered the narrator's voice as totally enclosed within the fictional structure, directed solely to expounding and advancing the narrative, and the author's voice as having some kind of extra-curricular intention, speaking directly to the reader, above the heads of the characters and outside the narrative. In Dickens they are often not to be distinguished. The situations are flooded with pathos, indignation, irony, humour, facetiousness; and these come from CD, a composite author-narrator who is partly immersed in his fictional task, partly obsessed with feelings and intentions that exist outside it.

French realism at its most vigorous in Balzac, even before it turned to the Flaubertian ideal of dispassionate objectivity, always embraces some commitment to the mere facts of the case, to letting them speak for themselves. Balzac's intruded commentaries are additional items of information, intended to instruct us more fully about the way the world works. CD, Dickens, as narrator, exists in indissoluble union with the objects of his narration :

Into a beastly scrap of ground which a Turk would reject as a savage abomination, and a Caffre would shudder at, they bring our dear brother here departed, to receive Christian burial.

With houses looking on, on every side, save where a reeking little tunnel of a court gives access to the iron gate – with every villainy of life in action close on death, and every poisonous element of death close on life – here, they lower our dear brother down a foot or two: here, sow him in corruption, to be raised in corruption; an avenging ghost at many a sick bedside: a shameful testimony to future ages, how civilisation and barbarism walked this boastful island together.

(Chapter XI)

Here the whole thing has been lived through : we cannot separate the facts from the narrator's experience of them. An attempt to wish this quality away in the interests of objectivity or aesthetic discretion would be impossible; it is a quintessential character of the writing.

This narrator-author has obviously read Carlyle and been deeply influenced by his social-historical sensibility; he hates shams, and sees them in the same places as Carlyle did. The picture of the legal world and the Dedlock world in *Bleak House* would not be as it is if it were not for the naked House of Lords and the naked court of justice in *Sartor Resartus*. The sense of a teeming, uncontrolled collective life surrounding the individual life would not be as it is without *The French Revolution*. This narrator-author is filled with passionate indignations; he feels profoundly for the dispossessed and the rejected but at the same time he delights in the mere existence of much that exasperates him; he delights in his own virtuosity, which displays itself in rhetoric, romantic irony and the grotesque. We feel no sense of an objective or social norm against which the characters are measured, but rather a huge personal, more than personal, almost demonic presence, emotional, unstable, passionately engaged, urging the story on, forcing certain aspects of it upon our attention. The language attacks our feelings directly, not merely through the objects represented; arresting images, repetitions, strongly marked rhythms play directly on the nerves. And this ceaseless manipulation of the reader's attention only stops when the characters themselves, in dialogue, take over. Then we find that this restless emotional narrator has an enormous capacity for empathy, can submerge himself completely in the Other, in personages entirely outside his own subjective experience.

4

This would be enough for the making of an ordinary novel, but of course it is only half of *Bleak House* – less than half, for I have hardly yet spoken of the central characters and the central situation. The rest is in Esther Summerson's narrative. Attentively considered, this is a very peculiar device. Esther is the central character; yet she is absent from half the book, for she never appears in the anonymous narrative. This means, what is more, that we have only her authority for her own actions, adventures and sentiments. Indeed we have only her authority for the whole central group of characters – Ada, Richard, and Mr Jarndyce. So far as *Bleak House* is a story of private life, involving the destinies and relations of a small group of persons in whom we are to take a special interest, it is all in her hands. And she is not matched in the rest of the novel with an equal collaborator, with another internal character presenting another point of view, but with an all-seeing anonymous narrator who subsists on a different imaginative level. There are therefore deep intrinsic differences between the two narratives, apart from those introduced by the idiosyncrasies of Esther's voice. The difference is clearly marked at the beginning of her tale :

I have a great deal of difficulty in beginning to write my portion of these pages, for I know I am not clever. I always knew that. I can remember, when I was a very little girl indeed, I used to say to my doll, when we were alone together, 'Now, Dolly, I am not clever, you know very well, and you must be patient with me, like a dear!'

This modest simper was doubtless more attractive to readers of Dickens' day than to those of ours; particularly as it is followed a few lines down by phrases which suggest that Esther is pretty well satisfied with her mental powers after all. But we must take courage to brush these misgivings aside, and consider the purpose of such an opening. It is of course a clear indication that we are dealing with a limited consciousness. CD is a titanic figure, with an immense sweep of awareness; Esther is a gentle one, moving in a restricted sphere. CD is masculine in his approach; his rhetoric is dominant and commanding. Esther's femininity is emphasised – a modern reader would say to excess; but the mid-nineteenth century liked these distinctions to be unambiguous. It is indicated then at the opening that some of the things to be found in other parts of the book will not be found here.

What are the things that are not found? First the highly wrought descriptive passages, with their marked departure from the rhythms of common speech and their purposeful manipulation of the reader's response. 'On such an afternoon, if ever, the Lord High Chancellor ought to be sitting here – as here he is – with a foggy glory round his head. [. . .] On such an afternoon, some score of members of the High Court of Chancery bar ought to be sitting – as here they are – mistily engaged in one of the ten thousand stages of an endless cause [. . .]' When Esther says she is not clever she probably means that she could not write sentences like that. Indeed she cannot, and she never tries. She hardly knows what the Lord High Chancellor is, the High Court of Chancery bar is not a concept for her; she merely sees dried-up gentlemen in wigs, whose motives she vaguely suspects. CD's generalising grasp of social institutions is entirely beyond her. She is a faithful witness to things whose essence she does not even offer to understand. Similarly CD's fiery social indignation is out of her range. She can be touched by particular misfortunes, she can register the mistakes and indirections that come before her eyes. But the law as an idea, cupidity and chicanery as pervasive social motives, crime and poverty as part of the fabric of the world, do not enter her consciousness.

Her own idiolect – the feminine vocabulary, with many tender expressions of feeling (Ada is constantly referred to as 'my darling', Mr Jarndyce as 'my dear, kind guardian') – is regularly sustained. There is much domestic self-approval – 'my tidy housekeeperish ways'. Occasionally she is intruded upon by the subjectivity of the narrator – in speaking of herself, in explaining her own intentions. Occasionally she expresses rather suspiciously well-formed opinions on general matters, as she does on public-school education in Chapter XIII. But these always spring from specific encounters, specific situations. She never generalises except from her own experience; but evidently she is extremely aware of herself and of her own point of view. Her language has nothing in common with that of the limited narrators in modern fiction – in *The Member of the Wedding* or *The Catcher in the Rye*, for example – and quite rightly, for its purpose and direction are entirely different.

When Esther comes to present a scene, however, it is fully dramatised. She uses dialogue in the same way as the anonymous narrator, with the same bizarre virtuosity. Mr Boythorn and Mrs Jellyby, who are Esther's creations, are as eccentrically vivid as any of CD's. The only observable difference, as far as dialogue is concerned, is even to Esther's advantage. In scenes where shades of character are to be developed through conversation, or incomprehensions registered, Esther's handling is apt to be more delicate than CD's, for there is a less obtrusive commentary, and its imagery is less exuberant. The development of Richard's character, or its failure to develop, is rendered almost entirely through his own speech. Esther regards him far too tenderly to parody his irresponsible utterances; her comments on them are restrained by affection; and the result is a quieter and sadder picture of degeneration than we should have had in the anonymous narrative. It is a remarkable instance of Dickens' capacity for empathy that when he tells a story through the voice of another character he almost acquires a different set of narrative skills.

The fullness with which the scenes are dramatised would alone forbid us to suppose that Esther is doing anything like writing a diary. And there are of course simpler evidences of this. She uses the past tense, the tense of completed action. There are many indications that she knows the end of the story while she is telling us the beginning or the middle; and it is eventually made clear that her narrative was written seven years after the events it describes. In fact Esther is writing an autobiographical novel, and in doing so she possesses many of the novelistic skills of her creator, of Dickens in his own person.

There is no conflict between the two narratives. They describe the same world, and so far as the observations and judgments overlap they are in consonance with each other. We are not disposed to inquire into Esther's status as a narrator or to question her reliability. Dickens is obviously behind her; the whole weight of the book is behind her. Anyone who does not believe that Esther Summerson is good and that it is better to be good than wicked is not capable of reading Dickens at all. It is worth noting how her authority and reliability are internally guaranteed. It is not by conformity to a norm established outside her own discourse. She is alone in her own narrative; and the anonymous narrative is so varied, so blown by contrary winds, and so much occupied with the dark underside of the *Bleak House* universe that it cannot provide the standard by which she is measured. She obviously approves of herself, and for this un-neurotic trait she is disliked by some modern readers. She is equally obviously approved by the other characters; they all love and trust her. It is not simply that we have her word for it; the whole course of events makes it clear that they do so. And they are right to regard her as they do, for her affections and her judgments are borne out by the event. In the novel we are not, as we often are in poetry, left alone with the language : what the language says is either confirmed or disproved by the events to which the language points – which are also the creation of language, but in another dimension. Yet the language as it presents itself to us immediately is always central; and Esther Summerson's is consistently admirable. The observation is close, the judgment is shrewd; none the less just and rational for being tempered with kindness and affection. On Richard and Mr Skimpole, for example :

I began seriously to think that Richard could scarcely have found a worse friend than this. It made me uneasy that at such a time, when he most required some right principle and purpose, he should have this captivating looseness and putting-off of everything, this airy dispensing with all principle and purpose, at his elbow. I thought I could understand how such a nature as my guardian's, experienced in the world, and forced to contemplate the miserable evasions and contentions of the family misfortunes, found an immense relief in Mr Skimpole's avowal of his weaknesses and display of guileless candour; but I could not satisfy myself that it was as guileless as it seemed; or that it did not serve Mr Skimpole's idle turn as well as any other part, and with less trouble. (Chapter XXXVII)

In Esther's presence even the obsessed and the misguided are liable to talk with some degree of rationality and self-awareness, as Richard does when she goes to visit him at Deal. Her language is not only the

language of the affections; it works everywhere for clarity and understanding. The self-knowledge which Esther displays is accompanied
by a knowledge of others, and of how far that knowledge can be of
any avail :

I will not repeat what I said to Richard. I know it was tiresome and
nobody is to suppose for a moment that it was at all wise. It only came
from my heart. He heard it patiently and feelingly; but I saw that on
the two subjects he had reserved, it was at present hopeless to make any
representation to him. I saw too, and had experienced in this very
interview, the sense of my guardian's remark that it was even more
mischievous to use persuasion with him than to leave him as he was.

(Chapter LXV)

The undisguised affectivity of Esther's language does not exclude
judgment, and it is not a mere authorial self-indulgence. It has a
significance beyond the meaning of Esther's words in a given context:
it signifies that her judgments have been lived through, that they
come from her experience, not from a canon of behaviour imposed
from outside. 'I saw too, and had experienced in this very interview,
the sense of my guardian's remark [. . .]' The language here is not
relying simply on the assumed authority of Esther's good heart. It
appeals to something seen, to something experienced in an encounter
just recorded, and to the judgment of another person whose presence
has already been abundantly established. It is by such means that
Esther's authority in the novel is assured. It is often felt that in such
characters as Esther Dickens is drawing on a fund of ready-made
sympathy. This may be, and more so perhaps in other places than
here; but it is important to observe that he has provided plenty of
backing for it within the substance of the novel itself.

5

We are now in a position to inquire more closely into the relation
between the two narratives. Is it that the norm, the standard of value
to which all must be referred, resides in Esther's voice? Certainly her
story is never criticised, her values are never undermined or seen to be
deficient. Yet, as we have shown, there are things in the novel that
are outside her range. The author is entirely behind her, but he does
not endow her with all his perceptions and powers. Even within her
own narrative she has occasional competitors. At the Jellybys', Esther
is resolutely thinking the best of everyone and everything as usual,
but is abruptly cut short by a blast of realism from Caddy. And she

can learn the truth from ridiculous persons. Mrs Bayham Badger, after some sublime absurdities about her opportunities for observing youth at the scientific conversaziones of the late Professor Dingle, suddenly comes up with some perfectly lucid and reliable information about Richard's application, or want of application, to his medical studies; which Esther agrees to accept. With a wholly normative character, one who is the complete spokesman for the totality of the work, this never happens. No one puts Mr Knightley to rights, or tells him anything he did not know.

A juster view of Esther's narrative is that it is there to *confirm*, to confirm by experience, the values implicit in the total structure. The all-knowing, opinionating, fulminating report of the anonymous narrator is attested by Esther's quieter tones. CD knows more, sees more, feels more than Esther Summerson; but it is immensely important that his vision should be supported by hers. Important for two reasons : first that a narrator so tendentious, so profuse, so passionately involved with his story, so little capable of distance and objectivity, stands in need of validation from one of the internal characters. This is a weak point in some of Dickens's fictions : the characters chosen for this role are mere tokens – symbolic children or anima figures without sufficient identity of their own to support the part they are supposed to play. Esther with her busy domesticity, her gentle but firm good judgment and her strong affections, has a very definite identity and a fully developed style of discourse in which to express it. She is not a Little Nell or a Florence Dombey, an object to which the reader's emotions can be attached – emotions which could be refused. She is a living and experiencing subject, and even a reader who declines to feel for her as the author does cannot refuse her experience. The two narratives become genuinely complementary, and the whole structure thereby becomes very strong.

The confirmatory role of Esther's narrative is brought out by the tense-system. Things can only be confirmed *a posteriori*, and Esther's narrative is accordingly in the past tense. CD's historic present immerses us in the immediate scene and the narrator's spontaneous reaction to it. He is intensely volatile; he hurries us from the grave to the comic, from the sinister to the pathetic, from the dignified to the grotesque, in a few pages; and the involvement in each mood is total. Esther's retrospective narrative, with the continuity of a more limited vision, and the sense of completion given by its placing in the past, comes as it were to say, Yes, so it was; and so it still appears now that the whole story is over.

The second reason that Esther's confirmatory role is important lies deeper; it is nearer to the heart of the novel. Esther is not placed in a superior position to the anonymous narrator; she is perceptive, she is loving, she is good; but she is not a heroic or extraordinary character. It is essential that she should not be; the ultimate rationale of her part in the dual structure of the book is to show that a simple and single-minded girl, with little experience and no theoretical knowledge, with nothing but deep affections, a good heart and sound native perceptions, can see *almost* all the truth about a complicated world. The appeal is not to experience, the conventional wisdom, or the authority of the social order; it is to the wisdom of the heart. But in saying this it is necessary to stress 'wisdom' as much as 'heart'. The modern American novels that present a limited consciousness in a cruel and bewildering environment nearly always show their protagonists in a state of hopeless confusion, a confusion that is partly linguistic. They do not understand their experience because they have no language capable of realising it. This probably corresponds to a real debasement of communication in American life; but it is very far from Dickens's way of seeing things. The whole drive of his novels is to suggest that a very slender worldly equipment, a quite rudimentary conceptual apparatus, can, if directed by natural feeling, be a sufficient guide through the difficult and horrifying labyrinth of the world. In the case of hopeless deprivation such as Jo's even the elementary conditions are lacking; and Dickens shows this to be so, without compromise. Apart from the physical misery of his condition it is Jo's pathetic ignorance that is always emphasised. 'I don't know nothink' is his perpetual refrain.

It must be a strange state to be like Jo! To shuffle through the streets, unfamiliar with the shapes, and in utter darkness as to the meaning, of those mysterious symbols, so abundant over the shops, and at the corners of streets, and on the doors, and in the windows! To see people read, and to see people write, and to see the postmen deliver letters, and not to have the least idea of all that language – to be, to every scrap of it, stone blind and dumb!   (Chapter XVI)

But above that condition Dickens takes the essentially hopeful view that men's minds are in some sense adequate to their experience; and this is realised in the extreme articulacy of his characters. Eccentric, ill-educated, formally chaotic, comically eclectic as the speech of the Flites, Guppys, Caddy Jellybys, *et al.* may be, it is living, energetic and capable of effecting its purpose. Whatever tragedies we may find in Dickens they are not tragedies of non-communication. And Esther, in her far more favourable situation, is not inadequately equipped to comprehend and communicate her experience. Esther's strength comes from love; but it would be quite wrong to suppose that love for Dickens means a warm feeling about the heart, vague and undifferentiated. His loving characters are also capable of discernment and understanding; and we are not asked to take this on trust, for their discernment and understanding is expressed in their language.

It would not have done, however, to let Esther Summerson stand alone. This would have been to assert that Esther's simplicity and goodness was adequate to understand *everything* in the world around her. As it is, Dickens goes perhaps dangerously near to giving Esther more weight than she can carry. To credit her with the insight needed to sustain the whole vision of the novel would have been a really damaging sentimentalism – the false assertion that the Esther Summersons of this world can comprehend everything in a disordered and complicated society. *Bleak House* does not commit itself to this wholesale assertion; and the two narratives, with their partial correspondence and their partial divergence, are the true structural representation of Dickens's vision.

6

Bleak House does not show us, as Jane Austen's novels do, a young girl growing up to accept the best judgment of the best society of her time : it shows us a young girl, by native goodness and uncorrupted natural judgment, enabled to criticise and supply a corrective for a society that she only incompletely understands. The conventions and mannerisms attending this presentation are those of Dickens's age and class, which we may accept or not as we like. But the possibility of this situation is something that we must accept if we are to read Dickens at all. In showing us this, *Bleak House*, like all Dickens's fiction, commits itself to another position – the denial of social determinism. Consider Esther's ancestry, birth and upbringing. She is the illegitimate child of a mother who later sold herself into a loveless marriage. She is taken away from her mother at birth and brought up, entirely lovelessly, by an aunt who only once speaks to her of her origins, and then with unmitigated harshness. In terms of a psychological text-book this would be a complete recipe for the production of a psychopath. On any social-determinist philosophy Esther could never have become what she becomes. She *chooses* herself as she is, as much as any Sartrean hero. The conventions are those of bourgeois romance and melodrama, but the underlying assertion is the assertion of human freedom. This assertion would not be at all powerful if within the same fiction were not included the squalid complexities of the social order – the crime, the physical misery, the ignorance, the power of the system. But all this is equally present. And then Dickens shows, here as in other novels, something physically and materially weak, even morally rather slender and fragile (for those who win out in his novels are not cast in the heroic mould) that is nevertheless able to stand as a criticism of all this hectoring, blundering confusion, and in some degree, locally and partially, to change it. We may or may not want to hear this said, but it is undoubtedly what Dickens is saying.

Quite remarkably 'unrealistic', in one frequent usage of the term. For by a common deflection of its significance 'realism' is often called upon to imply an unresisting subordination of the individual to collective forces. But this is a quasi-political vulgarisation. The great realist literature always depends on a historical situation; but it depends equally on a relative freedom of the individual within that situation. And the reading of such literature, in any sense of reading that is worth consideration, depends on our spontaneous capacity for feeling our way into other lives – other lives with their own degree of autonomy and individual expression. Many methods and devices can lead the reader to this end, but the power to compass a wide range of the variety and idiosyncrasy of human utterance, to show the play of light on this variously textured surface, is among the most enduring.

This is something different from the self-conscious attentiveness to language implicitly demanded by the tenor of modern criticism. Dickens has a great range and variety of linguistic equipment, but it is not displayed for our notice. His typical mode is not the deliberation of *écriture* but the spontaneous creativeness of speech – his own or that of his characters. Vivid and arresting as the language is, it is only temporarily arresting. We see through the language to the life behind it, and it is only by a wilful mutilation of response that the *connaissance du langage* can be the terminus of the reader's journey. We see indeed through the medium of language, but what we see is not language – it is all that to which language bears witness. That is the reason why it is the great realistic literature that in our day at least has been the most successful in transcending linguistic boundaries, passing beyond the prerogative of scholars and the dogmatisms of learning, and becoming truly a common heritage.

The problem of nineteenth-century German realism

MARTIN SWALES

In an essay devoted to the problematic character of nineteenth-century German realism, Wolfgang Preisendanz writes the following :

Legt man [. . .] den Beitrag zur Ortsbestimmung ihrer Gegenwart als Massstab, an, so erscheint der [. . .] of zu hörende Vorwurf ziemlich berechtigt, die Behauptung der 'Reichsunmittelbarkeit der Poesie' [. . .] habe den Rückzug oder wenigstens den Kontaktverlust mit den unmittelbar drängenden, brennenden Problemen und Realitäten des politisch-sozialen Lebens mit sich gebracht, habe wieder einmal die Einbürgerung des deutschen Dichters verhindert. Will man ein anderes, positives Verhältnis zu diesen Erzählern gewinnen, so muss man wohl oder übel einen anderen Massstab wählen.[1]

Preisendanz here expresses the crucial critical malaise in respect of German prose literature : it is a literature, so we are told, that is so much in love with 'poetry' as the redeemer of mere 'prosaic' facticity that it offers not an engagement with the workaday world but rather its aesthetic transcendence. The phrase Preisendanz quotes about the autonomy of poetry ('Reichsunmittelbarkeit der Poesie') is Gottfried Keller's. And Preisendanz sees Keller as the greatest and most persuasive advocate of that dictum 'man shall not live by prose alone', to which the finest creative talents of German realism would all have subscribed. Preisendanz' own work on Keller leaves us in no doubt that he views him as a prose writer of the very first rank. Yet, in the passage cited above, this admiration seems to be tinged with a degree of bad conscience. He tells us that, if we wish to achieve a juster estimation of German prose writing, we will have – 'wohl oder übel' ('whether we like it or not') – to apply different criteria from these that we know from the major classics of European realism. 'Whether we like it or not' is a very strange phrase, implying as it does that generous (perhaps even excessive?) allowance *has to* be made for the timidity and provincialism of German prose. Preisendanz, like so many other critics, has no difficulty in demonstrating the aesthetic quality of German prose : in its density of structural patterning, of symbolic intimation, of narrative suggestiveness, this corpus of writing

68

is of unmistakable stature. But precisely there the bad conscience makes itself heard. The values are, it seems, aesthetic rather than referential : and, when viewed in European company, German writers seem to have skill enough – but not any 'world' to speak of.

In this paper I wish to suggest that, while German prose writing may indeed need an apologist, we do not need to be apologetic about it. And I hope to show that, precisely in its aesthetic character, it partakes of a realistic enterprise – although of one that is different from that which informs the narrative universe of Balzac or Dickens.

J. P. Stern, in two weighty studies, has charted some of the territory for us. His book *On Realism*[2] has very little room for German litera-ture because German writers have not, for the most part, shared in that creative love affair with the palpable world which, for him, constitutes the 'perennial mode' of literary realism. Stern suggests that there are three principal ways in which that love affair manifests itself thematically : first, there is the sense of sheer material abun-dance, the narrative cherishing of the material world in its straight-forward 'thereness'; second, there is the tribute constantly paid to the mental and material weightiness of man's being in the world; and third, there is the principle of consistency whereby a fiction operates with certain extra-literary expectations of experiential coherence which must be respected by the fiction unless and until they are shown to be inappropriate. Now these criteria do admittedly only accommodate very few pieces of German fiction. But Stern him-self has also written with marvellous sympathy and perception of that 'non-realistic' German tradition. I am thinking of his study *Re-Interpretations*.[3] The essays that form that volume spell out the distinct-ness (and the distinction) of the German tradition : Stern suggests that that tradition offers a re-interpretation of the world as commonly interpreted and inhabited. The 'gedeutete Welt' is called into question, then : but not in a simple act of transcendence, of supplanting worldly values by spiritual ones. Rather, the German writers remind us that what human beings call reality is not simply a set of concrete circumstances and facts, an unmediated *donnée*: reality is facts bound together by a set of common assumptions or 'readings', and those readings can be shown to be that and no more: assumptions, and not inalienable givens.

If, then, we accept Stern's case in *Re-Interpretations*, and if we apply it (in a way that he does not, as far as I can see) to *On Realism*, one particularly suggestive conclusion emerges. If the reality which a culture inhabits is a set of assumptions, of agreements not to ask certain questions, then it would follow that one legitimate area of the realist's concern could be the processes by which, day in day out, those assumptions are made and confirmed such that they take root in the hearts and minds of individual men and women. Stern is quite right in *On Realism* to cherish the referentiality by which a text acknowledges the substantiality of institutions, houses, streets, families, jobs, money, clothes and so on. But one must ask if there cannot also be a referentiality which acknowledges ideas, values, concepts, the aggregate of assumptions that inform the affective and ethical life of the individual members of a particular society. To put the matter polemically, German literature, precisely because it does not take for granted what the great writers of the realistic tradition assume (without knowing that they are making – and confirming – assumptions), is able to develop a referentiality in respect of those intangible, but effective (and therefore 'realistic') forces which constitute the corporate identity of a given society.

I want now to take a number of specific points which Stern makes in *On Realism*, and to suggest that they could legitimately be applied to the – admittedly different – fictions that make up the German tradition of prose writing. It will be remembered that the first exemplary text which Stern discusses in *On Realism* is taken from *The Pickwick Papers*. Sam Weller's attention is caught by a Valentine card in a shop window: he enters the shop, purchases some expensive notepaper, and then repairs to the Blue Boar where he sits down and begins to write. The scene that follows is, as Stern rightly says, neither grandiose nor weighty: nor is it charged with any significance (whether allegorical or symbolical) in excess of the simple narrative constatation of the shapes and textures of everyday experience. Such scenes are 'the signs of the *eros* that binds him [the narrator] to this world. They are the signs not of a deprivation, not of a want of reassurance, but the emblems of plenty.'[4] This argument is one to which Stern attaches considerable importance. And he is not alone in this. Barthes and Hamon[5] stress the tribute paid by the realistic novelist to redundant 'thereness'. Now that principle of superabundance applies most obviously to the physical world – to ink and paper. But it can also apply, as Stern's discussion of the conversation about a chair shows, to the speech habits of a particular society. Stern reminds us of the charm of a narrative act which can fix the way people lived (and talked) at a particular time. As he puts it: 'a writer who condemns his world to the extent of rejecting its *parole* [. . .] cannot be a realistic writer'.[6] This surely is right. But we need to extend the argument and to say that that literary exploitation of the *parole* can consist in more than a mimetic closeness to the cadences of everyday speech : for that *parole* is also constituted by the public currency of certain concepts, values, images, metaphors, by the corporate linguistic arsenal on which the individual members of a society draw even when they are seeking to formulate private, perhaps intimate, experiences. Willibald Alexis and Theodor Fontane are masters in the narrative mode of sustained eavesdropping. In one sense, their art is close to the Dickensian love affair with the speech patterns of individual characters. Yet in another sense, it should be noted that Alexis and Fontane are less concerned with individual characterisation than with the corporate characterisation of a whole social ethos. And something similar applies also to Raabe. Raabe is so in love with loquacious characters that garrulousness becomes his prevailing novelistic mode. Often we find ourselves listening to a monologue : and, as Fritz Martini has acutely pointed out,[7] it is a monologue that is spoken rather than thought. Raabe is not in any precise sense a precursor of stream of consciousness. Rather, he is the chronicler of those moments when characters seek to explicate themselves to a (notional or actual) public. The result is often a slightly stilted soliloquy. And these soliloquies are all in the service of a novelistic credo which runs 'by their *parole* shall ye know them'. The stylisation derives from a certain self-stylisation on the part of the characters. And from an act of narrative stylisation : critics have not been slow to detect the patterned *Leitmotive* of *Im alten Eisen* or *Stopfkuchen*. And this patterning means that Raabe is less concerned to offer a transcript of particular (and individualised) speech acts than he is to record value-heavy (and value-explicit) acts of self-explanation. All of which may be at a great remove from the Dickensian 'emblems of plenty' with which we began. But this should not lead us to assume that the German writers are enticing us into a realm of fastidiously embattled inwardness. What we hear is an extensively socialised, indeed institutionalised, subjectivity.

To invoke the category of inwardness – 'Innerlichkeit' – is to acknowledge that quality which has so often been claimed as the birthright of German prose and as the disabling ideology which has constantly militated against the emergence of literary realism in Germany. German prose literature, it has been said, is too thoughtful, too 'philosophical' to be realistic. Once again a formulation of Stern's can help us. 'Realism', he writes, 'is philosophically incurious and epistemologically naive.'[8] This may well be true. But a great deal of

German fiction displays an epistemological curiosity that is not incompatible with a kind of literary realism. Much German novel writing from Goethe to Thomas Mann is, indeed, concerned with ideas. But we have to ask what form this concern takes. In my view, the narrative charting of the life of the mind which so amply fills the pages of *Wilhelm Meisters Lehrjahre* or of *Der grüne Heinrich* functions not as an invitation to us to enter some timeless realm of conceptual sophistication : rather, the mental life of the characters is historicised, is shown to be the psychological – and above all cognitive – precipitate of the culture to which those characters belong. Judged as dialectical debate, the verbal battles between Naphta and Settembrini in Thomas Mann's *Der Zauberberg* are singularly uneconomical and undisciplined. Judged as historical material, those debates afford a fascinating insight into the cultural temper of Germany in the years immediately preceding the First World War. I come back to the point with which I began : German prose fiction is able to historicise the life of the mind, and thereby it retraces the assumptions on which a society was grounded. It spells out the assumptions *as assumptions* – but without transcending them in a higher, philosophically rigorous, discourse. Ideas can as much be part of the bric-à-brac of an age as are chairs, inkwells, or hats. Inwardness need not be a bastion erected against the historical age: it may be less a piece of private property than the characters themselves wish (perhaps even need) to believe.

None of the arguments which I have advanced so far will have the effect of assimilating German prose literature of the late eighteenth and nineteenth centuries into the 'mainstream' of European realism. But I may at least have been able to suggest that this German tradition was not conceived on a different planet. Moreover I hope that, at the very least, I have been able to redeem German prose from the taint of being the (at best) questionable or (at worst) pernicious accompaniment to the dark course of German history which, it has sometimes been argued, leads with pathological inevitability to the Third Reich. The difficulty here is that the historiography of the European nineteenth century is often sustained by a strangely normative thinking. And because Germany before 1871 does not conform to the norm – the unified nation state within which the bourgeois revolution carries all before it – it is held to be necessarily questionable. Of course, the German-speaking lands are characterised by the legacy of the Holy Roman Empire whereby particularism provides a powerful socio-psychological inhibitor to the possibility of national unity. And the upshot of this is that, for the writer of prose fiction, there is no capital city which provides the palpable enactment and expression of the stresses and strains of economic change. Before 1871 there is no equivalent in German writing to the Petersburg of a Tolstoy, the Paris of a Balzac, the London of a Dickens. Yet if one criterion for literary realism is the commitment of the creative artist to the exploration of the social experience of his times, it would necessarily follow that the German Confederation would call forth a different kind of prose fiction from that which issues from France or England. A number of commentators have helped us to identify the distinguishing features of the German situation.

Raymond Williams's study *The Country and the City*[9] serves to point up a crucial distinction between Germany and England; not least because England enshrines the 'norm' of which I have spoken. Williams draws attention to the early development of agrarian capitalism in England which ensures the irrevocable demise of open-strip farming. As a result of this, market towns spring up which provide the economic focus for the marketing of agrarian production. The functional contrast between country and town is then exacerbated by the Industrial Revolution whereby the urban community moves even further away from the rhythms of 'natural life' – all of which serves to intensify the nostalgia for a pre-capitalist, pre-urban world from which large numbers of the population have been banished. Now this disjunction between rural and urban does not apply to the German lands as W. H. Riehl showed in his crucial study *Land und Leute* (for which George Eliot evinced such enthusiasm).[10] It is vital to notice that pre-industrial society in Germany was not simply dominated by a rural economy with the market town as the repository of the monetary infrastructure. Mack Walker's study *German Home Towns*[11] puts the historical argument with exemplary clarity, for he shows the extent to which, both factually and imaginatively, the German social consciousness was anchored in a pre-industrial urban culture. In the sixteenth century, the German lands do not lack for trading centres inhabited by the entrepreneurs of early bourgeois capitalism, moneylenders, speculators and so on. But in the seventeenth and eighteenth centuries the emphasis in European trade and commerce moves to the North and to the maritime West. And the German towns change their character. Particularly in German lands between Prussia in the north and Austria to the south the towns become enclosed, tied to the relatively stable, institutionalised framework of the guild economy. The skilled master craftsman becomes the élite figure : the 'hometown' is not dynamic, expansive, growth-conscious. It is inward-looking, distrustful of foreign capital, it is sustained by custom, convention, familiarity, rather than by impersonal laws or economic principles. The 'hometowns' of Riehl's 'individualised land' – such as Ulm, Regensburg, Nürnberg – were frequently viewed by the mercantile centres and the princely residences as strangely anachronistic relics of feudal society. Certainly, from the 1840s on, they are increasingly threatened by the growing dominance of Prussia, by the 'Zollverein', the pressure for 'Gewerbefreiheit' – and by the slump of 1857 and the extensive emigration that followed. Wagner's *Die Meistersinger von Nürnberg* is the great monument to the ethos of the 'hometown'.[12] Yet, however much one may need to call into question his Romantic, 'mythologising' view of the past, Wagner was not simply creating a mirage : for his imagination did capture a particular form of urban life which was sustained by a complex corpus of economic and emotional underpinning that was simply without equal in the rest of Europe. The German lands are late in joining the European norm of the nation state, and when they do unite to form that 'verspätete Nation' which has become such a topos in subsequent historiography, they do so as the bearers of a particular legacy. It is a legacy that is both spiritual – in the sense that before 1871, the nation only existed in its language and culture and not in a physical (demographic) sense; and psychological – in the sense that there had been a knowable model for communal life that was both urban and intimate, indeed familial. And even though the 'hometowns', as an historical phenomenon, were confined to the non-Prussian and non-Austrian lands, they marked the German cultural consciousness indelibly. If in England, nostalgia for a pre-industrial world was necessarily a longing for a rural, 'natural' world, in Germany such nostalgia could envisage an urban community that was exempt from the abstraction and anonymity of the industrial world. When Ferdinand Tönnies established his famous distinction between 'Gemeinschaft' and 'Gesellschaft', he was, at one level, arguing with 'ideal types' (in Weber's sense). But the 'ideal type' of 'Gemeinschaft' was not simply a figment of the imagination, a chimerical utopia. It was a tribute paid to a particular ethos of urban living that the particularism of the Holy Roman Empire had made possible.

What are the consequences of this legacy for the tradition of German prose literature that concerns us here? I am not for a moment claiming that that literature is largely set in 'hometowns' –

although it should be noted that the works of Jean Paul, or the late Tieck, or Eichendorff may be more 'realistic' than we now realise. But there is one crucial point that does emerge from the foregoing excursus into German social history. The European 'norm' implies, and many commentators have stressed this, a radical disjunction between public and private experience. The development of nineteenth-century bourgeois society, it is said, means that increasingly the public realm becomes merely the competitive marketplace in which enterprising individuals are locked in a struggle for survival, whereas the private realm (of family and home) shelters the deepest affective needs of the personality. The public realm is that of the self-regulating market : the private realm is the repository of compassion, gentleness, love. Yet it was absolutely central both to the reality and to the myth of the 'hometown' that there was no such sharp separation of private and public persona. In other words, the public realm was not inimical to the affective needs of the individual personality, and the private realm bore the imprint of the institutional function. I have no wish to set up some kind of paradisal model in which conflicts are necessarily relegated to mere psychological failings on the part of particular inadequate individuals. German prose literature is full of conflicts between public and private such as we find in the literature of European realism. Jürgen Habermas has, for example, drawn attention[13] to the distinction which Goethe's Wilhelm Meister makes between the bourgeois whose public persona is defined by what he produces, whereas the nobleman's public function is simply to represent what he is. Habermas argues, rightly, that this perception is a cardinal moment in the shifting definitions of public and private realms which characterise the development of bourgeois society. I am not claiming for German social experience a prelapsarian exemption from the tensions of bourgeois life. But what I do wish to suggest is that the commerce between public and private is conceptualised differently within German prose fiction. There is a different signature to the discussion of public and private : Wemmick, with his 'aged p', is a character from another world.

Stern writes : 'realism imposes a balance between public and private meanings'.[14] This is true. But both the definition and the weighting of public and private meanings are at issue here. Such meanings are not givens. They entail assumptions made and acted upon. And it is possible that private meanings can be (or can be shown to be) public meanings. By which I mean more than the simple

Marxian contention that any statement of the resolutely private necessarily tells us something about the public realm – precisely by refusing to have anything to do with it. Rather, I have in mind the possibility that the private self may harbour the assumptions that constitute the 'gedeutete Welt' of the corporate realm. Stern on one occasion refers to narrations in interior monologue as 'those oubliettes of private experience'.[15] That may well be the case. But we should not forget that the first great interior monologue in Western European literature is written in German : it is Arthur Schnitzler's *Leutnant Gustl.* And it is precisely the point of that monologue that we hear not private experience, but the tissue of assumptions – in this case prejudices – that fill the mind of a witless officer of the Austrian army. Indeed, it is part of the unforgettable comedy of that tale that Gustl, confronted by the prospect of his imminent death, is simply unable to find a corner of his subjectivity that is not institutionalised. It is no accident that the tradition of German prose narrative is peculiarly rich in such insights.

Indeed, one should note that precisely those German novels and stories which are 'on the map' as far as European literature is concerned have important insights to offer in respect of the commerce between public and private. At the risk of oversimplification, one could say that the German prose tradition claims European attention with Goethe's *Werther* and (to a lesser extent) with *Wilhelm Meisters Lehrjahre,* and then vanishes from the European consciousness altogether until we come to Fontane's novels (at the end of the nineteenth century) and to Thomas Mann's *Buddenbrooks.* From that point on, German fiction (with Mann, Kafka, Hesse, Musil, Grass) is an established part of the European mainstream. One familiar argument is used to account for this : it is said that when the essential tenets of realistic fiction come under attack in the early years of the twentieth century, the time is ripe for German literature to assume more than parochial significance. There may be an element of truth in this : but I would want to argue that in fact the cardinal achievement of those German fictions which have become European classics resides not in their offering the kind of inwardness which suddenly acquires the cachet of European endorsement : but rather that these German fictions historicise that inwardness, and reveal it to be part and parcel of the assumptions of the culture at large. Often the defenders of the German tradition have sought to validate it in terms of its philosophical depth and richness. I would rather put it differently and say that the 'philosophy' is made novelistic in the precise sense that the ideas, the very discourse of values, are shown to be part of the historical temper of the age. This is surely true of *Werther*. At one level, Goethe's amazing novel demands to be read in psychological terms, as the study of a particular kind of uncompromising, and threatened, sensibility. But *Werther* was also, in formal and linguistic terms, both a cardinal document – and a critique – of the age of *Empfindsamkeit*. It is inseparable from the public culture that attributed great value to letter writing, to keeping – and sharing – a diary of the inner life. Within the fiction of that novel, the 'Herausgeber' or editor figure publishes (that is he makes public) the letters that have come into his possession. The degree of – public – assent which he thereby invites was exceeded by the reception that the novel was actually accorded. And part of that reception had to do with the fact that the 'private' circumstances that went into the making of the novel – Goethe's affair with Lotte Buff, Jerusalem's suicide – were *also* public property. Moreover, Lionel Trilling has taught us to read *Werther* as a major document of the European quest for sincerity of soul and purpose.[16] Similarly, it could be argued that *Wilhelm Meisters Lehrjahre*, although it is concerned with the growth and development of the individual self, documents the contribution made to that process by key features of the cultural life of the age : the theatre, the pietistic confession, the (masonic) secret society. The cultivation of the self is, then, enacted with reference to the institutionalisations of subjectivity that were part of the society.

When German prose literature re-appears to European view, it does so with Theodor Fontane, who is the novelist par excellence of Berlin life in the last two decades of the nineteenth century. In one sense, of course, Fontane's realism is made possible by the age in which Germany becomes a unified nation state and thereby acquires that social and cultural focus on which European realism is grounded. One does not need to plead for the European stature of Fontane's art. But one all-pervasive characteristic of his fiction should be noted. The point has often been made that Fontane's novels lack the energy and passion of, say, Stendhal, Balzac, Dickens, or Tolstoy. And that lack of passion expresses itself not only in the experiences that he puts before us, but in the very mode of his writing. In a word, Fontane seems more conciliatory (his detractors would say timorous) than his European counterparts. I think it is important not to misread this complex of theme and mode as half-heartedness. For certain of the implications of Fontane's art are devastating. He suggests to us that neither the individual mind nor the individual heart are, in fact, private property : rather, the very modes of thinking and feeling are part of the discourse of their age. Fontane's characters are ill equipped to be rebels : and this is because they lack the alternative cognition – and discourse – that could make such rebellion possible. The inner life – and this is part of Fontane's shattering modesty – is not, and cannot be, insulated from the corporate realm in which it lives, moves, and has its being. In this perception Fontane is unequalled, as far as I am aware, within European literature. Never has the commerce between public and private been viewed so thoughtfully – and unsentimentally. One could advance a similar claim for Thomas Mann's first novel, *Buddenbrooks,* which is, in so many aspects of both theme and style, close to Fontane. The conciliations are less in evidence, of course. Thomas Buddenbrook's debilitating incapacity to serve the mercantile values in which inwardly he cannot believe becomes, in his son Hanno, the uncompromising rejection of anything to do with the life of a grain merchant. The increasing inwardness of successive generations of Buddenbrooks militates against worldly success. Yet even here – in its concern for the corroding inwardness that is causally linked to the 'decline of a family' which the subtitle announces – the novel does not spirit us away into the realm of privileged and inviolate subjectivity. For Mann is at pains to historicise the knowing mind, to show his characters as thinking the thoughts of their age (Thomas's Nietzschean reverie on Schopenhauerian doctrines), as creating the artistic themes and forms of their age (Hanno's Wagnerian improvisation on the senatorial grand piano). And much later in his career as a novelist, Thomas Mann will tell a story of the proudly isolated creative self and will seek (as in the closing sentence of the book) to link the creativity of the narrator's 'friend' to the political fate of the narrator's 'fatherland'. The novel, of course, is *Doktor Faustus.* However much the parallelism between music and politics has been disputed by critics, what is beyond doubt is the cogency and resonance with which Mann explores the cultural specificity – the historicity – of even such a non-referential art as music. The composer whose life is at the centre of the book is no Nazi ideologue, is in no way directly involved in Germany's slide into barbarism. Yet the novel unremittingly insists on the cultural chemistry that links the imaginative realm to the historical. And, in one shape or form, this argument, or something like it, recurs in German novels of the twentieth century, from Musil's unforgettable portrait of the Vanity Fair of the mind that characterises Austria-Hungary on the eve of the

First World War (in *Der Mann ohne Eigenschaften*) to Günter Grass's extraordinary attempt to historicise his own – and his characters' – riotously exuberant imagination.

For whatever reason, German novel fiction of the twentieth century stands in need of no special pleading. But between Goethe's *Werther* and Fontane's Berlin novels there is a gap of some hundred years in which German prose literature disappears from the European scene. I cannot attempt, in the brief compass of this paper, to do justice to the range and scale of the narrative achievement that emerges in those years. But I want at least to sketch in the parameters of that corpus of narrative fiction. The writings of the 'Jungdeutschland' period are both significant in their own right – and symptomatic of the problematic condition of German realism. It was a generation that was, with Heine, aware that Goethe's death marked the 'Ende der Kunstperiode'. And Heine suggests that this age of post-classical art will be marked by a different kind of culture : one that is characterised by a concern for the public realm of journalism, of polemical and political debate. Time and time again – and particularly in respect of the novel – the demand is heard for a literature that will, in the wake of the Walter Scott vogue, address the historical situation of the German lands. The demand does not go unheeded : but no œuvre of the size and scope of Scott's emerges, although Willibald Alexis's *Ruhe ist die erste Bürgerpflicht* is remarkable for its diagnosis of the frivolity and corruption of Berlin in the first decade of the nineteenth century. Alexis in a sense explores those factors which militate against Prussia's being able to experience, and therefore to make, history in a way that could justify the manner of a Walter Scott novel. *Ruhe ist die erste Bürgerpflicht* consists essentially of conversations which incarnate the disunity of the society : the historical totality which the novel seeks to invoke is but a loose aggregation of discrete groups. Far more suggestive for our purposes, however, are three novels which appear within some five years of each other : Gutzkow's *Wally die Zweiflerin* (1835); Immermann's *Die Epigonen* (1836) and *Münchhausen* (1838–9). All three novels are characterised by an overt literariness. And indeed this literariness is part of their theme. For they are all concerned with a society in which personal experience is strangely bereft of anchorage. So many of the characters are painfully aware that their experience is no longer in any inalienable sense, theirs. Rather, they find themselves living out certain cultural images and stereotypes. The 'Kunstperiode' may, it seems, be over : but it will not relinquish its hold. The shades of Goethe's *Werther* and *Wilhelm Meister* are omnipresent. There is a discursiveness to these novels. But, at their best, they imply that that discursiveness is the curse of their age, that the characters are doomed, in a world bereft of meaningful activity, to lead a vicariously literary existence. The profoundest insight of all three novels entails a quite precise sense of characters living within – and with – the cultural bric-à-brac of their time. Once again, as in so much of the fiction I have been discussing, the signature of the age is shown to reside in certain concepts, ciphers, even clichés : the assumptions of the social reality are conditioning presences in the psychic life of the characters.

We have admittedly come a long way from J. P. Stern's starting point in *On Realism* : those Dickensian 'emblems of plenty' that so richly animate the scene in which Sam Weller settles himself to compose a letter. There is one final point about this scene which needs to be highlighted. Stern observes that this passage, like so many in Dickens, offers us 'physical details, some of the "bric-à-brac" of the age, but not from very close by, and with no emphasis on their symbolical quality'. And he goes on to insist that 'these abundant scenes from the social and physical world are not very carefully arranged, not "highly structured" '.[17] The point is an important – and a familiar – one : realism offers an acknowledgment of the physical world's 'thereness' – what Barthes and Hamon will see as a redundancy beyond the process of artistic structuring and symbol-making. It is the purpose of such details that they are not – and that they do not need to be – 'recuperated' into any artistic significance above and beyond their physical existence in the extra-literary world. The difficulty with such an argument is that it can petrify into a critical ideology which says that realism needs to exhibit this principle of superabundance, and that realistic fictions should have the feel of 'loose baggy monsters'. Or, to put the point negatively, the ideology asserts that careful artistic shaping, that a density of pattern, *Leimotiv*, and symbol of necessity militates against literary realism. All of which brings us back to the 'German problem' : to the view that asserts that German prose literature is all too assiduously concerned to recuperate prosaic facticity into the 'poetry' of literary statement. Under this aspect, form, metaphor, symbol are not explorations of the workaday world but rather artistic victories over its recalcitrant, resistant matter.

This seems to me misleading in the extreme. One example will have to suffice. The first volume of Gottfried Keller's *Die Leute von*

Seldwyla (1857) contains a story entitled *Romeo und Julia auf dem Dorfe*. It is a tale which exhibits a scrupulous – almost claustrophobic – density of artistic pattern. It is no exaggeration to say that almost every critical discussion of this tale necessarily refers to the subtle process of symbolisation at work in so much of its descriptive detail. The ploughing scene with which the work opens shows the beauty and the catastrophic rigidity of the two farmers. The two children play in the disputed field, a wilderness between the ploughed land, and the motif of 'wild', 'verwildert', 'Wildnis' will continue to sound throughout the story as the two children are crushed by the enmity of their fathers. Yet paradoxically their love is marked by the longing for the orderliness enshrined in the opening scene. When they are older, Sali and Vrenchen meet in that disputed field : there they will be confronted by the 'schwarzer Geiger' who cannot establish his entitlement to that field. His bohemian existence offers an escape to the lovers that proves unimaginable and therefore unworkable. The colour symbolism underpins the symbolism of locality. There is, I think, no need for me to itemise further the richness of symbolic statement in Keller's tale. Yet all too often critics have been content to trace the symbolic connections, and to imply (or to state) that the symbolism of the story lifts it above a humble record of village life. Such critics often invoke the title as symptomatic of the ethos of German 'poetic realism' : for that title – 'A Village Romeo and Juliet' – so it is said, implies a will to transfigure the modest *donnée* of the characters' lives by invoking the supremely 'poetic' model of Shakespeare's 'star-crossed lovers'. But this, in my view, is to misunderstand both the title and the artistic logic of the story. For the point of the Shakespearean model is to highlight the contrast between two kinds of tragic experience. In Shakespeare's play we are not told the cause of the feud that separates the Capulets and the Montagues. In Keller's tale, the feud is given a quite specific socio-economic motivation : it has to do with land, with property. The motif of destiny sounds frequently in Keller's tale : but it is a destiny that is made, not in the stars, but in the modest, socially and economically determined consciousness of two young people. Keller's lovers are simply not capable of the lyrical, *poetic* rapture of Romeo and Juliet. When, in a scene that recalls Sam Weller's glimpse of the Valentine card, they buy each other gingerbread pastries, they read the verses which are inscribed on them. The narrator quotes these verses – they are little better than jingles. He then comments : 'nie ist etwas Gereimtes und Gedrucktes schöner befunden und tiefer empfunden worden',[18] ('never has anything printed in rhyme been found more beautiful or felt more deeply'). This narrative comment is in no sense to be taken as patronising : but Keller's narrator is at pains to identify the cognitive and emotional limitation of the two young people. And that limitation is his theme : Sali and Vrenchen have so internalised the shapes, and sounds, the very values of their upbringing that there can be no escape for them. They carry their society with them. And to this insight Keller directs the whole range of his narrative and linguistic skills : the symbolism does not transcend the social destiny, it articulates it. And the delight which we take in Keller's artistry is inseparable from our comprehension of the ways in which – and the extent to which – society has become part of the very selfhood of the characters.[19]

One concluding observation on this issue of 'poetic' symbolism versus 'prosaic' constatation. In Keller, as in Fontane, we find a density of symbolic argument which is scrupulously in the service of a precise exploration of society seen not just as a profusion of physical details but as a set of assumptions that are enshrined in the linguistic and psychological life of individual characters. Within the 'loose baggy monster' ideology this might seem a somewhat surprising – perhaps even unworthy – employment of the art of literary symbolism. But a moment's reflection will convince us that this need not be so, for the simple reason that the literary symbol is particularly attuned to tracing the psychological anchorage of social life. The symbol works by implication : and it can therefore express the processes by which an individual consciousness is implicated in the linguistic and cultural existence of a society. And it can implicate us, the readers, in that process of sharing, in that 'hum and buzz of implication' (the phrase is, I believe, Lionel Trilling's) which is the corporate existence of an age.

I hope that I have been able in the foregoing to suggest the importance of the tradition of German prose writing in the nineteenth century, a tradition that is valuable both in its own right and also because it can differentiate and deepen our comprehension of the varieties of literary realism. In a sense, I am envisaging the confluence of Stern's *Re-Interpretations* and *On Realism*. I have no wish to dispute Stern's case for the 'perennial mode' of realism. But that perennial mode is necessarily enacted through history : and, as Stephan Kohl has so acutely observed,[20] part of that perennial character has to do with the recurring process whereby each age challenges what it apprehends as an outworn literary convention in the name of a greater truthfulness to life, 'realism'. What is entailed in that process is the sense that reality, as constituted and inhabited by the human species, by *homo significans*, is a set of corporate assumptions, an agreement to define and interpret the character of man's being in the world in a quite particular way. I am not thereby saying that all art is realistic. But for us, as twentieth-century readers, the achievements of nineteenth-century prose fiction constitute not simply *a* period of realistic art, but a particularly immediate and durable mode whose truthfulness we still acknowledge. But, even so, it can be helpful for us to remind ourselves that even that canonical realism is a set of assumptions and not an inventory of givens. The Brecht/Lukács debate focussed these issues with particular clarity. And if, in that debate, Brecht's voice was valuable in that it challenged certain assumptions by revealing them to be, precisely, assumptions, then nineteenth-century German prose may be able to perform a similar function in respect of the realistic Pantheon from which it has so long been excluded. Above all, it may be the one prose literature that most richly and fruitfully helps us to understand the Brechtian dictum that realism is not the way real things are, realism is the way things really are.[21]

NOTES

1. Wolfgang Preisendanz, *Wege des Realismus* (Munich, 1977) p. 90. See also *Bürgerlicher Realismus*, ed. Klaus-Detlef Müller (Königstein/Ts., 1981).
2. London, 1973.
3. London, 1964.
4. *On Realism*, p. 5.
5. Roland Barthes, 'L'Effet du réel', *Communications* 11 (1968) pp. 84–9; Philippe Hamon, 'Qu'est-ce qu'une description?' *Poétique* 12 (1972) pp. 465–88.
6. *On Realism*, p. 76.
7. Fritz Martini, 'Wilhelm Raabe's *Prinzessin Fisch*' in *Begriffsbestimmung des literarischen Realismus*, ed. Richard Brinkmann (Darmstadt, 1969) p. 312.
8. *On Realism*, p. 54.
9. London, 1973.
10. George Eliot, 'The Natural History of German Life', *Westminster Review* 66 (July 1856) pp. 51–79.
11. Ithaca and London, 1971.
12. See Timothy McFarland, 'Wagner's Nuremberg' in *Richard Wagner: 'The Mastersingers of Nuremberg'*, ed. Nicholas John (English National Opera Guides, 19) London, 1983, pp. 27–34.

13. Jürgen Habermas, *Strukturwandel der Öffentlichkeit* (Neuwied and Berlin, ²1965) pp. 22ff.
14. *On Realism*, p. 84.
15. *On Realism*, p. 114.
16. Lionel Trilling, *Sincerity and Authenticity* (London, 1974) pp. 47ff.
17. *On Realism*, p. 5.
18. Gottfried Keller, *Sämtliche Werke*, ed. Jonas Fränkel 7 (Erlenbach-Zürich and Munich, 1927) p. 167.
19. See my article 'Keller's Realism: Some Observations on *Romeo und Julia auf dem Dorfe*', in *Formen realistischer Erzählkunst* Festschr. Jolles, ed. Jörg Thunecke (Nottingham, 1979) pp. 159–68.
20. Stephan Kohl, *Realismus: Theorie und Geschichte* (Munich, 1977).
21. See Bertolt Brecht, *'Katzgraben'-Notate*, Werkausgabe, 16 (Frankfurt am Main, 1967) p. 837: 'Wir müssen nicht nur schildern, wie die Wirklichkeit ist, sondern wie die Wirklichkeit wirklich ist.'

Proust's Balzac

SHEILA STERN

Despite the existence of various groups of enthusiasts, readers of Balzac are generally rare both in England and in France, though until recently one of his works was usually 'done' in the course of a school career in either country. Assisted rather than impeded by this latter fact, a generation of French and French-influenced critics have been able to use Balzac as an Aunt Sally on the fair assumption that they would meet with no serious resistance when they presented his writing as usurping the status of a mirror of the world, as the naive monologue of intrigue, observation and factual information. The need for such an object to set against the new enlightenment led to their turning 'the Balzacian novel' into a monolith as compact and solid as one of Rodin's statuettes of the man himself, easy to handle and all of a piece when viewed from whatever angle.

Whatever conclusions may be drawn from the enormous range of critical opinions of Balzac, it is clear that the monolithic view is not tenable in good faith for long. Paul Bourget, who in his *Le Disciple* drew heavily on Balzac's novels *Le Lys dans la vallée* (which he alludes to) and *Louis Lambert* (to which he does not), wrote at a later date in a letter of the 'roman de mœurs, (issu) de Balzac par Flaubert' having effectively deprived the novel of 'toute étude des phénomènes intérieurs'. This is perhaps dishonest, certainly unacceptable; but in our own time painstaking but irreconcilable assertions have been made about Balzac by Alain Robbe-Grillet, whose concern (in *Pour un nouveau roman*) was not with 'les phénomènes intérieurs' but with 'making-visible' and freeing objects from the envelope of human reference, or from the human significance seen as underlying them, which cause them to be apprehended as either muffled or transparent. Neither of these views is of assistance in explaining how Balzac comes to be named among the precursors of Proust, who names him so often.

I would like to be able to show that there is a fundamental kinship between the art of Proust and that of Balzac, not reposing on the obvious analogy between Balzac's interlinking of lives through several novels and Proust's long pursuit of characters all supposed acquaintances of a single narrator. Something more essential is intended by Gérard Genette when he writes, after devoting a few pages to Balzac: 'De Balzac à Proust, par exemple, il y a moins loin qu'on ne pense – et Proust, d'ailleurs, le savait mieux que personne' ('Vraisemblance et Motivation', *Figures* 2 (Paris, 1969) p. 86). Whether this kinship should make us hesitate to call Balzac a realist, or contemplate the possibility that Proust is one, is a question that will not be in my power to answer here.

Proust's admiration for the fiction of the nineteenth century is well attested. Of Balzac, both in the novel and in essays, Proust speaks at times with an almost incredulous mingling of love and exasperation that is easily sympathised with. A preoccupation with theme and matter, rather than manner, is clear in many of the incidental comments on literature throughout *A la recherche du temps perdu*, and there are obvious respects in which Balzac and Proust share the subject matter of their writing: the facets of character perceived from different view-points, the reversals of status and in relationships brought about by time. M. du Châtelet and Mme de Bargeton in *Les Illusions perdues* undergo metamorphosis when they move from Angoulême to Paris – he, like Swann, because past events surround him with prestige and even glamour for the society of the capital, and she by virtue of powerful cousins and her innate ability to learn. Both, seen through the astonished eyes of Lucien de Rubempré, throw off what he has just time to recognise as provincial absurdity, and acquire, or reassume, Parisian coolness, decisiveness and chic. In *Le Colonel Chabert*, after winning honour and a career by his courage, a man has been robbed of his identity by the report of his death in battle and by years as a prisoner of war. 'Je suis le colonel Chabert – celui qui est mort à Eylau' – these are the words with which he attempts to convince the authorities of his claims when he turns up, a living scarecrow, after begging his way across Europe. The Baron de Charlus reduced from the arrogant security of his social position to abject dependence on panders and to public humiliation, Mme Verdurin – close kin to Mme de Bargeton as a pretentious patroness of artists – later transformed into the Princesse de Guermantes, the possessors of youth and strength decayed into senile helplessness, are examples of Proust's incomparably more intense and leisurely scrutiny of the same themes of time and mutability. This well-studied thematic closeness is too large for our attention here. We may first try to locate a few slighter echoes of Balzac in Proust's text before turning to links long established by Proust's own critical comments.

Most nineteenth-century novelists, for example, hint at the effect produced on an involved listener by the musical sound of a beloved voice. In *Le Lys dans la vallée* Balzac gives an analytical account of Mme de Mortsauf's manner of speaking while his hero, Félix de Vandenesse, is in the act of falling in love with it :

Sa façon de dire les terminaisons en *i* faisait croire à quelque chant d'oiseau; le *ch* prononcé par elle était comme une caresse, et la manière dont elle attaquait les *t* accusait le despotisme du cœur. Elle étendait ainsi, sans le savoir, le sens des mots [. . .] Combien de fois n'ai-je pas laissé continuer une discussion [. . .] pour étreindre cette lumière parlée.

A similar spell is cast on Proust's narrator by the voice of the Duchesse de Guermantes, when her blue eyes seem to reflect 'le ciel de l'Ile de France ou de Champagne évoqué par son parler [. . .] une vieille chanson'. In his first extended conversation with Albertine he detects in her speech the remote influence of an English governess, an affected immobility of the facial muscles, and a degree of nasal catarrh – and simultaneously succumbs, despite this objectivity, to the overwhelming enchantment of the voice; when he is alone he is impelled to summon it up by mimicry, and repeats with fervid delight 'On ne vous voit jamais au golf' as nearly as possible in the way Albertine said it.

The region of the 'arbitraire', which Genette defines in the psychological procedures of Balzac, also has its counterpart in Proust. In the Casino at Balbec (*Sodome et Gomorrhe II*), watching the women he sees as his rivals for Albertine, the narrator is made aware of a form of signalling between them. The scene continues, with the words 'Une fois je vis [. . .]', to describe the meeting of two young women instantly understanding each other without a word being exchanged. Then, in a sudden withdrawal from the position of onlooker into that of third-person narrator, mediated by the phrase '[. . .] on aurait pu voir bientôt [. . .]' (mistranslated, I think, by Scott Moncrieff and Kilmartin as 'one could presently see') we are given a short story in four sentences, ending '[. . .] an incident they laughed about later, as they did over the husband they had fooled, with an enjoyment that led to new caresses'. No 'sans doute' to preserve plausibility; it is a kind of *arbitrary* hiatus to be bridged by intuition, comparable to those phrases in which Balzac telescopes what is told and what is yet to tell. The story *Facino Cane*, about a blind Venetian exile, has two examples : 'Et il fit *un geste* effrayant de patriotisme éteint et de dégoût pour les choses humaines', and '[. . .] *un accent* qui annonçait que ses regrets ne portaient pas seulement sur la perte de sa vue, mais sur quelque grand pouvoir dont il aurait été dépouillé' (my italics). In the first part of *A la recherche* the narrator, as a boy, sees through a window the scene between Mlle Vinteuil and her friend, in which their amorous game seems to summon the spectator they are unaware of, and uses as a substitute the photograph of Mlle Vinteuil's late father. There is an air of timidity about the narrator's comment that the fictional situation is too much like melodrama to be easily credited : 'c'est à la lumière de la rampe des théâtres du boulevard plutôt que sous la lampe d'une maison de campagne véritable qu'on peut voir une fille [. . .]' etc. It is a gloss precisely in Balzac's manner, illustrating too the typical unselfconscious use of *véritable* (as, also, of *réel, réalité*) in both writers, and continuing into a kind of *maxime* ('[. . .] il n'y a guère que le sadisme qui donne un fondement dans la vie à l'esthétique du mélodrame'), equally familiar in its psychological perfunctoriness.

Comments such as this reference to the theatre are inevitably understood as 'spoken' aside to the reader. Rather a mannerism than a device, they are usually associated with a certain artlessness of nineteenth-century writing. Yet in some contexts the effect is deliberately integrated in the undertaking, linking candid selfconsciousness with the quicksilver digressiveness, the now-you-see-me-now-you-don't fluidity of Laurence Sterne. To apologise for long-windedness, or for disappointing expectations of continuity or indeed of narrative itself, is to recall *Tristram Shandy* and much earlier modes of story-telling, even to the desperately motivated artfulness of Scheherezade.

'Joliment tragique ce soir !' exclaims Emile Blondet in a transparent attempt to stem the flow of total recall on which Raphaël de Valentin has embarked at a drunkne party (*La Peau de chagrin*). But he, and the reader, are doomed to submit to this recital before the action can proceed. Proust's reader too has to suffer similar *longueurs*. Embarrassed by the fact that he has not been introduced to his host, Proust's narrator at the Princesse de Guermantes' party is fobbed off by five or six acquaintances he successively approaches, who all evidently feel the responsibility of presenting him is too great. Each encounter and each personage is brilliantly detailed, digressions of all kinds interpose, and we are surprised to receive an overt acknowledgment of our own presence, and possible impatience (so improbable in fact that there is a hint of coquetry in this apology) in the form of a dialogue in which the 'lecteur' remonstrates with the narrator for his brief inability to recall Mme d'Arpajon's name. The wit and range of this interlude exemplify the uses to which Proust could put any conventional device, however threadbare or unpromising, by a combination of dislocation, mimicry and pastiche.

It is unlikely that Proust was on oath when he asserted that Hardy's *A Pair of Blue Eyes* was the novel he would most like to have written, but in that novel we can find a succinct expression of our next point of comparison between Proust and Balzac :

It is with cliffs and mountains as with persons; they have what is called a presence [. . .] A little cliff will impress you powerfully; a great one not at all. It depends, as with man, upon the countenance of the cliff.

We are here concerned with what Keats in a letter calls 'the tone, the colouring, the slate, the stone, the moss, the rock-weed; or, if I may so say, the intellect, the countenance of [. . .] places'.

In Balzac's *Le Médecin de campagne* (1833) Dr Benassis, a vigorous and despotic benefactor, is showing an army officer, Genestas, what his methods have achieved in a poor valley of the Dauphiné. Near sunset a mysterious distant singing causes them to leave their horses and follow a path that leads them to the scene of conditions not amenable to disciplined organisation. 'Est-ce une femme ou un homme, est-ce un oiseau?' asks the visitor, 'est-ce la voix de ce grand paysage?' and the doctor answers that each of these suppositions has some truth :

[. . .] un sentier bordé de deux haies d'épine blanche en fleur qui répandaient de pénétrantes odeurs dans l'humide atmosphère du soir. Les rayons du soleil entraient dans le sentier avec une sorte d'impétuosité que l'ombre projetée par le long rideau de peupliers rendait encore plus sensible, et ces vigoureux jets de lumière enveloppaient de leurs teintes rouges une chaumière située au bout de ce chemin sablonneux. Une poussière d'or semblait être jetée sur son toit de chaume ordinairement brun comme la coque d'un châtaigne, et dont les crêtes délabrées étaient verdies par des joubarbes et de la mousse. La chaumière se voyait à peine dans ce brouillard de lumière; mais les vieux murs, la porte, tout y avait un éclat fugitif, tout en était fortuitement beau, comme l'est par moments une figure humaine, sous l'empire de quelque passion qui l'échauffe et la colore [. . .] Ce paysage semblait avoir en ce moment une voix pure et douce autant qu'il était pur et doux, mais une voix triste comme la lueur près de finir à l'occident; vague image de la mort, avertissement divinement donné dans le ciel par le soleil, comme le donnent sur la terre les fleurs et les jolis insectes éphémères . . .

'C'est le chant du cygne' dit Benassis [...] 'Hâtons-nous, il faut l'empêcher de chanter!'

The wordless melody is the tune of *Malbrouk s'en va*, the singer a consumptive boy of fifteen, forbidden this use of his voice by the doctor; he excuses his disobedience, when they come upon him alone in the farmyard in the last sunlight, by saying 'Je me suis écouté moi-même, parce que ma voix ressemblait presque à celle du flûtiau de votre berger.' (The narrative frame is completed when Benassis and his young patient die at the same time a few months later, and are the first to lie in the new cemetery the doctor has had prepared, in accordance with recent legislation, at a hygienic distance from the church.)

For all the energy of the 'récit', with its narrative-bound pathos, this episode brings it to a halt; as Proust's narrator does, in Bergotte's novels, we linger over 'une invocation, une apostrophe, une longue prière' in which he comes to recognise, after all, their principal hold on him, which he first believed to be linked with the charm of their subject. The golden dust and mist of the slanting light render the outlines of the cottage both hard to discern and instantly familiar as a theme of early Impressionism, or, with its mosses and house-leek, as related to Samuel Palmer's very tumbledown *Cottages at Harble-down*. With the 'impétuosité' of the rays of light intensified by the shadow of the curtain of trees, and the precision of 'crêtes délabrées' for the half-rotten thatch, we may feel that this pause itself is intensi-fied by a certain haste, the dynamism of the decline of day – a discovery is to be made, and moreover the light is going. This haste merges into the perception of the transitory energy of a human countenance in the 'fleeting accidental beauty' of the whole scene, which with its human voice is conjuring and mourning its own ending.

A passage such as this (and, for instance, the descriptive letter that opens *Les Paysans*, or the landscape high on the Mont Dore that responds to Raphaël's need for serenity in *La Peau de chagrin*) may tempt us to a comparison with the accounts in the early parts of *A la recherche* of delight in natural surroudings, with their evocations, almost emanations, of an imaginary country-girl, 'criblée de feuillages' – a kind of Green Woman, 'produit nécessaire et naturel de ce sol' – whom the narrator might clasp in his arms. A truer counterpart of Balzac's perceptions of human qualities in the inanimate are the metaphors and anologies to which Proust resorts in some of these same intensely contemplative descriptions, such as the 'sourire' of the sun after rain, on water or on walls. These analogies form themselves into an instrument in the narrator's exploration of the 'essences' he seeks beyond what his senses tell him. One of the most celebrated instances is the 'petit morceau' scribbled in pencil in the doctor's carriage on a drive from Combray, his first success, as it seems to him, in noting something of the fresh life of an impression rather than, as earlier, 'collecting' it and allowing it to wither unused in his mind. The view of the twin church-towers of Martinville, with the single one of Vieuxvicq now superimposed on them and now separate as the road winds, evokes visual comparisons – '[. . .] comme trois oiseaux posés sur la plaine [. . .]' '[. . .] comme trois pivots d'or [. . .]' '[. . .] comme trois fleurs peintes sur le ciel [. . .]' – till, as they are lost to sight after sunset,

Ils me faisaient penser aussi aux trois jeunes filles d'une légende, abandonnées dans une solitude [. . .] je les vis timidement chercher leur chemin et après quelques gauches trébuchements de leurs nobles silhouettes, se serrer les uns contre les autres, glisser l'un derrière l'autre, ne plus faire [. . .] qu'une seule forme noire, charmante et résignée, et s'effacer dans la nuit.

'Penser' is the necessary intervention between vision and its object before this last comparison is arrived at; the birds and flowers were merely what the towers 'looked like'.

It is not, however, only in the early, lyrically subjective books of *A la recherche* that landscapes assume human characteristics. The contrast between the mysterious directness, point to point, of rail travel and the new experience of finding the way by automobile, 'incertain de sa route', but finally charging down upon the destination, after looping round it like a hunter encircling the prey, yields the satisfaction (in *Sodome et Gomorrhe* II) of 'sentir d'une main plus amoureusement exploratrice, avec une plus fine précision, la véritable géométrie, le belle "mesure de la terre" '. This topographical eroticism seems to re-deploy Donne's metaphor of 'my America! my new-found-land'; the traveller shares the lover's need to possess by 'knowing'.

Parfois dans le ciel de l'après-midi passait la lune blanche comme une nuée, furtive, sans éclat, comme une actrice dont ce n'est pas l'heure de jouer et qui, de la salle, en toilette de ville, regarde un moment ses camarades, s'effaçant, ne voulant pas qu'on fasse attention à elle.

Here, in Combray, the image arrived at is so sophisticated, in fact urban, as to administer something of a shock. The familiar but mysterious apparition of the moon in daylight is at an immense distance in our minds from this mondanity, and we are inclined to rebel. It seems a process at the opposite pole from that described as Elstir's method of working on a painting : 'L'effort [...] pour se dépouiller en présence de la réalité de toutes les notions de son intelligence [...]' and 'Elstir tâchait d'arracher à ce qu'il venait de sentir ce qu'il savait – aggrégat de raisonnements que nous appelons vision.' Yet paradoxically this freedom of reference between different types of experience that Proust permits his fictional self is capable of producing a result not dissimilar to the total visual honesty at which Impressionism aimed. It is the declaration of our right to assemble on one plane fleeting or trivial sensations and profoundly strenuous intellectual insights; part of the unity of flesh and spirit, 'the premise of a single, undivided reality', to quote J. P. Stern (*On Realism* §49).

An intense response to the world of nature, only to be conveyed by being equated with the response of our sympathies to other human beings, characterises Balzac and Proust in a rare degree. 'Nous croyons d'une foi profonde à l'originalité, à la vie individuelle du lieu où nous nous trouvons', the narrator tells us of his walks near Méséglise; it is a very Balzacian use of the first person plural, and the dell on the Mont Dore is a full exemplification of the statement.

Of two notable passages of discourse on the novel in general to be found in *A la recherche du temps perdu*, one has Balzac as its prime example, and the other recalls him by implication. It can hardly escape us that on both occasions a kind of description of Proust's own work is offered in the guise of the narrator's thoughts about other writers. There is no question of comprehensiveness in these descriptions, but in the aspects they touch upon they have validity for *A la recherche* as much as for the works named.

First, Proust's narrator reflects on Wagner's method of composition. Putting to use a motif perhaps created long before, suddenly aware of its appropriateness to a particular figure he wishes to equip with its own melodic phrase in the opera, Wagner reminds the narrator of 'all the great works of the nineteenth century' with their caractère d'être – bien que merveilleusement – incomplètes; [...] du dix-neuvième siècle dont les plus grands écrivains ont manqué leurs livres, mais, se regardant travailler comme s'ils étaient à la fois l'ouvrier et le juge, ont tiré de cette auto-contemplation une beauté nouvelle et supérieure à l'œuvre, (lui imposant rétroactivement une unité, une grandeur qu'elle n'a pas.)

I place these last words in parentheses because in the context it seems possible that they represent the point at which the thought diverges towards an aspect of Balzac not central to the earlier part of it, but now becoming so; since, after a glance at Hugo and at Michelet under the heading, as it were, of the words in brackets, Proust's text explicitly compares Wagner's retrospective discovery of the unity of his mythological enterprise with Balzac's perception of his work as a 'Comédie humaine', a cycle rather than a number of scenes, and speculates that Wagner must have experienced 'un peu de la même ivresse'. Balzac, it continues, cast on his works 'le regard d'un étranger et d'un père' and thus suddenly arrived at the idea of recurring characters. There is a suggestion here I think of the argument going off at a tangent, or at least of some 'incompleteness'; can this grouping operation be all that was intended by the comment as it was formulated?

For the first part of the sentence quoted above, with the words 'l'ouvrier et le juge', belongs to a train of thought that arises, as we read Balzac, at innumerable moments unconnected with the attempt to impose overall unity. It is precisely the quality of tentativeness, the appeals for participation, and the extent to which Balzac is simultaneously creator and critic of his fictions that the reader remembers when the word 'incompleteness' is applied to them. 'Auto-contemplation' is not simply the writer's final glance over proofs or preparations for a new edition; it is fundamental to their composition, and we are conscious of it whenever we find Balzac at our elbow pointing out an effect, asking advice, making sure we do not miss a parallel in Shakespeare or an analogy with an item of art-history, questioning his own achievement – threatening, it really seems at times, to start on an immediate revision of the text before our eyes and pressing us into service. 'Lire, n'est-ce pas créer à deux?' is Balzac's succinct, and typically interrogatory, comment on this provisional tone. If we can reply 'No' to this question we had better find something else to read, for others like it will constantly be asked, and while some are plainly rhetorical, many clearly convey that we are being consulted on matters of technique :

Pourquoi les noms des deux domaines [...] dont monsieur et madame de Mortsauf s'occupaient tant, la Cassine et la Rhétorière, m'émeuvent-ils plus que les plus beaux noms de la Terre-Sainte ou de la Grèce? [...] Ces noms possèdent les vertus talismaniques des paroles constellées en usage dans les évocations, ils m'expliquent la magie [...] ils me mettent dans cette heureuse vallée, ils créent un ciel et des paysages [...] Ne vous étonnez donc pas de me voir vous entretenant de scènes si familières.

(*Le Lys dans la valée.*)

'Pourquoi [. . .]?' 'Ne vous étonnez pas [. . .]' Questions and injunctions that convey or conceal others : 'can this be shared, raise an echo?' . . . 'search your own memory, interrogate your past'.

Towards the end of *Le Temps retrouvé*, approaching the recognition of his power to fulfil something of his arduous task, the narrator condemns the 'réalisme' that is a bleak account of the surface of things; and speaks of the immaterial essence of the past that things preserve for us, which we may experience again in the future with their aid :

C'est elle [this essence] que l'art digne de ce nom doit exprimer, et s'il y échoue, on peut encore tirer de son impuissance un enseignement [. . .] à savoir que cette essence est en partie subjective et incommunicable.

Souvent la perfection dans les œuvres d'art empêche l'âme de les agrandir. N'est-ce pas le procès gagné par l'esquisse contre le tableau fini, au tribunal de ceux qui achèvent l'œuvre par la pensée, au lieu de l'accepter toute faite?

The quotation is from Balzac's story *Gambara* at the point where the composer is playing part of his opera to an audience of two on an instrument of his invention, the Panharmonicon; it imitates several of the sections of the orchestra but is in dubious repair; the music is recognisably magnificent. Gambara sings the vocal parts himself, and

loin de nuire à cette riche mélodie, son organe l'expliqua, la fortifia, la dirigea, comme la voix atone et chevrotante d'un habile lecteur, comme l'était Andrieux, étendait le sens d'une sublime scène de Corneille ou de Racine en y ajoutant une poésie intime.

François Andrieux of the Collège de France was a Professor of literature whose lectures Balzac heard. Nothing separates the world from the fiction. Reference might easily be made, in a comparable medical context, to Bianchon; in a Proust passage, to Bergotte. But the whole paragraph indicates, briefly and with assurance, Balzac's idea of the space left, in a work of art, for the play of intelligence and imagination in our reception of it, the part fulfilled by our recognition of things not wholly stated or expressible even by what seems perfect achievement – our 'recognition' of them, that is, as to some extent familiar and our own. Not only this idea, but the manner, and even the example of 'the feeble and quavering voice of an accomplished reader' all bring Balzac here very close to Proust in his most fundamental preoccupations and his most characteristic tone :

il lui demanda de jouer [. . .] la petite phrase de la sonate de Vinteuil, bien qu'Odette jouât fort mal, mais la vision la plus belle qui nous reste d'une œuvre est souvent celle qui s'éleva au-dessus des sons faux tirés par des doigts malhabiles, d'un piano désaccordé. (*Du Côté de chez Swann*.)

Argument, manner and example also show us Balzac offering a perhaps half-conscious commentary on himself, an apologia for hesitancies, defects of tone and style, over-assertiveness – all the faults for which he was castigated by Sainte-Beuve; the Panharmonicon in dubious repair. And that first authoritative attack led of course to Proust's enthusiastic defence of Balzac and his castigation of Sainte-Beuve in his turn as an imperceptive unloving reader, a critic who consistently and on principle refused to distinguish between the writer and the man who wrote, one to whom it was more important to be considered 'un homme de bonne compagnie' (as Mme de Villeparisis describes him in her early appearance in *Le Balzac de M. de Guermantes*) than to give his whole energy to art.

The pianola was invented about the year 1900 and was still gratefully cherished by the most fastidious of listeners in the pre-1914 period. When Proust's narrator is unable to go to concerts, private or public, he often enjoys Wagner and Vinteuil at home in renderings re-created by himself, or by Albertine pedalling away in her little gold slippers copied from those of Oriane de Guermantes. It is one evening when they are thus engaged, towards the end of *La Prisonnière*, that from talking of Vinteuil with his repeated melodic phrases they move on to comparable hallmarks of identity in literature. The idea has a simplicity that would seem to equate it with the narrator's youthful musings about his reading in the first part of the novel; it rapidly turns out to have greater scope and complexity, as we begin to see with the remark that 'les grands littérateurs n'ont jamais fait qu'une seule œuvre, ou plutôt réfracté à travers des milieux divers une même beauté qu'ils apportent au monde.' (Writing of Balzac in *Contre Sainte-Beuve* Proust had noted the procedure of Sainte-Beuve in presuming to select as worth attention a few of the stories and novels, lumping the remainder together as 'un pêle-mêle effrayant'; and in *Le Balzac de M. de Guermantes* he adds the name of Emile Faguet to that of Sainte-Beuve for having labelled *Un Ménage de garçon* (later *La Rabouilleuse*) a masterpiece, and *Le Lys dans la vallée* as execrable. Proust adds 'I am unable to see very great differences between his [Balzac's] different works.' From the context it seems plain that these remarks are closely connected with the conversation in *La Prisonnière*.) As with the discourse on 'incompleteness', the narrator seems, in this second discourse on the novel in general, to give Albertine and us a commentary on some writers he admires with the underlying purpose of glossing the work in which this conversation appears. Not that we are attending a lecture; the discussion is part of the depiction of the daily life of the prisoner and her captor – its literary theorising interspersed with his anxious and anxiously dissimulated attempts to discover more than she wants to tell of her relations with Gilberte Swann – and it arises from a wider contemplation of art, in the form of Vinteuil's music, in which it is an interlude. The evocation of 'un monde unique' by that music, identified as 'the most authentic proof of genius', leads on to the literary parallel; the 'typical phrase' in Vinteuil's various compositions is compared with repeated themes ('une réalité cachée, révélée par une trace matérielle' in Barbey d'Aurevilly, the 'geometry of the stonemason' in Hardy, high places associated in Stendhal with the life of the mind) and above all with the repetition in Dostoevsky of female characters in whom goodness and charm co-exist with shocking cruelty and arrogance, and male characters who combine sly calculation with genuine kindness. What we are shown in such studies is an 'effect', the narrator continues, like the 'effects' of the painter Elstir where the sea appears to be in the sky – the Impressionist technique of reproducing what is seen, not what is known; the related 'cause' may be revealed to us later; it is not logically placed beforehand.

The notion of the 'typical repetition' bringing before us the mysterious but demonstrable identity of the cast of mind, the world-view, of the particular writer, and the ability to communicate something of the least communicable self by the nature of these repetitions (which we may assume from the context to be a choice only partly under conscious control) suggests the application of these remarks to *A la recherche* even more strongly than to the authors named or to Balzac, as we may see from one little example.

When Dr Cottard is implored by his wife to attend to their cook, who has just cut her hand and is bleeding severely, he replies that they must send for someone else because he has already dressed to go out to dinner – '[. . .] tu vois bien que j'ai mon gilet blanc'. The implacability of the social pleasure-seeker is delightfully encapsulated in this glimpse of the professional man's home-life. It is also like a tremor set up by the reverberations of the set-piece in which the Duc de Guermantes and his wife react similarly to the threat suspended over their complex programme for an evening of parties, not by some minor injury but by mortality itself – Swann's news of his incurable disease, and the footman's message that their cousin Amanien d'Osmond is not expected to live another hour. There is a poetry in the convoluted, reiterated self-revelations of egoism in this scene, which gives it some of the force and inevitability of a morality play; gorgeously dressed, Everyman and his Wife in the improbable guise of the Duc and Duchesse de Guermantes receive their admonition from the gentle, reluctant Charles Swann, are observed by their young friend the narrator, who will record their every syllable and play of feature in his Book, and go off to the splendid entertainments that await them, dismissing the footman with abuse ('Taisez-vous, espèce d'idiot [. . .]') and Swann with the equally brutal affectation of incredulity ('Vous vous portez comme le Pont-Neuf. Vous nous enterrerez tous !').

If 'typical repetitions' can characterise the identity of one author, perhaps they can also establish a relationship between two. It has, of course, often been remarked that the prototype of this episode is Delphine de Nucingen's terror of being prevented from going to Mme de Beauséant's brilliant ball by Eugène de Rastignac's announcement that her father, M. Goriot, is on his deathbed. Less often noticed is the kinship of both writers manifest here in the fluidity of Balzac's play with self-awareness. 'Les devoirs de famille', still paramount in Eugène's moral idea of the world, are, to his astonishment, without effect on Delphine; like the Duc de Guermantes, she has but one concern; that her partner should be dressed on time – 'If we get caught in the queue of carriages, we'll be lucky to make our appearance by eleven o'clock' – and he is hustled away by her maid. Eugène's reflections on his way to change present us with the reasoned version of what Proust's scene gives us in action; by showing us the response of the immediate spectator of this behaviour, rather than, like Proust in his parallel incident, allowing that spectator merely to convey to us what he saw and heard with the minimum of comment, Balzac pre-empts our own response. But he does so in the interest of further developing Eugène's understanding both of the world he is choosing and of himself, and it is Eugène who traces for us with full awareness of their speciousness the pretences that serve as a mask for the self against the onlooker and against the self :

Il se plut à penser que le père Goriot n'était pas aussi dangereusement malade qu'il le croyait [. . .] [and there follows a move into *style indirect*

97

libre entirely appropriate to the movement of his attempt to find a way into an acceptance of Delphine's attitude] Elle ne connaissait pas l'état dans lequel était son père. Le bonhomme lui-même la renverrait au bal, si elle l'allait voir. Souvent la loi sociale [and here Eugène by a considerable effort broadens his considerations into generality and embarks on a public tone, as though Balzac were converting one of his own pronouncements on things in general to quotational use, mocking the all-purpose journalistic diapason by putting it to the service of hypocrisy] implacable dans sa formule, condamne là où le crime apparent est excusé par les innombrables modifications qu'introduisent au sein des familles la différence des caractères, la diversité des interêts et des situations. Eugène voulait se tromper lui-même.

The trouble with this sentence (it too part of a morality play) is that it is a parody so close to the model as to pass unnoticed in hasty reading. It needs one of those signposts that its serious intention precludes; as when at a drunken dinner-party in *La Peau de chagrin* a discussion of philosophy leads to insults :

—Voleurs!
—Imbéciles!
—Fripons!
—Dupes!
—Où trouverez-vous ailleurs qu'à Paris un échange aussi vif, aussi rapide entre les pensées, s'écria Bixiou en prenant une voix de basse-taille [incidentally reproducing a Balzacian 'question' that might elsewhere be part of a solemn evocation of life in the metropolis].

An equally familiar critical juxtaposition is that of the first meeting of M. de Charlus and the violinist Morel, on a railway station, with the encounter on the road in *Les Illusions Perdues* that brings Lucien de Rubempré into the ambience of Vautrin, here disguised as a Spanish ecclesiastic. In itself this seems to me rather a forced analogy; it might be truer to say that Vautrin's behaviour to Lucien at this point is strongly anticipatory of an enormous number of other small incidents in which the Baron de Charlus reveals his uncontrollable desire for close physical contact and for moral ascendancy by his reactions to young men including the narrator, and both before and after the explanation of these incidents is available to the narrator. The almost involuntary reaching out ('ses doigts comme magnétisés') to caress the chin of his new acquaintance, with the attendant effect of a shared pretence that the young man is a great deal younger than is really the case; the habit of leaning on an arm or rearranging a coat-collar – these gestures become part of our mental picture of Charlus through reiteration, and are those used by the supposed Abbé

Herrera within minutes of his first sight of Lucien. Putting an arm through Lucien's, or about his waist, tweaking his ear 'avec une familiarité quasi-royale', kissing him tenderly on the forehead, are actions performed with the pretext of enthusiasm in the course of their first conversation and of the Abbé's joy at having frustrated his new friend's immediate project of suicide. What is more important is the nature of the discoveries that conversation affords which are responsible for this enthusiasm – all of the kind Charlus, too, would find most irresistible .

'Petit drôle !' exclaims Herrera to Lucien. 'Petite fripouille !' says Charlus to Proust's narrator early in their acquaintance (receiving, in the event, an indignant retort). Trying out the line of religious consolation at the very outset, Herrera learns that Lucien is an atheist.

Santa Virgen del Pilar ! ... s'écria le prêtre en passant son bras sous celui de Lucien avec un empressement maternel [...] Eh ! voilà l'une des curiosités que je m'étais promis d'observer à Paris. En Espagne, nous ne croyons pas aux athées. [...]

All the peccadilloes and betrayals Lucien has to confess arouse similar effusions and are countered with maxims of anti-social cynicism offered as the model of worldly behaviour and intended as a gauge of his corruptibility; his astonishment makes Herrera 'fear he had revolted Lucien's innocence' – as Charlus keeps watch for the reaction that will tell him he has gone almost too far; it is another game of the will, like the one we have glimpsed between Eugène and Delphine, where the weaker player is challenged, and fails, to commit the social gaffe of speaking condemnation.

At our first introduction to Lucien this development in his story has been foreshadowed by the description of his physique, like that of 'une jeune fille déguisée', slender, but with a suggestion of femininity about the hips – 'indice qui trompe rarement'. The change in Herrera's mode of address from 'vous' to 'tu' occurs at the moment when, as though yielding to an obsession, he asks if Lucien knows Venice Preserved – 'cette amitié profonde, d'homme à homme, qui lie Pierre à Jaffier, qui fait pour eux d'une femme une bagatelle, et qui change entre eux tous les termes sociaux ?' This, for the reader, is the clue to Herrera's identity, since Otway's play is cited in a precisely similar way by Vautrin in Le Père Goriot when he opens his heart to Eugène de Rastignac, and there as here with the aim of introducing themes often on the lips of Charlus – his solitude, his need to bestow affection, and his power to give worldly success too.

This reminiscence is of course underlined by Lucien's mention of Rastignac's name as an acquaintance in Paris. A little later the road on which Herrera's barouche is travelling brings them to the manor of Rastignac, which Lucien points out, and the 'priest' dismounts to get a view of it.

If *Venice Preserved* is, for Vautrin, a sacred text, it is this episode that makes *Les Illusions perdues* precious in its turn to the Baron de Charlus. His identification of himself with Vautrin turns it, for him, into 'la *Tristesse d'Olympio* de la pédérastie'. This phrase is also Proust's own, in the essay *Sainte-Beuve et Balzac*. With its glance at Hugo's fine lyric of nostalgia it further enriches the literary brew, but it is hard to see the relation between the poem and Balzac's crisp reticence here. However, the remarks about Dostoevsky we have noted in *A la Recherche* are relevant to the admiration Proust expresses (again in the essay), for Balzac's technique in reserving overt commentary on Vautrin-Herrera's motivation, while giving a precise account of all he does and says on this journey, up to a certain point in time. (A pact is mentioned, the large sum Lucien owes to his family is promised as the reward of 'obedience', and in sending the money to them he writes of Herrera 'je suis sa créature'.) Thus Proust can write of the 'profondeur admirable' by which 'chaque mot, chaque geste, a ainsi des dessous dont Balzac n'avertit pas le lecteur' in the same way in which, in the novel, he dwells on Dostoevsky's 'effects' obtained by juxtaposing uncommented actions and leaving us to make sense of them according to our ability to decipher the 'sous-texte', as he would no doubt have called it if the term had been available. Regarded as an admonition to anyone misled into hasty reading by the belief that there exists something called 'the Balzacian novel', this comment of Proust's is invaluable. Yet we may still feel that emotional closeness to the *theme* brings the critic to the verge of disequilibrium, indicated not only by the Hugo reference but also in the appeal to the well-known quip by Oscar Wilde, to the effect that the greatest sorrow he had known was Lucien's death in the sequel. Proust attributes this sentiment to the fact that Wilde and all other readers adopt the point of view of Vautrin, which is also that of Balzac. Wilde perhaps did so, but Balzac and most of his readers probably occupy a more generally available standpoint, and still find Lucien's history a moving one.

The truth is that, exactly as Vautrin might be considered to have rather missed Otway's main drift, so the Baron de Charlus as a lover of Balzac has to be listened to with caution; his judgment is not the objective appreciation or sense of intellectual kinship that makes most of us say we 'love' an author. It is closer to an effusion of gratitude for the long hoped-for validation of his own emotional inclinations by a writer whose reputation is not generally identified with them; a validation not consisting in any defensive stance Balzac might have taken on their behalf, but simply, in the recurring figure of Vautrin, and in *La Fille aux yeux d'or*, his recognition of the mere existence of homosexuality as a motive of human conduct.

If, following the example of Proust's narrator in *La Prisonnière*, we try to locate a thematic recurrence in his novel, it might be that of pursuit; of the woodland paths near Balbec he writes: 'They reminded me that it was my fate only to pursue phantoms, beings whose reality, for the most part, was in my imagination.' It is most characteristically, though, in the streets of Paris that the obsessive stratagems of the hunt are deployed; by Swann seeking Odette, by the narrator studying the habits of Mme de Guermantes; and towards the end of his quest, of his 'recherche', trailing Charlus and Saint-Loup through the blacked-out wartime city like a somnambulist in an inferno, although their motives and their destination have long been known to him.

Thus too (*Gambara*, *Ferragus*) Balzac leads us on the track of pursuers; and, in the muted, unmediated first-person reminiscence that opens *Facino Cane*, shows us himself at twenty, following and eavesdropping on working-class couples going home from the theatre in the poor quarter where he lodged, near the Place de la Bastille. Inconspicuous and unresented, because he was 'as badly dressed as they', this observer was not impelled by erotic or malevolent curiosity as the protagonists of his stories would be; he sought 'la distraction' of replacing his own perceptions with theirs, sharing their anxieties and grievances, studying their language, and delighting in what seemed to him a mysterious gift of entering into their lives, 'devenir un autre que soi'.

For all the circumstantial realism of its presentation (*récit* in Balzac, the at times effortful insistence on plausibility in Proust), this theme of the quest typically merges fictional beings with their creators. When we read, in Balzac's *Les Proscrits*, of the writer sitting down to his work, 'Il demandait des mots au silence, des idées à la nuit' – we are looking into the intensification of the hunter's solitude in the imaginative task. 'Les vrais livres', writes Proust towards the end of *Le Temps retrouvé*, 'doivent être les enfants non du grand

jour et de la causerie mais de l'obscurité et du silence.' If a barrier
can somewhere be drawn between realism and the 'literature of
inwardness', we will very often be obliged to admit that the true
encounter between Balzac and Proust takes place not at the barrier,
where the two domains touch, but beyond it, in the realm of 'inwardness' itself; and this, perhaps, is what Proust 'savait mieux que
personne'.

Realism, modernism, and 'language-consciousness'

STEPHEN HEATH

Debate about literary realism runs by now on well-established lines. The very nature of the term – one of aesthetic description and evaluation, like epic or lyric, but, unlike them, one that cannot be discussed simply aesthetically, suggesting as it does questions of the relations of a work to an outside, to the reality that a realism presumably involves – gives a certain range of inevitable topics and points of argument; and which are present too when attempts are made to exclude them, such exclusion itself being easily internal to the debate, so many positions and moves within it. Realism may be traced as perennial, a permanent mode of writing that is dominant or not throughout the ages, at the same time that it may be clearly identified as a particular literary-historical moment, that of the rise of the novel and the culminating achievement of nineteenth-century European Realism, which latter indeed powerfully underwrites the perception of that permanent mode of writing, determines our perennial recognitions. Auerbach's exemplary *Mimesis* explores the representation of reality in Western literature over three thousand years of a history that in the end finds its sense in Stendhal, Balzac, Flaubert; the realism they offer is a modern revolution, that of 'die moderne ernste Realistik', but is also the perspective of the exploration as it looks back to forge, from that realism, a literary-historical continuity, exactly this history that *Mimesis* is.[1]

Realism, moreover, is immediately political in its implications : a matter of literary politics – literary movements readily identify themselves as effecting a return from convention to reality ('Tous les écrivains pensent être réalistes', comments Robbe-Grillet)[2] – but then also of politics itself, of cultural-political struggle – as witness the clash between Lukács and Brecht in the thirties, arguably the most significant discussion of realism in the twentieth century.[3] How is reality to be understood? The question comes with realism and turns description into evaluation : the judgment of the realism of a work can be made conventionally, by reference to a particular literary standard of what realism is, but that conventional judgment cannot but bring with it an accepted version of reality, a given representation to the givenness of which the literary standard contributes. One vital stress and lesson of realism, that achievement of nineteenth-century European Realism, is history, social-historical awareness (Balzac, says Auerbach, grasps the present as history, 'die Gegenwart als Geschichte').[4] Stress and lesson, however, must then *include realism*, itself historical not just in its perception of its object-reality (a historical world) but equally in its construction and formulation of that perception and the object-reality with it (a historical representation of the world) : the production, recognition, definition of realism are themselves historical through and through.

Of course, realism can be reduced to, say, acknowledgement of a substantial world of things – 'One solitary plate, one knife, one fork, one glass !' as fundamental realist gesture[5] – but, though this is part of the history of the term and the literature, it is evident that what is at stake is far more complex, *is* a particular *representation* of the real as a *reality*, not the sum of a few separate and universal elements. This is why, indeed, realism is so quickly gathered up into positions of conservatism or revolutionism : realism as a given and known quantity-quality that can be grasped in a literary tradition and enshrined in an essential form (Lukács's championing of 'bourgeois critical realism' against the 'decadence' of modernism, the nineteenth-century realist novel as the available and necessary form for a new 'socialist realism' that would thus be a painless extension of it – 'Be like Balzac – but of today!' as Brecht sardonically put it);[6] or realism as an historical act of production that necessitates the shattering of old forms, accepted representations, in the interests of a new, effective hold on reality (Brecht's call for the description of a world in a constant process of transformation which ceaselessly demands new modes of expression, 'immer neue Mittel der Darstellung',[7] this determining his omission from Lukács's pantheon of potential realist writers in the thirties and forties). In short, realism is a major political, philosophical and practical issue (Brecht again, 'eine grosse politische, philosophische, praktische Angelegenheit').[8]

Much of this context of realism as a 'concept of literature' is finely stated and developed in J. P. Stern's *On Realism* which simultaneously argues its own position in the debate.[9] I take that position centrally to involve a basic idea of realism as 'perennial' (p. 52 and *passim*) and so to be seen as 'a literary tradition' (p. 150) though realised each time with some historical specificity, 'Every age has [. . .]

its own realism' (p. 89). Realism is thus 'a disposition of mind and pen' (p. 52), 'a condition not a content' (p. 147), with 'attributes' that include 'riches of the represented world', 'weightiness and resistance to ideals', 'consequential logic and circumstantiality' (p. 28). Overall, it 'designates a creative attention to the visible rather than the invisible, an unabating interest in the shapes and relations of the real world, the system that works' (p. 171). As *a mode of writing* (p. 52), it depends on a balance of 'making' and 'matching', with the balance 'on the side of the matching' (p. 75); and it must maintain 'the middle distance' which 'places individual people and their institutions in one working perspective ("gets them all into the picture" at any one time in history)' (p. 121): 'that middle distance at which realism portrays and preserves persons and their world in their time-bound, relative integrity' (pp. 125–6).

Presenting this account of realism, Stern proceeds descriptively: works which are not realist, those of Kafka for instance (pp. 129–30), are simply a different mode of writing, occupy a different place in the 'one field' of literature (p. 122). At the same time, his argument is clearly also evaluative, strongly so: realism shows a valued 'continuity of meaning' (p. 81), gives us 'all of our common reality' (p. 153), is democratic – if realism 'cannot be identical with any one coherent ideology' (p. 52), its 'exaggerations and omissions' being dictated not ideologically but 'by the convention and form of the work in which they occur' (p. 56), it nevertheless remains true that 'the democratic ideology' is 'a more natural habitation for the practice of literary realism' (p. 57). From this mesh of description and evaluation comes the concern with a modern loss of realism, 'a recession of realistic writing' (p. 158): the balance of the middle distance, the picture and its completeness, 'the total form' (p. 73), these have disappeared with modernism – 'Halfway between the Somme and Auschwitz, Virginia Woolf, the first of the *nouveaux romanciers*, describes the death of a pale-brown fieldmoth' (p. 176). Evidently, it is not just a question of neutral alternatives, this mode of writing and then that one. For all their differences, Stern comes close to Lukács; he too can see and regret in modernism a progressive dissolution of realism, could echo the thirties' cry: 'Es geht um den Realismus'.[10]

One crucial demonstration of the loss, the recession, is provided by what Stern calls 'the literature of language-consciousness' (p. 159), 'literature in the language-conscious mode' (p. 161): 'here fictions are dominated by language, or rather by an articulated consciousness

of the creative process, its psychology, technicalities, and institu-
tionalization' (p. 159). Such a dominance can only tip the balance
the wrong way, an extreme version of making over matching, and
be an end of realism : 'A realism composed of nothing but language-
conscious fictions is an impossibility, albeit a fashionable one' (p. 85).

That 'language-consciousness' brings a shift in realism is, I think,
correct; that it must come to the latter's impossibility is not. Of
course, if 'realism' were predefined to exclude attention to language,
there would be no argument, as neither would there be if it were
predefined to include it. But the point clearly does not lie in such
triviality; the issues at stake are real. 'Language-consciousness' shifts
realism *importantly*; it poses central questions for a contemporary
realism, with this last term in no way then becoming inappropriate
or merely arbitrary. Relations between literary work and world, that
is, are not broken, though understanding of those relations and of
reality with them may be recast, which recasting indeed might be
seen as fundamental for any significant activity of realism. What
Stern treats as 'the literature of language-consciousness' is to be
grasped as a specific historical moment in literature and the politics
of reality (the understanding of reality as human production and
hence as transformable), involving precisely the articulation of
modernism and realism, an avant-garde problem of changing reality,
changing representation – something of Brecht's 'Es verändert sich
die Wirklichkeit; um sie darzustellen, muss die Darstellungsart sich
ändern.'[11] That this is not fully brought out in Stern's treatment is
due not simply to his particular position but also to confusions and
difficulties in the work – mainly mine – from which he draws material
for his account of such a modernist-realist practice of writing.[12] That
work and that account are too closely bound up with the limited and
limiting phenomenon of the French *nouveau roman* in the fifties and
sixties, and with a time of what for want of better might be called
extreme semiotic reaction, an acute attention to language and signification at once essential in its focusing of issues and advancing of
theoretical awareness and potentially difficult in its practical developments, always open to formalist reductions. Which at least allows
scope here for some remarks towards a revised – hopefully clarifying
– consideration of realism, modernism and 'language-consciousness'.

The determining position of nineteenth-century European Realism
in our very conception of realism – it is only with that European
Realism after all that realism becomes a central 'concept of litera-

ture', that specific and sustained debate on its terms begins – makes any challenge to it hard to accept with reference to a continued idea of realism nevertheless. Modernism, which makes such a challenge directly, is thus quickly excluded from its field, as by Stern who on 'the deadly plains of contemporary literature' (p. 158) sees at best only 'alternative[s] to realism' (p. 143). Certainly, the directness of the challenge, its explicit statements of intention can easily support him : Proust writes against 'la fausseté même de l'art prétendu réaliste';[13] Woolf looks to novelists who in future will leave 'the description of reality more and more out of their stories';[14] and if Joyce offers *Dubliners* with 'the conviction that he is a very bold man who dares to alter in the presentment, still less to deform, whatever he has seen and heard', by the time we get to 'Work in Progress' we need only remember Beckett's appraisal, 'His writing is not about something; it is that something itself.'[15] Though, of course, there is then also here an appeal to a true reality, to, as it were, the reality of reality : Proust wants to write 'un livre extrêmement réel' that will give the essence of self and experience, 'notre vraie vie, la réalité telle que nous l'avons sentie';[16] Woolf seeks to grasp something 'so real (I do not by that mean so lifelike)', to 'give the moment whole', to 'convey this varying, this unknown and uncircumscribed spirit, whatever aberration or complexity it may display', to 'reach the dark places of psychology';[17] and Joyce after *Ulysses*, after what Pound calls 'an epoch-making report on the state of the human mind in the twentieth century', reaches in *Finnegans Wake* to those dark places, their reality, 'conscious, then semi-conscious, then unconscious'.[18] It is this movement against realism (the nineteenth-century novel form) and for a new demonstration of reality that works with a consciousness of and attention to language, pulling towards formulations suggesting the creation of autonomous linguistic wholes, the text with word as world : Proust stresses style and the book as the realisation of reality, its writing 'la seule vie par conséquent réellement vécue';[19] Woolf talks of 'the sentence in itself beautiful';[20] Joyce writes *Finnegans Wake* as a veritable 'polyhedron of scripture'.[21]

A familiar literary history, one that has its rightness, understands and contains this fact of the novel and modernism in terms of a switch from 'objective' to 'subjective', from world to consciousness – and below, the dark places. Evaluatively, this is a fall into 'solipsism' and thus the end of the middle distance, of the voice that 'caps' any 'subjective totality' and holds it within the overall view, the picture,

of the 'objective totality of the world' which it thereby maintains; the
'decision for realism' in the face of any 'solipsistic assessment' is
always 'to cap *that* once more by a realistic assessment, and to stop
at that point' (p. 144). Solipsism and 'language-consciousness' run
hand in hand (remember the final quotations above from Proust,
Woolf, Joyce), the latter to an extreme 'yet another form of inwardness' (p. 162): from the confident flourish of external naming and
reference, 'Au commencement du mois d'octobre 1829, monsieur
Simon Babylas Latournelle, un notaire, montait du Havre à
Ingouville [...]', we move to the self-reflecting fiction of the paper
voice, nowhere but in this moment of language on the page, 'Je suis
seul ici, maintenant, bien à l'abri.'[22] Yet the familiarity of the history
and the rightness it has should not be allowed to mask a different
understanding of modernism and realism, of the modernist possibility
of realism. One of the things that comes through from modernism –
unevenly, contradictorily – is a version of 'world, self, meaning, and
language' (p. 142), of reality, which is not a collapse of realism (into
'self', into 'language'), but a transformation of our grasp of their
conjunction – that transformation affecting the given opposition of
'subjective' and 'objective' itself. At which point it can also be said,
to mark the complex dialectic, that our perception of modernism in
these terms, our reading now of Proust and Woolf and Joyce, owes its
force to the semiotic reaction mentioned earlier, which brought out
and gave definition to the work of modernism in respect of realism.

Eisenstein, part of this history of modernism and realism, put it like
this: 'Absolute realism is by no means the correct form of perception.
It is simply the function of a certain form of social structure.'[23] The
achievement of nineteenth-century European Realism, however
much that monolithic literary-historical construction needs also to be
broken down so as to take account of the evident differences from
novelist to novelist and from country to country (the difference, for
example, between the French and the English novel, the latter said
by James in 1884 to lack the seriousness and theory of the former)[24]
and whatever the difficulties of the analysis (the whole Marxist
problem of determination), can be seen in relation to a class and to
developments of capitalism, urbanisation, democracy (or the struggle
for it). Realism, in function of that social reality, undercuts traditional forms and values in the interests of a prosaic world, visible,
matter of fact ('As to the book, 'tis for the most part, matter of fact,
and all transacted within these three months').[25] Its world is secular
and secure in the voice of the 'objective totality' that homogenises

the disparate actions and dramas its narratives reveal – ' "gets them all into the picture" ' (p. 121). The sole arena of value is that social-historical world, only there can fulfilment lie; or rather, it is there that fulfilment is sought and that the pressure of its difficulty is given and confiningly felt.

Realism, in fact, is produced in the novel as a social narration of the individual as problem : what, where, how is the meaning of the individual in this prosaic world, confronted thus by society, by history? The novel ceaselessly makes sense for the individual, brings him or her – hero or heroine but also simultaneously the reader as its addressed agent – into this new field of reality, into recognition, knowledge, meaning. Crucially, its realism is a response to instability: the novel coincides with the development of a new form of social organisation, that of capitalism, in which, precisely, society and the individual become the terms of reference, in which the social relations of the individual – 'the individual and society', as we have learnt to say – become a problem as such. The point now is a society which, dependent in its economic instance on the relations of people as individual agents, producers and consumers assuring a circulation of commodities and capital in the 'free market', institutes human being as individual being, with the latter the corresponding realm of given private freedom and endeavour for fulfilment; 'the various forms of the social texture', writes Marx in the year of the trial of *Madame Bovary*, 'confront the individual as merely means towards his private ends, as external necessity [als äusserliche Notwendig-keit]'.[26] Freedom and necessity run together here as the reflection and definition each of the other in the form of 'the individual and society'. There is then a powerful work of *social* representation of 'the individual', the socially cohesive realisation of the latter, people given that sense : so many patterns of recognition through the repeated account of the social as meaning for the individual, the stabilisation of a continually achieved and maintained representation in those terms.

Which representation is, again, both *of* – the represented world and agents – and *to* – the reader addressed, put in the picture. The seriousness of realism is not just what it says but also, and this is then part of the saying, what it does in a society in which literature is becoming a commodity for mass private consumption, the work for the individual serialised reader, for his or her 'entertainment' and 'culture'. The world that confronts the individual, hero or heroine, in the book's fiction confronts the reader as the knowledge, the property of the book that gives him or her the representation of life, the novel 'being everywhere an effort at *representation* – this is the beginning and the end of it'.[27] World and book are enclosed and totalising wholes, with realism as their relation, their truth; buying the book is buying – literally and figuratively – the world it contains, the coherence of its picture and the stability of meaning, the overall view, that coherence entails. When James attacks Trollope for betraying the 'sacred office', for failing the seriousness of the novel's realism, it is precisely for breaking into the picture, shattering the necessary coherence of the representation : 'He admits that the events he narrates have not really happened, and that he can give his narrative any turn the reader may like best' but the novelist is historian and 'must speak with assurance', that middle distance – 'as the picture is reality, so the novel is history'.[28]

Picture, history, reality : *representation*. When Stern says of realism that 'It gives us all of our common reality' (p. 152), we must understand that it produces it, contributes to its production and to the very situation of that 'us' and 'our', constructing a subject-site of identity from and for the picture, history, reality given. This is the crux of the representation : realism is realism for someone, for the some *one* that the capping voice places in its perspective. Representation, that is, involves not just an imaging or portraying ('of life') but always also an argumentation – a position, a case, is represented to me – and a deputation – I am represented by this imaging-argumentation that stands for and gives back the sense of identity, my intelligibility. As representation, the novel's realism is a system – and not 'a luxurious independence of rules and restrictions'[29] – that includes the reader as the subject-position of its coherence, the point of its view, the knowledge of the common reality.

The common reality must needs be constructed, depends on its representation, is a question of knowing. For all the imagery of mirror and reflection so characteristically present in the defining statements of realism and the novel, realism is never intended as a simple copy of reality – whatever that could mean – but always, and modernist writers are in a way only more radically explicit on this, as a demonstration of reality, getting through to what it really is; thus Balzac's sociology (the aim to give a scientific typology modelled on the work of Cuvier and Saint-Hilaire, Balzac as 'docteur ès sciences sociales')[30] or George Eliot's morality (the aim 'to give no more than a faithful account of men and things as they have mirrored themselves in my mind' is also, and derives from, the aim to show the moral fabric that is the truth of human reality, the necessity for that 'deep human sympathy' of which realism, teaching us to see and understand 'commonplace things', is the confirming vehicle).[31] Realism is reality as intelligibility, the real made sense; it is there to provide knowledge and truth, and, like science to which it so often referred in the nineteenth century, 'would be superfluous if the outward appearance and the essence of things directly coincided'.[32]

The problem – but also the stuff of the greatest nineteenth-century realist novels – is then that reality is not coherence and single truth but process and contradiction, is available not reflectively but dialectically in a specific production of understanding that cannot be merely conceived as a matter of vision and essence in the way that realism in the nineteenth century classically proposes and that continues in certain critical arguments. Lukács makes of realism the presentation of totality, its end would be to give an image of reality in which the contradiction between phenomenon and essence, particular case and law, immediacy and concept and so on is resolved in an indissoluble unity : 'dass beide im unmittelbaren Eindruck des Kuntswerks zur spontanen Einheit zusammenfallen, dass sie für den Rezeptiven eine unzertrennbare Einheit bilden'.[33] But such a totality – the resolved oneness of reality–reflection–knowledge – is the dead weight of a 'realism' that the finest novelists, those indeed whom Lukács praises, challenge in their works which show the understanding of reality as difficult and contradictory, as heterogeneous, exactly in its understanding. Balzac and Eliot know a reality that they produce–reproduce in their novels, a reality set over and against hero or heroine and reader who are brought – 'capped' – into its terms, gaining that knowledge; but then the action of the novels, their writing, exceeds, gives the difficulty of knowing, the limits, impasses, overrunnings of the given picture – the panic of *La Fille aux yeux d'or*, the tensions of *Daniel Deronda*.

Realism's 'creative attention to the visible rather than the invisible' (p. 171) is in fact for the nineteenth-century novel (and this very way of putting it is from *that* realism) an attempt to hold the two together as one, to make, impossibly, reality visible as such, to make it the source of its knowledge and coherence. The result is a literature in which reality is transparent, knowable, *and* opaque, troubled; with all the figures of that visible–invisible attempt, the patterns of narrative discovery and revelation, and with all the problems increasingly of confidence in its terms, the failure of those patterns to give a unity. From Balzac's mosaic-pieced world that, wishfully, might perhaps be put together in an overall 'comédie humaine' by some complex process of continually present narration but that is so difficult to hold still ('Il n'y a rien qui soit d'un seul bloc dans ce monde, tout y est mosaïque. Vous ne pouvez raconter chronologiquement que l'histoire du temps passé, système inapplicable à un présent qui marche. L'auteur a devant lui pour modèle le XIXe siècle, modèle extrême-ment remuant et difficile à faire tenir en place')[34] we move to James's 'house of fiction' with its 'number of possible windows not to be reckoned', so many views on the incalculable myriadness of life ('reality has a myriad forms')[35] and thence to the impossible – 'queer' – 'multiplicity' of, say, Huxley ('the essence of the new way of looking is multiplicity [. . .] no picture can be queer enough to do justice to the facts').[36] The visible–invisible becomes a relation of the novel to the fragmentary and the secret, as Conrad talks of the novelist's task as that of holding up 'the rescued fragment' and disclosing 'its inspir-ing secret'. [37] The resolution of the visible and the invisible fails, breaks down in its fiction; vision, realism's metaphor of reality and its knowledge, cannot contain the fact of realism, its writing, the activity of its *production.*

Stern writes of 'riches', the plethora of George Eliot's 'common-place things', as 'signs of the *eros* that binds [the realist] to this world': 'what informs his evocations is always an unabating *interest* in this world and in this society as a thing real and, as to its reality, wholly unproblematic' (p. 5). But the *eros*, the desire that permeates the rela-tions of realism, produces a particular and problematic world. The existence of things is not in doubt but then that existence is a *mode* of existence : what realism produces is not a recognition of a world of things (though we may make that a concomitant of any realism); it is a version of reality in which things have a *specific* existence. The resistance of things and world in realism is not just that of materiality (Dr Johnson kicking the stone); it is that of Society, History, an overstanding force in respect of which desire, the individual, has its measure, his or her history – and the writing too, giving measure and history.

Realism, that is, is not 'a perennial mode', however much this or that realist attribute might be traced back and forth over the ages; it involves always a politics of reality, reality as 'reality', a *representa-tion,* and for and to and of a particular subject-position. The attempted homogenisation-stabilisation of nineteenth-century realism (still with us today in much novel writing) as a mode of meaning the world – of representing reality – cannot be allowed by virtue of its accepted 'naturalness', exactly its 'realism', to mask the facts of its construction. To say which is not to detach it from any connection with an external reality nor to make reality linguistic in some simple – and ludicrous – sense. It is, though, to stress in any reality as we understand and know it, reality for us, the inextricable presence of language : reality is not accessible outside of the codes of observation, perception, recognition through which we grasp it and without which it could not be conceived as 'reality'. To turn realism into its writing is to remember this, to attend to its representation, reality as 'reality' – 'le réel sous sa forme jugée,' as Barthes defines a writing.[38]

Consider together these two passages from English nineteenth-century novels, both describing a man just as he is about to leave his house on Chartist business :

'Oh! father, don't go yet . . .'
But he pushed her away, and was gone. She followed him to the door, her eyes blinded by sudden tears; she stood there looking after him. He was so strange, so cold, so hard. Suddenly, at the end of the court, he turned, and saw her standing there; he came back quickly, and took her in his arms.

. . . he released himself from the hand of his daughter with abruptness. Sybil looked up to heaven with streaming eyes, and clasped her hands in unutterable woe. Gerard moved again towards the door, but before he reached it, his step faltered, and he turned again and looked at his daughter with tenderness and anxiety.[39]

The writing of the first passage may well be more skilful than the writing of the second but they are both the same writing, both from within the same generally and naturally available mode, the stock ways of conceiving – of contriving – a reality which these passages repeat, sustain and confirm. In both passages, which come from 'social fact' novels whose whole stress is on the realism of the picture they give, the innocent gentleness of the daughter acts as a demonstration of the coldness of the father drawn into Chartism, and the turning back, the faltering step, is the ratification of the demonstration, the admission of guilt. The writing, that is, proceeds through the assumption of specific figures – the pathetic heroine, the man as father, the focus through the family; it works by repeating the forms that make up the possible representation of 'reality', its space of discourse. This repetition, of course, from within that space, is then called 'realism'. In fact, in the Disraeli passage this repetition goes along with the manoeuvring of a deliberate ideological intervention, but in the passage by Gaskell it is the realisation of what is consciously intended as an extreme fidelity to fact, as supremely realistic writing. The juxtaposition of the two passages indicates clearly enough, however, the situation of that 'realistic' writing within an area of generally accepted, and acceptable, forms. It is those forms that allow the middle distance, the stable view : when Gaskell attempts to write her novel close up to the experience of the working-class John Barton representation fails her, there is no given resolution; the switch to the form of the heroine and the plot of daughter and father puts things back into focus, the coherent perspective. The greatness – another realism – of the novels of her contemporary Dickens is bound up exactly with their dramatisation of this problem of representation as increasingly they lack middle distance, overall position, unifying sense. Sense is made – by the Christian rhetoric of overt commentary or by the genre recall of melodramatic pathos – but *alongside*, going on amidst a whole host of effects and turns of language, a restless movement of words and things and agents, a panic of representation that turns back on the given forms, disrupts them – gets them askew – as part of the novels' awareness of reality : the figure of the pathetic heroine fails to stabilise and protect in *Bleak House*, the conventional inheritance offers no conclusion in *Little Dorrit*, the revelations of identity and transformations of character at the end of *Our Mutual Friend* are simply grotesque, the mark of the lack of any responsible – availably 'realistic' – perspective. Mention is made at one point in this last novel of people becoming 'infected with [. . .] fiction'[40] and it is just such an infection that Dickens's novels begin to see in the conventional seeing, in the given realism (hence, unsurprisingly, the criticism of a lack of realism so frequently directed by reviewers at his later novels).

The history of realism is a history of writings – discursive modes of the organisation of a representation of reality – and the judgment as to a work's 'realism' must be understood accordingly. Reproaching Lukács for the timeless formalism of his literary tradition of realism, Brecht suggests that one cannot judge a work's realism by the yardstick of what passed for realism at the time: 'Ob ein Werk realistisch ist oder nicht, das kann man nicht feststellen, indem man nur nachsieht, ob es bestehenden, realistisch genannten, für ihre Zeit realistisch zu nennenden Werken gleicht oder nicht.'[41] One way he is wrong: the recognition of realism depends conventionally precisely on fidelity to a given mode of representation, on repetition; so that it can be determined rather after the fashion of the restaurant-owner in *A la recherche du temps perdu* who 'avait l'habitude de comparer toujours ce qu'il entendait ou lisait à un certain texte déjà connu et sentait s'éveiller son admiration s'il ne voyait pas de différences'.[42] Another way he is right, the point being to break the circle in which judgment as to realism depends on an idea of reality, a picture, itself derived from the given realism, the existing representation to which the realism of literature contributes, and to pose a politics of reality in which literature is implicated, with writing – 'realism' – the place of that implication.

A history of writings . . . Stern comments : 'It is clear that realism is exceptionally sensitive to the movements of social and political history; and that, more than other modes of writing, it is dependent on its literary antecedents. The literary history of realism would [. . .] have to be a sequential account of ever new areas of worldly experience becoming available to literature – that is, a sequential account of ever new possibilities of fiction and sentence-making within the *données* of changing historical situations' (p. 99). Along with which we can put Barthes : 'On pourrait imaginer une histoire de la littérature, ou, pour mieux dire: des productions de langage, qui serait l'histoire des *expédients* verbaux, souvent très fous, dont les hommes ont usé pour réduire, apprivoiser, nier, ou au contraire assumer ce qui est *toujours* un délire, à savoir l'inadéquation fondamentale du langage et du réel.'[43] Stern seems to hesitate (and in that hesitation we can also see the sign of the complexity of any realism) : on the one hand, realism is dependent on its literary antecedents (but why more so than other modes of writing, pastoral say?); on the other, it appears to follow social and political history and the availability of new areas of worldly experience; while on a third hand, if that expression be permitted, it is a matter of new possibilities of fiction and sentence-making. Barthes shifts the stress clearly to language, to language-productions : a history of realism would be part of an overall literary history, engaging that set of verbal expedients that seek particularly to tame or deny – rather than to assume – the fundamental inadequation of language and real. Which is where Stern would see the signs of 'language-consciousness', a stress that effectively leads away from realism.

'Language-consciousness' is described by Stern in two forms : a 'relatively naive form' involving 'the "artist and society" theme', 'the self-conscious story of artistic creation', the consummation of this form being *Finnegans Wake*; and a more sophisticated form, 'an altogether different mode', 'where this self-conscious "wording" of the creative process becomes a major theme, drawing all others into itself', 'all language "is about" language', with this form characterised by the *nouveau roman* (p. 159). This description seems wrong, though to a certain extent plausible on the basis of formulations made in the context of the semiotic reaction and on that of the practice of the accompanying literature.

Symptomatic here, and crucial, is the reference to *Finnegans Wake*. That work certainly reflects on the story of artistic creation and uses 'the artist and society' (the corrosive 'going over' of *A Portrait of the Artist as a Young Man* in the 'Shem the Penman' section) but is certainly also an altogether different mode of writing, language about language. But then again, what Joyce produces is not language about language in the mere sense of 'complex language-games' (p. 159); rather, the book, contemporary with Freud and psychoanalysis, explores the intricate mesh of subjectivity, sexuality, language, the history of the individual in a way that has become readable from the theoretical developments of the sixties and seventies, the attention to language given in the semiotic reaction.[44] That this represents 'the progressive loss of realism' (p. 159) is true historically (*Finnegans Wake* is not like *Middlemarch*) and true in effect in as much as social-historical determination is lost sight of in Joyce's universal history (a problem in psychoanalysis too) but not in any automatic sense in relation to language, not simply because it is about language.

Everything hinges on how 'language' is understood here (and 'language about language'). The great defining versions of modern linguistics – Saussure's, Chomsky's – split language into enclosed formal system and actual individual use, *langue* and *parole* or *competence* and *performance*. What is at stake in the work of modernism and language, 'language-consciousness', is not the abandonment of the taken-for-granted individual use of language for attention to an abstract autonomous system as such; on the contrary, it is a focus on the productivity of language, its determining role in the very fact of 'reality', that recasts the understanding of language, looks at its construction of social and subjective, all the orders of meaning that are in play at any moment in the construction of our reality. The semiotic reaction to which I have been referring was a theoretical grasp of this (Barthes after all in *Le Degré zéro de l'écriture* introduced 'writing' from the very start as a concept to give an awareness of language quite different from the linguistic split and then gave in *S/Z* a specific analysis of a realist writing) but through a semiotics that was itself easily caught up in a closed systematisation that evacuated the social-historical, the grounds of realism : the study of – in Saussure's famous phrase – 'la vie des signes au sein de la vie sociale',[45] could turn merely into the description of abstract structures, with on the literary side the development of a technicist 'structuralist poetics'. What pulled semiotics forward from this was a practice of writing, an avant-garde literature, that worked as a reflection not on 'artistic creation' (or, at least, not in those conventional terms) but on the forms of representation and their construction of subject and 'reality'. If such a practice could collapse into 'play' (Robbe-Grillet's slide into pornography, the 'playful' quotation and combination of mass cultural stereotypes), it could also offer a critical – realist – attention to 'reality', grasping its orders, envisaging its transforma-tion. Some of the work of Sollers would serve as example here (*Lois, H*) but the more striking developments were in film – the politically semiotic cinema of Godard, for instance : modernism and Brecht and the pressure of the contemporary social-historical from May 1968 on.

Stern quotes Barthes as quoted by me : 'Le réalisme, ici, ce ne peut être la copie des choses, mais la connaissance du langage; l'œuvre la plus "réaliste" ne sera pas celle qui "peint" la réalité, mais qui, se servant du monde comme contenu (ce contenu lui-même est d'ailleurs étranger à sa structure, c'est-à-dire à son être), explorera le plus profondément possible la *réalité irréelle* du langage' (p. 165).[46] And he is right to draw back from 'the world as a mere occasion for setting the exploration of language in train' (*ibid.*). Barthes's formu-lations, the seminotic *reaction*, often go this way : 'le discours n'a aucune responsabilité envers le réel : dans le roman le plus réaliste, le referént n'a pas de "réalité".'[47] That the referent has no reality in a realist novel is saying that such a novel is impracticable in the sense that, say, a cookery book is not (one can *do* the recipes). But this is not to say that the novel loses all referentiality, however difficult the relations of fiction and reference may be. The point is that no referent can *guarantee* a novel, that the novel is representation, bound up in a responsibility of forms. The stress in all this falls, indeed, on *form*, language as forms, the social forms of language as discourse, as writing. The formalism of Barthes as quoted by Stern is, in fact, not an eviction of content but the emphasis on its formation, its construc-tion : 'Le formalisme auquel je pense ne consiste pas à "oublier", à "négliger", à "réduire" le contenu ("l'homme"), mais seulement à *ne pas s'arrêter* au seuil du contenu (gardons provisoirement le mot) : le contenu est *précisément* ce qui intéresse le formalisme, car sa tâche inlassable est en chaque occasion de le reculer (jusqu'à ce que la notion d'origine cesse d'être pertinente), de le déplacer selon un jeu de formes successives.'[48] The concern with language is not to sever it from the world but to stress the interrelation of the two, the relations of meaning that everywhere hold, the whole reality of representation. What is then at issue is not a loss of realism but a contemporary redefinition of it to include the awareness – the 'language-consciousness' – of the terms of its production. Realism becomes a question of forms rather than simply of contents; but then, Barthes's formalism, those words no longer quite fit, suggesting as they do some clear separation, signifier and signified, where the crux on the contrary is the formal fact of 'content', its forms – including those of any 'realism'.

To acknowledge that is to allow new questions to be inserted. Think of Virginia Woolf's writing, her novels. Stern was quoted earlier on their loss of realism, of the middle distance, the pale-brown fieldmoth between the Somme and Auschwitz; again not too far from Lukács for whom Woolf's doubling of objective time with subjective time loses all continuity and connection, 'jede Kontinuität und jeden Zusammenhang'.[49] Woolf's writing lacks the coherent, balanced picture, the overall view, turns in on the trivial. But there is another way of seeing this that does not take realism for granted, a fixed and known vision; a way that sees the limits of that vision, and, for instance, in respect of sexual difference. Dorothy Richardson, Woolf's contemporary and praised by her for the development of 'the psychological sentence of the feminine gender',[50] talked of the problem for the woman writer of 'attempting to produce a feminine equivalent of the current masculine realism'.[51] An equivalent, however, is perhaps itself still within the same currency : there can be no mere 'completing' the picture, 'annotating the male novelists, filling out the vast oblivions in them';[52] the need is to *change* the picture, in that sense 'to be rid of realism', as Woolf herself put it in a review of Richardson's *The Tunnel*.[53] The terms of the representation must be understood and transformed, and *that* is a matter of 'language-consciousness' *for realism*, of 'language-consciousness' that can produce awareness of, say, 'the current masculine realism' and raise questions of the gender of sentences for a writing, a new realism, that includes in its representation the reality of sexual difference.

Brecht saw this, and saw it with regard to women, the impossibility of 'old form new content' : in the New York or the Moscow of his day 'die Frau weniger vom Mann "geformt" als im Paris Balzacs',[54] so the forms of the old realism will no longer work, their 'reality' is challenged as such, a new montage of forms must be created, giving and finding and bringing into being the reality of this experience, its representation.

The necessity for realism is then clear; we need a realist art. Its guidelines, the terms of 'einer praktikablen Definition des Realismus', cannot be found simply in literary antecedents, cannot be got from literary works alone.[55] That way lies conservative formalism, whereas the problem is that of social content – 'die Weiterentwicklung des sozialen Inhalts'.[56] We can remember Marx's comment in *Der achtzehnte Brumaire des Louis Napoleon* to the effect that the content can go beyond the phrase. Which is not, though, to make of the necessary realism a mere reflection of a simply pregiven social reality: going beyond the phrase, the old modes, the content is a directly formal problem of realisation, of the production of reality; realism too as combat, 'Realistische Kunst ist kämpferische Kunst'.[57] The point, famously, is to change reality; realism is about that, the politics of reality again.

Brecht's thesis brings us back to realism as a question of form distinct from the accepted opposition of 'form and content'. Realism is indeed, and we started from this, quickly conservative or revolutionary, repetition or transformation, the latter the breaking of the *possession* of 'reality', cutting through its *thickness* – the unified overall view. Historically after all, this radical stance was the function of what has now become classic – the standard of – realism, the force of which was that exactly of throwing off old patterns, articulating the new field of secular, social-historical bourgeois reality. That this was bound up with a political idea of freedom and democracy is not in doubt but that idea is not then to be taken as ideal, as democracy achieved without further question, and without further question for realism. The middle distance and the completeness of the picture were formal, gave limits. How in the end could Gaskell write John Barton? Democratically, to be sure, but that democracy is specific, politically bound; hence all the tensions in the writing of her novel. Middle and completeness look less likely if you are marginal to the centre, the consensus of the established realism. Which is Richardson's problem as she sits down to write; with realism then to be created elsewhere, perhaps even in writing the fieldmoth.

The sixties–seventies semiotic reaction importantly connected with Brecht; remember his initial and continued significance for Barthes, 'le formalisme de Brecht [. . .]'.[58] That reaction gave a new political formalism as well as an old literary one, the version of 'language-consciousness' as 'complex language-games' to which Brecht had already premonitorily replied, it being clear of writers of that version that they had shed grammar, not capitalism : 'sie sich nur von der Grammatik befreit hatten, nicht vom Kapitalismus'.[59] Not that that reply itself can be allowed to be read as a dismissal of work on language, attention there; on the contrary, and for Brecht, exploration, demonstration, criticism of the terms of representation are now fundamental to any consequential realism.

So, 'a recession in realistic writing'? Yes, in as much as the old model and assumption of realism have been challenged. No, if one looks at the new writings that pose explicitly different questions of reality, make different representations. Realism is not a property of reality nor of any given literary form; it is always to be fought for, achieved. Only the major realists, argued Lukács, are capable of forming a true avant-garde, 'eine solche wirkliche Avantgarde der Literatur'.[60] To which we must add that the avant-garde is ahead, not behind in an old form. Realism importantly is a utopia of writing and reality : a new, transformable world grasped in and against the modes, meanings, orders of this one present and presented as reality. 'Language-consciousness', I think, is part of that possibility of realism.

NOTES

1. Erich Auerbach, *Mimesis: dargestellte Wirklichkeit in der abendländischen Literatur* (Berne, 1946); tr. Willard Trask, *Mimesis: The Representation of Reality in Western Literature* (New York, 1957); phrase quoted, p. 409; trans., p. 408.
2. Alain Robbe-Grillet, 'Du réalisme à la réalité (1955–63), *Pour un nouveau roman* (Paris, 1964) p. 171.
3. For details and references, see Werner Mittenzwei, 'Die Brecht-Lukács Debatte', in *Wer war Brecht*, ed. W. Mittenzwei (Berlin, 1977) pp. 361–402.
4. Auerbach, *Mimesis*, p. 426; trans., p. 424.
5. Laurence Sterne, letter to Elizabeth Lumley ?1739/40, *Letters of Laurence Sterne*, ed. Lewis Perry Curtis (Oxford, 1965) p. 11.
6. Bertolt Brecht, 'Über den formalistischen Charakter der Realismustheorie' (c. 1938), *Gesammelte Werke* 19 (Frankfurt, 1967) p. 307.
7. Brecht, '[Notizen zur Arbeit]' (c. 1939), *Gesammelte Werke* 19 p. 416.
8. Brecht, 'Über den formalistischen Charakter der Realismustheorie' p. 307.
9. J. P. Stern, *On Realism* (London, 1973); page references to this work will be given in brackets in the main body of the present essay.
10. Georg Lukács, 'Es geht um den Realismus' (1938), *Essays über Realismus* (Berlin, 1948) pp. 128–70.

11. Brecht, 'Volkstümlichkeit und Realismus' (1938), *Gesammelte Werke* 19 p. 327.
12. Stern refers to S. Heath, 'Nathalie Sarraute and the Practice of Writing', *Novel* III, 2 (1970) pp. 101–18; cf. Stern, *On Realism*, pp. 159–67.
13. Marcel Proust, *A la recherche du temps perdu* 3 (Paris: 'Pléiade' edition, 1954) p. 881.
14. Virginia Woolf, 'The Mark on the Wall' (1919), *Monday or Tuesday* (Richmond, 1921) p. 84.
15. James Joyce, letter to Grant Richards, 5 May 1906, *Letters of James Joyce*, ed. Richard Ellmann 2 (London, 1966) p. 134; Samuel Beckett, 'Dante ... Bruno. Vico ... Joyce', in *Our Exagmination Round His Factification for Incamination of Work in Progress* (Paris, 1929) p. 14.
16. Proust, letter to René Blum, cit. Léon-Pierre Quint, *Proust et la stratégie littéraire* (Paris, 1954) pp. 50–1; *A la recherche du temps perdu*, 3 p. 881.
17. Woolf, 'Mr Bennett and Mrs Brown' (1924), *Collected Essays* 1 (London, 1966) p. 325; *A Writer's Diary*, ed. Leonard Woolf (London, 1969) p. 139, entry for 28 November 1928; 'Modern Fiction' (1919), *Collected Essays* 2 p. 106; *ibid.*, p. 108.
18. *Pound/Joyce*, ed. Forrest Read (London, 1968) p. 199; Joyce cit. Max Eastman, *The Literary Mind* (New York, 1931) p. 101.
19. Proust, *A la recherche du temps perdu*, 3 p. 895.
20. Woolf, *A Writer's Diary*, p. 188, entry for 2 October 1932.
21. Joyce, *Finnegans Wake* (1939) (London, 1964) p. 107.
22. Honoré de Balzac, opening words of *Modeste Mignon* (1844), *La Comédie Humaine* (Paris: 'Pléiade' edition, 1951–65) 1 p. 358; Robbe-Grillet, opening words of *Dans le labyrinthe* (Paris, 1959) p. 9.
23. Sergei Eisenstein, 'The Cinematographic Principle and the Ideogram' (1929), *Film Form* (London, 1963) p. 35.
24. Henry James, 'The Art of Fiction' (1884), in *The House of Fiction: Essays on the Novel by Henry James*, ed. Leon Edel (London, 1962) p. 23. ('no air of having a theory, a conviction, a consciousness of itself behind it').
25. George Farquhar, Preface to *The Adventures of Covent Garden* (London, 1699) n.p.
26. Karl Marx, 'Einleitung [zur Kritik der Politischen Ökonomie]' (1857), *Marx Engels Werke* (Berlin, 1964) 13 p. 616; tr. 'Introduction', *A Contribution to the Critique of Political Economy* (Moscow, 1977) p. 189.
27. James, 'The Lesson of Balzac' (1905), *The House of Fiction*, p. 76.
28. James, 'The Art of Fiction', pp. 25–6.
29. James, 'The Future of the Novel' (1899), *The House of Fiction*, p. 53.
30. Balzac, *La Cousine Bette* (1846), *La Comédie Humaine* 6 p. 183.
31. George Eliot, *Adam Bede* (1859) (Harmondsworth, 1983) pp. 221–4.
32. Marx, *Das Kapital*, Buch III, *Marx Engels Werke* 25 p. 825; tr. David Fernbach, *Capital*, Volume 3 (Harmondsworth, 1981) p. 956.
33. Lukács, 'Kunst und objektive Wahrheit' (1934), *Probleme des Realismus* (Berlin, 1955) pp. 13–14.
34. Balzac, 'Préface' to *Une Fille d'Ève* (1839), *La Comédie Humaine*, 11 p. 374.
35. James, 'Preface' to *The Portrait of a Lady* (1907), in *The Art of the Novel* (New York, n.d.) p. 46; 'The Art of Fiction', p. 31.
36. Aldous Huxley, *Point Counter Point* (1928) (Harmondsworth, 1961) p. 196.

37. Joseph Conrad, 'Preface' to *The Nigger of the Narcissus* (1897) (Harmondsworth, 1965) p. 13.

38. Roland Barthes, *Le Degré zéro de l'écriture* (Paris, 1953) p. 21.

39. Elizabeth Gaskell, *Mary Barton* (1848) (Harmondsworth, 1983) p. 250; Benjamin Disraeli, *Sybil* (1845) (Harmondsworth, 1984) p. 360.

40. Charles Dickens, *Our Mutual Friend* (1864–5) (Harmondsworth, 1975) p. 161 ('the Veneering guests become infected with the Veneering fiction').

41. Brecht, 'Volkstümlichkeit und Realismus', p. 330.

42. Proust, *A la recherche du temps perdu* 2 p. 406.

43. Barthes, *Leçon* (Paris, 1978) p. 22.

44. Cf. S. Heath, 'Ambiviolences: notes pour la lecture de Joyce', *Tel Quel* no. 50 (summer 1972) pp. 22–43 & no. 51 (autumn 1972) pp. 64–76; and 'Trames de lecture', *Tel Quel* no. 54 (summer 1974) pp. 4–16.

45. Ferdinand de Saussure, *Cours de linguistique générale* (1916) (Paris, 1968) p. 33.

46. Barthes, 'La littérature, aujourd'hui' (1961), *Essais critiques* (Paris, 1964) p. 164; cit. S. Heath, 'Nathalie Sarraute and the Practice of Writing', p. 117.

47. Barthes, *S/Z* (Paris, 1970) p. 87.

48. Barthes, 'Digressions', *Promesse* no. 29 (spring 1971) pp. 18–19.

49. Lukács, 'Das Spielerische und seine Hintergründe' (1955), *Thomas Mann* (Berlin, 1957) p. 93.

50. Woolf, 'Romance of the Heart' (1923), *Contemporary Writers* (London, 1965) p. 124.

51. Dorothy Richardson, 'Foreword' to *Pilgrimage* (1938), *Pilgrimage* (London, 1979) 1 p. 9.

52. Richardson, *Dawn's Left Hand* (1931), *Pilgrimage* 4 p. 240.

53. Woolf, review of *The Tunnel* (1919), *Contemporary Writers*, p. 122.

54. Brecht, '[Bemerkungen zu einem Aufsatz]' (c. 1938), *Gesammelte Werke*, 19 p. 312.

55. Brecht, 'Über den formalistischen Charakter der Realismustheorie', p. 307.

56. Brecht, 'Über reimlose Lyrik mit unregelmässigen Rhythmen' (1939), *Gesammelte Werke* 19 p. 403.

57. Brecht, '[Über sozialistischen Realismus]' (c. 1954), *Gesammelte Werke*, 19 p. 547.

58. Barthes, 'Les tâches de la critique brechtienne' (1956), *Essais Critiques*, p. 88.

59. Brecht, 'Über den formalistischen Charakter der Realismustheorie', p. 304.

60. Lukács, 'Es geht um den Realismus', p. 155.

Nietzsche and the 'middle mode of discourse'

NICHOLAS BOYLE

I

> Now you see me, now you –
> *Rosencrantz and Guildenstern are Dead* (Act III)

Qu'on s'imagine un nombre d'hommes dans les chaînes, et tous condamnés à la mort, dont les uns étant chaque jour égorgés à la vue des autres, ceux qui restent voient leur propre condition dans celle de leurs semblables, et, se regardant les uns et les autres avec douleur et sans espérance, attendent à leur tour. C'est l'image de la condition des hommes.[1]

If there is realism anywhere in Pascal's *Pensées*, then it would seem to be here. J. P. Stern tells us that between the language of poetry with its concern for particulars and the language of philosophy with its concern for the general, between concrete and abstract, metaphor and concept, there lies a middle or hybrid mode of writing, practised in particular by Nietzsche, but with antecedents, which include the Book of Proverbs, Pascal, and William Blake.[2] Can this mode, which, we are told, it was Nietzsche's greatest achievement to devise and to bequeath to many successors in the twentieth century, also be a realistic mode? The example from Pascal might seem to suggest that it can. There is certainly something hybrid about this aphorism. On the one hand it is overtly concerned with conceptual matters, with representation ('l'image') and the representation of something very general (the human condition). On the other hand it is an elaborately and climactically constructed analogy – strictly speaking, a synecdoche – which opens and closes with two different kinds of rhetorical appeal to the reader. It is both philosophical and poetical – and it is both together, not separately. For the insight – the thought – which this particular *pensée* communicates, the *point* of the remark, does not lie in the conceptual content of the literary analogy which the second sentence invites us, as it were, to decipher (all men, not just a handful in chains, live in pain and without hope, and in the presence and knowledge of death). The point lies in the shock of the revelation that the second sentence makes, in the process, which is neither simply literary nor dispassionately conceptual, by which we are invited in, deceived, and surprised by the revelation that we have been deceived, as we learn that what we had taken for an exercise of the imagination was in fact an analogy, or that what we had taken for a fiction about others was a truth about ourselves. But is this 'realism'? For it may be admitted that the knowledge which makes up the conceptual content of the paragraph is common knowledge, though it is a knowledge which we, like the men in the story, read in one another's eyes but prefer not to utter (there are three references to sight in the *pensée*, and none to speech). And it may be admitted that the imagined story itself has a theme that, for all its atrocity, has to be called realistic, as has the way in which it is narrated, for all its sophistication (the emphasis on sight and the absence of speech reinforcing the allusions to impotent and inactive constriction). There is here, then, both realism 'of assessment' and realism 'of description', in Watt's terms. But can the shock which is the point of the *pensée*, and in virtue of which the *pensée* can be assigned to a middle or hybrid mode of writing, also be regarded as itself a 'realistic' device? Realism presumably involves the presentation of a reality and it is not, or not quite, in the presentation of the reality of our own necessary death that the shock communicated by Pascal's aphorism consists, though the aphorism makes use of that reality to give itself weight, to put momentum behind its 'point'. 'Thou art the man', said Nathan the prophet (2 Sam. 12.7) when he had finished the story in which he presented to King David the reality of his crime. But the prophet said those words *when he had finished*, and his saying them was part of another story than that which he had just recounted. So it is with Pascal. The shock conveyed by his second sentence derives from our recognition of the identity of two images which we had thought distinct, and references to which frame the obviously 'realistic' vignette ('Qu'on s'imagine [...]', 'C'est l'image [...]'). It derives, that is, from a recognition of our own intellectual failure to acknowledge the nature of our condition, a failure which is a major episode in the 'other story' which Pascal is telling, and from which we have so far regarded this *pensée* as detached. But it will not allow itself to be so detached. In its purposeful, shocking, address to its reader this *pensée* proclaims itself a fragment of Pascal's apology for Christianity, a story in which the principal role is occupied by the reader himself :

Les hommes n'ayant pu guérir la mort, la misère, l'ignorance, ils se sont avisés, pour se rendre heureux, de n'y point penser.   (No. 168)

The reality with which Pascal's story of the men in chains endeavours to confront us is not that we are wretched and shall die (a reality that we can anyway confront only individually), but that Pascal's scheme applies to us – that we are what he (his Apology, his 'other story' in which the fragment is situated) says we are.

Aphoristic or quasi-aphoristic writing has at its disposal a number of devices which enable a short passage – be it *pensée*, paragraph or even short essay – to culminate in the miming, the apparent enactment, of a confrontation with reality, the transition from the 'word-world'[3] that signifies, to the world of things, whether thoughts or objects or passions or deeds, that is signified. There is not only shock and paradox, there is authorial self-reference and 'the second look at language',[4] there are even the humbler devices of syntactic incompleteness, rhetorical questions and dots or dashes, more tellingly known as *points de suspension, Gedankenstriche*. By all of these means, and also by the monolithic self-confidence of the maxim, the silence that supervenes at the end of an aphoristic thought and that largely defines its aphoristic nature (the gap on the page between one thought and the next) can be made into an image of the silent world of signified things, on the brink of which the signifying words of the aphorism either stand in defiant awareness of difference, or tremble and spill. Aphorisms in short always raise, implicitly, the question of their *application* – and if they raise the question explicitly, they also raise implicitly the question of the application of that explicit question. Pascal raises the question of the application of his first sentence with the words 'C'est l'image [. . .]'. Then, asking ourselves what is the application of that *second* sentence, we discover that we have been caught in the toils of his Apology and that our thoughts have followed the course Pascal defines for them elsewhere.

Even though all aphorisms raise the question of their application it does not follow that all aphorisms are realistic. It is a second defining feature of the aphorism, even if one largely unremarked,[5] that though surrounded by silence it is gregarious : aphorisms appear in collections, in books of aphorisms. Lines, relations, patterns are set up between individual remarks as between the stars in a constellation, and it is of those patterns that we should ask whether they are realistic, rather than of the individual insights of which the pattern is composed. From an early stage in European literature aphoristic collections offer, in a peculiarly acute form, a choice between a referential and a non-referential use of language. Is the world into which the concluded aphorisms discharge us an open world, unpredictable, finite, yet unbounded, over which words have a certain limited (if undefinably limited) hold, and which the reader shares with the aphorist on more or less equal terms? This, I believe, is the case with the aphoristic collections of La Rochefoucauld and Lichtenberg and in their hands the modern, i.e. post-Renaissance, European aphorism becomes a realistic genre. These aphorisms always raise the question of their application, but they do so on the assumption that that to which they apply or might apply is a world known to their readers through many other channels besides themselves, literary and non-literary, linguistic and non-linguistic, and that it is by that knowledge, external to and independent of the aphoristic collection, that we, the readers, know whether the aphorism 'applies', whether the phrase tells, the shaft sticks, the story illuminates.

Or is the world beyond and between the aphorisms a closed world, defined and even constituted by the aphorisms themselves, by their vocabulary and their trains of thought? Is it a world in which the reader may think only what the aphorist directs him to think? In which he may experience the shock of reality not through making on his own initiative numerous, determinate 'discoveries' (Jonson's term), but only through applying the words of the aphorism to his (in respect of the aphoristic collection) wholly indeterminate self, or in recognising the inapplicability of any words at all to the (therefore equally indeterminate) body of what the aphorisms do not say? Such aphorisms also raise the question of their application, but they assume that application itself, and even perhaps that to which application is made, is defined and described and known within, or by projection from, the aphoristic collection only, and not otherwise. Some aphoristic collections are referential and some – the rest – are self-referential, and the moment the decision for self-reference is made, the middle mode of discourse is born, a mode in which 'reality' can be invoked, but in which determinate real things are not, and cannot be, discussed. This I believe to be the case of the nascent proto-aphorisms of Montaigne, Pascal's aphoristic fragments, and the numerous collections of Nietzsche, who saw himself as the master of the German aphorism (II 1026)[6] and Pascal as his principal adversary (III 1335, cp. I 1139). And the more loudly Nietzsche appeals to 'reality',[7] the less it is possible to regard his hybrid and aphoristic mode of writing as a form of realism – on the contrary, it appears as the predecessor, perhaps even the progenitor, of a kind of writing which, in both literary practice and critical theory, is hardly compatible with realism and may actively seek to supplant it.

2

> Half of what he said meant
> something else, and the
> other half didn't mean any-
> thing at all.   (Act II)

In an unpublished essay of 1873, which contains several allusions to Pascal, the young Nietzsche seizes on one of the *Pensées* ('Les rivières sont des chemins qui marchent, et qui portent où l'on veut aller')[8] as a prime example of the activity of an intellect that has freed itself from the established metaphors and conventional concepts that make up ordinary, contemptible, functional language. The description that follows of a de- and re-constructive, paradoxical, zeugmatic and ironical play with an accepted linguistic and conceptual structure 'contains the most accurate account we have of Nietzsche's own future philosophical and literary undertaking [...] of the discontinuities, *aperçus* and aphoristic turns that will come to characterize his writing'.[9] The argument of the essay, *On truth and falsehood from the extra-moral point of view*, is that language is doubly metaphorical, doubly a metaphysical (rather than a moral) lie. For language consists of words which have only an arbitrary or conventional relation to thoughts, and thoughts have no rational or systematic relation to the physical objects to which they are simply the response of the human nervous system. Whatever the coherence of this argument, Nietzsche draws from it the conclusion that language is a system of self-sustaining metaphors that cannot be firmly bedded down into non-metaphorical referentiality, in short, that linguistically expressed 'truths are illusions, whose illusory nature has been forgotten' (III 314). This belief that language is distinct from, can gain no purchase on, 'a silent cosmos or world of unworded experiences, to which all utterances are intended – but fail adequately – to refer', is a belief that Stern has shown to be shared by Schopenhauer, Nietzsche and the early Wittgenstein (*A Study of Nietzsche* pp. 95, 193). This belief is the premiss of all Nietzsche's critical and aphoristic engagement with the metaphysical and moral vocabulary of his time. In 1873 he still thinks it possible that a freely creative, artistic spirit might, even if only through 'an intimatory translation, a halting interpretation', mediate between the subject and object he believes to be so completely sundered, though to do this would require 'a

middle sphere and a middle force of free poetry and free invention'
(III 317). In 1888, at the end of a literary career which has turned
him (he tells us, with almost metaphysical seriousness) from a meta-
physician into a moralist, Nietzsche finds that 'middle sphere' of
language, however poetically creative, to be self-condemned, in virtue
of the very metaphor that denotes it :

Die Sprache, scheint es, ist nur für Durchschnittliches, Mittleres, Mit-
teilsames erfunden. Mit der Sprache *vulgarisiert* sich bereits der
Sprechende. – Aus einer Moral für Taubstumme und andre Philo-
sophen. (II 1005)

Language, it seems, was invented only for what is average, middling,
mediable. Simply through language the speaker *vulgarises* himself. –
Extract from a theory of morals for deaf-mutes and other philosophers.

What sort of language is written then by the philosopher who can
neither speak nor hear the medium through which the herd (III 868)
think truth and truthfulness to be communicable? It is a language
which, even in 1888, even in *Twilight of the Idols* (to which I shall
here give most attention), still conforms to the pattern laid down in
1873 for any language whatever. It is an (in principle) endless
sequence of mutually sustaining, mutually parodying and mutually
criticising, metaphors (which is not to say that Nietzsche's total repertoire of metaphors does not *in fact* have a limited and specific
character). That principle is given to us *in nuce* when Nietzsche tells
us, for example, that the phrase 'peace of mind' may be synonymous
with

der Anfang der Müdigkeit, der erste Schatten, den der Abend, jede
Art Abend wirft. (II 967)

the beginning of weariness, the first shadow cast by evening, any sort
of evening.

'The beginning of weariness' looks a fairly literal, physiological,
phrase (though it need not be – it might have a cultural-historical
sense, for example), certainly it looks sufficiently literal for 'the first
shadow cast by evening' to seem an elucidatory metaphor. Yet the
addition 'any sort of evening' makes the first reference to evening
seem in retrospect to be fully literal, while at the same time opening
an endless perspective of further possible metaphorical applications.
Indeed, this is but one item in a brilliantly ingenious – and not in that
at all unusual – enumeration of different possible more or less metaphorical synonyms for the initial metaphorical phrase. The list
accumulates with such ease and rapidity that it seems it could go on

for ever, though it in fact ends – if it is an end – in an application
to the very work Nietzsche is writing :

Götzen-Dämmerung: wer weiss? vielleicht auch nur eine Art "Frieden
der Seele" . . .

Twilight of the Idols: who knows? perhaps also just a sort of "peace of
mind" . . .

Any term in the sequence can be seen as 'just a sort of' some other
term, and each term stands at the head of another potentially endless
sequence consisting of 'any sort of' itself. By the end of this reflection
the distinction between 'literal' and 'metaphorical' meaning has
practically ceased to exist. Nietzsche has said as much in the preceding reflection, where he referred to 'those natures that need la Trappe,
metaphorically speaking (and non-metaphorically)' – 'im Gleichnis
gesprochen (und ohne Gleichnis)'.

Even that – by public convention? – most real world of public,
institutional, history is for Nietzsche only one more moral-
psychological conformation metaphorically related to many others,
whether philosophical, personal, physiological or mythical, in a
sequence whose first, or last, term is likely to be his own work. In
Twilight of the Idols the section 'The "Improvers" of Humanity' (II
979–82) begins and ends with a programmatic statement of
Nietzsche's aims and beliefs. There are, we are told (in italics), no
moral *facts*, moral judgments are never to be taken literally, they are
'merely sign-language, merely symptomatic'. Signs, symptoms, of
what? Nietzsche gives a first example taken from the medical, or at
any rate veterinary, area to which his word 'Symptomatologie' has
perhaps already directed our attention. Instead of the 'improvement'
of humanity we should speak of its 'domestication', its 'breeding':
'only these technical zoological terms express realities'. Not that
Nietzsche seriously means that his two words 'Zähmung' and
'Züchtung', which look even less technical than their English equiva-
lents, have a special non-metaphorical status. It becomes apparent
from the continuation of his argument that 'reality' is simply a part
of his own affective and polemical vocabulary, a term which points
to the metaphorical – that is, the deceitful – status of the vocabulary
of his adversaries. 'Domestication' and 'breeding' he says are 'realities
of which, to be sure, the typical "improver", the priest knows nothing
– and does not *wish* to know anything' – but they are also the beginnings of a metaphorical chain in Nietzsche's text which cannot by any
catachresis be called 'zoological'. 'Domestication' applies to what goes
on in menageries, Nietzsche says, 'improvement' does not, so we

should not apply 'improvement' to the moral history of humanity, which *as history*, as raw event, justifies another metaphor, another sign-language. The early medieval church 'was' a menagerie.

It is even more difficult to give a sense to the word 'was' than to the apparent claim that zoology is non-metaphorical. 'Was' is not just a harmless copula in a self-contained witticism. Nietzsche is invoking the real past of contemporary public institutions and he develops his metaphor as purposefully as if it were a historical explanation. Menageries need to be filled with wild beasts – what beast was hunted to fill the early medieval church? – the 'blond beast', the Teuton. To be sure, a superb flight of metaphorical fancy sovereignly dismisses any philistine, literal (e.g. eugenicist) notion of what Nietzsche might mean. The captive Teuton, he says :

stak im Käfig, man hatte ihn zwischen lauter schreckliche Begriffe eingesperrt.

sat in a cage, locked away behind rows of terrifying concepts.

(The further development of the metaphor of the sickness of the caged animal need not concern us here.) It seems ridiculous, after such a sentence, to bother one's head too much about what Nietzsche means by 'was'. But a serious question is still raised by Nietzsche's claim – whether we call it sovereign, or whether we call it heedless – for the truth of one description of human society (the 'zoological') rather than another (the 'moral') and by his refusal to acknowledge any distinction between the historical and the moral realms – each the object of metaphorical interpretation *ad libitum*. May he not then, in the eyes of those (who may include ourselves) who continue to believe in the more or less distinct existence of a public, institutional and historical world, appear – when he says for example that human society is a matter of 'breeding' – to be asserting a truth about that world, even though he believes neither in the possibility of asserting truth nor in the separate existence of that or any world other than the totality? In the remainder of the section 'The "Improvers" of Humanity', Nietzsche praises what he believes to be the Indian caste system, with its institutionalised contempt for its lowest class, calling it an 'Aryan humanity' which contrasts with the Jewish hostility to the principles of 'breeding' and 'race'. Now it is clear, if we accept the totally metaphorical nature of Nietzsche's style, its middle course between all accepted notions of truth-telling, that Nietzsche is here simply drawing on the intellectual vocabulary of contemporary German anti-Semitism to create another extended quasi-historical, quasi-sociological metaphor in criticism of the hated system of Christian morality (to which of course many an anti-Semite might still adhere). As when he asserted briefly the non-metaphorical status of zoological terms, Nietzsche in elaborating this cultural counter-example is concerned principally for the critical and polemical relation of what he says to the positions of his adversaries. But does he not run the risk of appearing – not to use for his own purposes, but – to *adopt* the principles of anti-Semitism and Teutonism? And, more importantly, does he not run the risk – whatever he himself may mean (though of course he does not *mean* anything at all) – of furthering those principles, in the public, institutional, historical world in which books circulate?

> Quite as much as Wagner I am a child of this time, i.e. a *décadent*: only that I understood that, only that I resisted it. The philosopher in me resisted it [...] For such a task I required a special self-discipline – of taking sides *against* everything about me that was diseased, including Wagner, including Schopenhauer, including the whole of modern 'humanitarianism'. – A profound alienation, dispassionate, disenchanted, in respect of everything temporal, of the time: and as supreme desire the eye of *Zarathustra*, an eye that from an immense distance can look over the whole human phenomenon – look *down* on it.   (II 903)

Nietzsche's dependence on his own time, of course, is a matter of more than Schopenhauer, Wagner, and the anti-Semitism of his own sister and brother-in-law. Stern says that Nietzsche's work 'is the biography of a soul but [...] it is a biography that abounds in articulated consciousness of world and time – his time and world, and ours. The work has a broad realistic base.' But this extract from the preface to *The Wagner Case* (1888) shows not only that Nietzsche believes his conscious relationship with his time to be essentially, and wholly, negative, but more importantly that he has nothing to put in the scales against the weight of his time and place and culture beyond the picture of himself as the 'Aryan' Christ, Zarathustra, at an immense distance of empty space from it all. He has only the power of his *own* denial, his *own* contempt, the power to make small – in relation to himself. There are no resources of reference to other times, other cultures, other human achievements, such as those, for example, which build up the shoulders and peaks of Goethe's Olympus. Such references – above all of course to Greece – are absorbed by Nietzsche's metaphorical style and transformed into allotropes of contemporary issues, for historical and cultural distinctions are after all only linguistic fictions. As a result, though negated and diminished, and against his will, Nietzsche's own time continues to speak and operate through his work. We may see this in little matters, such as the assumption that certain issues are important and deserve treatment (such as 'the question of marriage' or 'the question of the workers' (II 1015–17), or indeed the question of '*décadence*' itself), or even in rare moments of endorsement of contemporary attitudes (as when Nietzsche shows a certain complacent enthusiasm for the first principle of Bismarck's foreign policy (II 966) or speaks approvingly of the military character of contemporary German society (II 983)). We see it in great matters however when we consider the reputation of Nietzsche's work in Germany in the first half of the twentieth century, which cannot simply be dismissed as a fortuitous misinterpretation : 'More than once [Nietzsche] tells us that communication is not what he is concerned with, that he wishes to be misunderstood [. . .] *Zarathustra* [. . .] *was* misunderstood [. . .] yet *that* was a misunderstanding we may be sure he did not wish for' (Stern, *A Study of Nietzsche*, p. 197). But this is to ignore the extent to which Nietzsche's works, and not only *Zarathustra*, offer no resistance to misunderstanding, because the only counterweight to their overwhelming destructiveness, all that they assert beyond metaphoricisation, fictionalisation, unmasking, reduction and critique, is either the common, even vulgar, attitudes of his age or Nietzsche's own indeterminate self, indeterminate because deliberately stripped of all determinants of time and culture and interest and loyalty, and reduced at the last to a pseudo-historical mythico-theatrical metaphor – 'the eye of Zarathustra'. Can we be so sure that Nietzsche would not have wished for the misunderstanding if he had known it was coming? It is all too easy to imagine a concluding fifty-second paragraph in the section 'Skirmishes out of season' from *Twilight of the Idols* : 'Yes, in my *Zarathustra* I gave humanity the profoundest book it possesses. And I rejoiced that it was misunderstood and bestially misused by the National Socialists. For did I not thereby help to bring about the destruction of what I hated most – *Germany*! And did not Germany *deserve* its destruction? – for having *thus* misunderstood me?...'

There is perhaps the material for a realistic achievement in Nietzsche's writings. But that material is not made to serve a realistic purpose, it cannot be made to for as long as it remains dissolved into the medium of discourse in the middle mode. Stern (*A Study of Nietzsche*, p. 186) isolates a telling, since probably unconscious, 'linguistic tic' which at times lends a certain monotony to Nietzsche's style : his over-frequent linking of nouns and phrases by means of the particles 'als', 'as', – 'moral judgment as semiotic sign' (II 979), 'man as reality' (II 1008), 'freedom as something one acquires by conquest' (II 1015), 'the world as an aesthetic phenomenon'. 'Als' is the representative within the sentence of the theory that language as a whole is disjoined from reality. 'Als' is the universal linguistic solvent through which 'a never-ending interchange in the function of words' (Stern, *ibid.*) suspends all images, concepts, facts and arguments in a state of metaphoricity, always only reinterpretations of one another, never pinned down – or abandoned – in the finality of the singular, the historical, or the real.

The process intensifies in the course of Nietzsche's career. Nietzsche is at his finest as a critic of individual writers and thinkers, an analyst of specific phrases. But as time goes on he succumbs increasingly to the temptation to make these individual phenomena signs of something other than themselves, their critique part of some larger scheme. No. 22 of the 'Words and Arrows' section in *Twilight of the Idols* deals with a piece of received moral wisdom and inventively sets it in a public, even a political setting :

"Böse Menschen haben keine Lieder." – Wie kommt es, dass die Russen Lieder haben? (II 946)

"The wicked have no songs" – How does it come about that the Russians have their songs?

Were it not for the series of consequential thoughts laid down by the rest of the collection this question would seem limp. The limitations of a proverb are a subject hardly worth even two lines of Nietzsche's prose. But the representation of themselves as a singing nation is a part of the specifically German ideology (cp. No. 33, II 947). So the Russians are not wicked in themselves but are only called so by the Germans, who fear them – the 'sign language' of moral judgment here represents a relationship of 'will to power'. But in fact the Russians are rightly called wicked *by modern Germans* because the Russian state is built on such different principles from the German. Russia is 'the *only* power that nowadays has duration in its belly' because it is 'antiliberal to the point of malignity (Bösheit)' (II 1016).[10] Liberty of course is something that Nietzsche personally loathes (II 1018) because, like the German state, which he has already publicly denounced, it is a symptom of decadence (II 1016). Not that that decadence can be put into reverse (II 1019) – but that should not trouble 'us', greatness need not fear infection from surrounding decadence, for the belief that great men are dependent on their age, are made by their milieu, is another 'neurotic' belief with the stench of decay about it (II 1020). Russia is 'the diametrically opposite concept' to the 'neuroses' of the other European states (II 1016), and the great man, the genius, is the antithesis of his age : he is strong, the age is weak; he is necessary, the age is contingent (II 1019). The strength of the genius consists in his existing and acting for *himself*, not for any extraneous purpose, not for his age or his fatherland or some public cause. Posterity may see him as its benefactor, but that is 'all misunderstanding'. The great man – necessarily misunderstood – is not a beginner of, a contributor to, anything – he is an 'explosive' 'end', a terminus (II 1020). Nietzsche's sequence of thought reaches a conclusion outside the moral and public and political world in which it began, in the contemplation of a genius figure cut off from his own time and from posterity by the explosion in him of the accumulated energies of preceding centuries.

It is noteworthy that of the nearly 1,400 remarks which make up Nietzsche's least programmatic collection, the collection in which he comes nearest to being a simple *moraliste*, perhaps even a simple realist, namely *Human, All too Human* (1878–80), over 1,200 end with an unqualified full stop. In the whole collection (excluding the prefaces to the later edition) there is not a single case of a thought ending in *points de suspension*. However, in the later works extracted from the corpus of notes towards the *magnum opus*, *The Will to Power*, the position is dramatically different : some 60 of the 144 reflections in *Twilight of the Idols* end with three dots, and 37 with a dash.[11] The thoughts spill over at the end of the aphorisms, but into what? Into the endless circular flow of redefinition and reinterpretation in which the only unreinterpretable reality, the self-authenticating metaphor, the terminus of any argument remorselessly pursued, is the pose of complete detachment, the stance of Zarathustra. In *Thus spoke Zarathustra* that stance was prophetic metaphor, in the permanently promised future synthesis, in *The Will to Power*, it would have been eschatological reality (cp. II 1026, 1032). Nietzsche's aphorisms, at any rate in his later years, direct his readers only to the thinking of his thoughts, and ultimately to the thinking of his self (itself a metaphor : Nietzsche-as-Zarathustra). They correspond to the pattern of the aphorisms not of La Rochefoucauld and Lichtenberg, but of Pascal : whether they conclude in shock or in insinuation they do not discharge us into the late 19th-century German world of which they speak, but make of the confrontation with reality an element in their own intellectual scheme.

3

we can do you rapiers or
rape or both, by all means,
faithless wives and ravished
virgins – flagrante delicto
at a price, but that comes
under realism for which
there are special terms.   (Act I)

Nietzsche and Pascal, of course, unlike Lichtenberg and La Rochefoucauld, were not married. Of Nietzsche it may perhaps be true that
'mulierem numquam attigit' (Stern, *A Study of Nietzsche*, p. 4). In
no area of his writing is the cultural ballast of his age more obviously
an unperceived and uncriticised hindrance than in what he has to say
about 'das Weib'. Nietzsche's references to women would not therefore seem to be the most promising starting point for a study of his
thought, but that is the starting point chosen by Jacques Derrida for
his essay *Éperons. Les styles de Nietzsche*.[12] Point indeed, for the
reason for Derrida's choice, and the likely tenor of his argument, are
apparent from the moment that he tells us that 'La question du style,
c'est toujours l'examen, le pesant d'un objet pointu' (p. 36). The
argument – if that is the correct word for an exegetical structure of
such virtuoso ethereality – is that in Nietzsche's texts, particularly
Twilight of the Idols, the question of the style is inseparable from, nay,
is inscribed into, the question of woman. The style, or stylus, is not
only the instrument of writing, and so of public thought, it is also, as
a long, hard (though in some cases collapsible) pointed object, an
instrument of penetration or, as a stiletto, for example, an instrument
of defence, for keeping a threat at a distance. If 'style' may be
regarded as masculine, what is feminine then would be veils, sails,
curtains, the hymen, whatever may be cut, penetrated, torn aside or
kept at a distance by the style, or even (in the case of a spar or sprit,
or for that matter an umbrella) extended or erected by it. On the basis
in particular of the comparison between woman and a sailing-ship in
paragraph 60 of *The Gay Science* (II 79–80), and of the parable
'How the "true" world finally became a fable' in *Twilight of the Idols*
(II 963), Derrida uses these reciprocal terms to analyse Nietzsche's
expressed attitudes to women and to truth. Like Stern, Derrida finds
in Nietzsche's thought a tripartite progression, but his scheme is
significantly different from Stern's in respect of its last stage. While
for Stern Nietzsche's thought characteristically proceeds from the
description of an existing phenomenon (*a*) to its rejection (*not-a*) to

the reinterpretation and reassertion of what was described, but in a
new sense (A) (*A Study of Nietzsche*, pp. 160–1), Derrida finds the
following pattern : 1. woman is condemned as a figure or power of
untruth (Nietzsche 'was, and feared, some castrated woman' – the
assertion that there is such a thing as truth being psychoanalytically
equivalent to the threat of castration); 2. woman is condemned as a
figure or power asserting truth – e.g. philosophical or Christian truth
– by contrast with the artist-actor who rejoices in masks and deception (Nietzsche 'was, and feared, some castrating woman'); 3. woman
is recognised and affirmed as a dionysiac affirmative, artistic power
(Nietzsche 'was, and loved, some affirmative woman', having recognised that the threat of castration, like the assertion of truth, is a
phantom) (*Éperons*, pp. 96, 100). Nietzsche's final 'affirmation' (the
category of course is notoriously Nietzsche's own – e.g. II 969) is
tantamount to the denial of sexual difference, that is, the denial of
the difference between truth and non-truth : the grounds for the
original distinction between style and veil, truth-seeker and truth-
concealer, male and female (the female being, psychoanalytically
speaking, the castrated male), have been eliminated. Derrida con-
cludes (if we except the witty interpretation of Nietzsche's isolated
note ' "I have forgotten my umbrella" ' as the key to all his writings)
with an exercise in Heideggerian epistemology, Heidegger having
been taken to task for ignoring the phrase 'Sie wird Weib', 'It becomes
female', in Nietzsche's parabolic description in *Twilight of the Idols*
of the Christian transformation of the notion of the 'true world'.
Beyond the distinction between male and female, true and not-true,
we enter the 'régime [. . .] des guillemets' (p. 106) : all concepts that
rely on such antithetical distinctions now have only hypothetical,
citational, status, and among these belongs the concept of the given,
the *datum*, the *donnée* :

De même qu'il n'y a pas d'être ou d'essence de *la* femme ou de *la*
différence sexuelle, il n'y a pas d'essence du *es gibt* dans le *es gibt Sein*,
du don et de la donation de l'être [. . .] Il n'y a pas de don de l'être à
partir duquel quelque chose comme un don déterminé (du sujet, du
corps, du sexe [. . .]) se laisse appréhender et mettre en opposition.
(p. 120)

Just as there is no being or essence of Woman as such or of Sexual
Difference as such, so there is no essence of the *es gibt* in *es gibt Sein*,
of the gift and giving of being [. . .] There is no gift of being on the
basis of which something like a determinate gift (of the subject, of the
body, of a sex [. . .]) could be apprehended or set up in opposition [i.e.
to being in general]

Derrida leaves it unclear whether this is his position, or his interpretation of Nietzsche's position. Perhaps, in the circumstances, there is no difference.

The most dubious feature of Derrida's analysis is its progressive quality, its own directionality (into the 'abysses of truth', to cite one of his subtitles) and its attribution of a progressive dialectic to Nietzsche. This is dubious, firstly, because Derrida leaves inexplicit the relation between terminus and starting point, for his conclusion has actually annihilated his starting-point. If there is no *datum*, not merely in the sense that there are no determinate 'styles' and 'veils' but in the sense that there is no given *distinction* between 'styles' and 'veils', it is difficult to see what was the justification for associating men and stilettos, or truth and castration, in the first place, or for distinguishing them from curtains, affirmation, or the coverings of umbrellas. True, Derrida asserts, at the end of his increasingly (as he tells us) cryptic and parodistic text, that in it there 'never has been' *'le style . . . la* femme. Ni *la* différence sexuelle' (p. 138). Like the early Wittgenstein, having ascended to mystical insight, he draws up behind him the ladder of dialectic leaving his reader with a text which it is the task of reading to acknowledge as superfluous. But, in all of this, he is simply miming the gestures and presuppositions of Nietzsche himself. Derrida's enactment of the various possible modulations of a belief in the total disjuncture of language and reality (including the only finality – that of self-reference and the total privacy of the great man) is misleading only if the progressive, directional, dialectical mode in which it appears to be couched is taken for more than an expository device – one style among the many styles that are available to the practitioner of the middle mode of discourse.

No sooner has Derrida attributed a progressive dialectic to Nietzsche than he acknowledges how dubious is his attribution. It is not possible, he tells us (pp. 106–8) to determine whether the denial of the distinction between truth and non-truth, style and veil, is not itself another act of unveiling, another act of penetration to the truth: this question, as ('en tant qua') question, 'reste – interminablement'. It is the acknowledgement of the *interminable* quality of Nietzsche's reflections that makes Stern's account of his dialectic preferable to Derrida's – that, and the fact that there seems to be no example of Derrida's third stage anywhere in Nietzsche's work. The third stage of Stern's *a – not-a – A* dialectic returns us, in some sense, to the beginning. Precisely because the 'sense' of the return is indeterminate (it is never *really* clear what is the relation between a 'value' and a 'transvalued value'), the process is not circular – let alone directional – but capable of being indefinitely prolonged. To pursue a Nietzschean concept, such as that of Russian wickedness, through its transformations, inversions, metaphoricisations and parallelisms until it strays too near the vortex of Nietzsche's self-consciousness and is swallowed up in the metaphor-as-reality of Zarathustra, is like nothing so much as listening to a Wagnerian endless melody, though one that can never give birth to drama.

But it is Derrida's presentation specifically of the third stage of Nietzsche's dialectic that is most questionable. Let us retrace the critic's steps through the subject matter that he has himself chosen :

1. Nietzsche certainly seems to accept without question or variation the equation of 'female' and 'castrated male'. Female sexuality and will to power are always derivative – negated, perverted, or more cunning (but for that very reason more successful) versions of the male original. To say that in Christianity the idea of 'the true world' becomes female (II 963) is synonymous with the statement that Christianity is the religion of eunuchs (II 965, 968). To say that Wagner – like the French – is surrounded by an aura of eternal femininity (II 992 cp. 'Postscript' to *The Wagner Case* II 937) is no different from saying that he is the Klingsor of Klingsors (II 931), the castrated wizard *par excellence*. If women allow themselves to be treated as the possessions of men it is because women know how best to bring men to furnish them with the possessions the women themselves want (*Beyond Good and Evil* §§ 238, 239, II 700–704). With the world of femininity and castration Nietzsche regularly associates falsehood and deceit, particularly the deceit that asserts transcendence, asserts that reality lies behind the appearances, asserts that what we do not have but desire to have will be given us somewhere else and at some other time (whereas according to Nietzsche we lack what we do not have only because we are incapable of taking it). Christianity is 'female', 'castrated', because it asserts that reality is transcendent, that the empirical world is unreal and should be discarded, and that those who are poor here will be rich in heaven. 'The whole counterfeiting business of transcendence and the Beyond has its most sublime advocate in Wagner's art [...] Music as Circe [...] You will nowhere find a more pleasant way to enervate your spirit, to forget your manliness under a rosebush [...] How he flatters every cowardliness of the modern soul with the tones of magical

maidens!' (II 930–31). Women exert their will over men by fostering men's erroneous belief in the wholly autonomous, independently non-masculine 'eternal feminine' (II 702). Against the falsehoods of women, priests and magicians Nietzsche asserts – and here we may certainly follow Derrida – the penetrating and unveiling power of knowledge, 'Erkenntnis', identified with masculinity (II 930) :

> *Unter Frauen.* – Die Wahrheit? O Sie kennen die Wahrheit nicht! Ist sie nicht ein Attentat auf alle unsre *pudeurs*? (II 945)

> *Woman to woman.* – Truth? Oh, you do not know what truth is! Is it not a violation of all our *pudeurs*?

The notion of a reality behind the appearances, of a thing in itself, is the *horrendum pudendum* of metaphysics (II 974), the deceitful assertion that behind the veil lies a centre of power which, when the veil is torn away, is revealed to be a vacuity. Behind the 'moral figleaf' (II 1010), the woman, the eunuch, the *décadent*, have nothing – only impotence of will, either incapacity (II 1010) or mere velleities, mere ideals : 'the history of what it has thought desirable has hitherto been the *partie honteuse* of the human race' (II 1008). The place of that vacuity, that is deceitfully called the 'true' or ideal world, is taken by masculine knowledge. The 'point' of a Nietzschean remark is directed at, or into, the femininity of his reader.

2. Occasionally – and some of the occasions are famous – Nietzsche does allow for a different response to the 'seductions' (II 930) of the feminine veils, the lure of the ideal, the transcendent, the promised or hidden 'truth', which is untruth. There is an alternative to the brutal, masculine, uncovering of illusion and imposition of knowledge. Occasionally, as Derrida says, Nietzsche takes the part of the masked actor, looking down disdainfully on the coarse and uncultivated passion for reality of those who are insensitive to the higher illusions of art. 'We have art, lest we should perish of the truth' (III 832). 'Lest the bow should break, art exists' ('Richard Wagner in Bayreuth' I 385). The best-known expression of the belief in life-protecting illusion (which is usually called art, but not always, see e.g. I 87, 213) is the cry of the Apolline dreamer in *The Birth of Tragedy*, for whom life has the coherence and grandeur of an epic. 'It is a dream! My will is to dream on!' (I 23). But the idea is expressed at all stages of Nietzsche's career : in *On the Genealogy of*

Morals falsehood (die Lüge) is said to 'justify itself' in art (II 892); in *Nietzsche contra Wagner* the 'will to truth' is the 'bad taste' that would unveil everything and see it naked (II 1061). It is in this context alone that we find Nietzsche 'affirming' woman, whose 'great art is lying, whose chief concern is appearance and beauty' (II 698), and who therefore – Derrida explains – is in her perfection a higher type of human being than the perfect man (*Human, All too Human* I § 377, I 647).

3. But the actor is sexually ambiguous, and the supreme example of the actor is Richard Wagner (II 919), the great eunuch before whom women unclothe themselves (II 931 cp. I 401). There has to be, as Derrida sees, a stage beyond the differentiation of male and 'female' (=castrated male), beyond the differentiation of truth and untruth, and beyond even the epicene (if elegant, 'vornehm') affirmation of illusion. That stage is indeed intimated for us at the end of the parable 'How the "true" world finally became a fable', when both the 'true' world and its complementary opposite, the 'apparent' world, are equally abolished. But this new state, after the negation of negation, after the abolition of differentiation, is not, as Derrida suggests, one of identification with and love for the affirmative woman. Nietzsche's dialectic terminates in no such synthesis, and anyway he nowhere acknowledges the existence of an autonomous femininity. Nietzsche's third stage is the *reaffirmation of the male* – 'INCIPIT ZARATHUSTRA'. In the world where truth and appearance are at one, art is no longer apolline illusion, the antithesis of reality; art is now dionysiac, 'die Realität noch einmal', 'reality repeated' (II 961) (the supremely artistic vision would thus be that of the eternal recurrence, of reality infinitely repeated). In the world in which castration has no place nothing is opposite or alien to the artist's creative, generative (II 1003) urge : all things rather are potentially flesh of his flesh, extensions of his power, forced by him, in his dionysiac, sexually initiated ecstasy, to partake of his character, to reflect his own tumescent will :

> Damit es Kunst gibt, damit es irgendein ästhetisches Tun und Schauen gibt, dazu ist eine physiologische Vorbedingung unumgänglich : der *Rausch* [...] vor allem der Rausch der Geschlechtserregung [...] endlich der Rausch des Willens, eines überhäuften und geschwellten Willens. – Das Wesentliche am Rausch ist das Gefühl der Kraftsteigerung und Fülle. Aus

diesem Gefühl gibt man an die Dinge ab, man *zwingt* sie von uns zu nehmen, man vergewaltigt sie – man heisst diesen Vorgang *idealisieren* [...] das Idealisieren besteht *nicht* [...] in einem Abziehn [..] des Nebensächlichen. Ein ungeheures *Heraustreiben* der Hauptzüge ist vielmehr das Entscheidende, so dass die andern darüber verschwinden.

Man bereichert in diesem Zustande alles aus seiner eignen Fülle: was man sieht, was man will, man sieht es geschwellt, gedrängt, stark, überladen mit Kraft. Der Mensch dieses Zustandes verwandelt die Dinge, bis sie seine Macht widerspiegeln – bis sie Reflexe seiner Vollkommenheit sind. (II 995)

For there to be art, for there to be any kind of aesthetic action and contemplation, one physiological pre-condition is indispensable: ecstasy [...] first and foremost the ecstasy of sexual excitement [...] finally the ecstasy of the will, of an overcharged and swollen will. – The essential feature of ecstasy is the sense of intensified strength and of plenitude. Out of this feeling one emits into things, one *forces* them to take from us, one rapes them – this process is named *idealisation*. Idealisation does *not* consist in an abstraction from the inessential. Rather, an enormous distension of the principal features is what is decisive, so that beside them the rest shrink to nothing.

In this state one enriches everything from one's own plenitude: what one sees, what one wills, one sees swollen, taut, strong, charged with energy. Man in this condition transforms things until they mirror his power – until they are images of his perfection.

Lest there should be any doubt about the essentially and exclusively masculine nature of dionysiac art, Nietzsche notes in a fragment 'On the genesis of art' that, 'physiologically speaking', the 'creative instinct of the artist' is equivalent to 'the diffusion of semen through the blood' (III 870). There is a role for woman in the mysteries of Dionysus but it is a separate, subordinate, and instrumental role, the role of pain and childbearing, which exists *in order that* the ecstatically swollen masculine will should contemplate and affirm itself into eternity :

only in the dionysiac mysteries, in the psychology of the dionysiac state, is the fundamental fact about the Hellenic instinct expressed – its 'will to life' ... *Eternal* life, the eternal recurrence of life ... *true* life as collective living on through procreation, through the mysteries of sexuality. Therefore the *sexual* symbol was for the Greeks the archetypal venerable symbol ... In order that there should be the eternal pleasure of creation, in order that the will to life should eternally affirm itself, there must also be to eternity 'the pangs of the child-bearer'.   (II 1031)

The production of art is, 'metaphorically speaking (and non-metaphorically)', a male affair, the female is merely its precondition. This acknowledgement, in a modified form, of the male–female distinction (woman giving birth to the 'real' world which art repeats and intensifies) is the moment at which the third stage in Nietzsche's dialectic can rejoin the first. The moment of transition itself is perhaps given in Nietzsche's modification of a thought which we have unambiguously assigned to the first stage: 'Art as practised by the artist – don't you women understand what that is? – a violation of all *pudeurs*' (III 622).

This then is the nearest that Nietzsche comes to an acknowledgement of complementarity, reciprocity or relationship in difference between male and female. We cannot say with Derrida that 'he was, and loved, some affirmative woman'. Throughout his life Nietzsche's passionate desire to identify with someone, to love someone, was frustrated at every turn by another, a supreme desire – that for 'the eye of Zarathustra' – and throughout his life his 'affirmation' remained solitary.

Similarly the delicate interplay in realistic art between truth and fiction ('illusion') always escapes Nietzsche's understanding. The realistic novelist and the realistic moralist have in common that they believe both that things are not quite what people like to think they are, and also that appearances save themselves, and cannot be totally resolved into some hidden reality (as, for example, Schopenhauer thought they could). For La Rochefoucauld as for Stendhal the appearances, as well as the realities which those appearances rather badly conceal, are equally part of 'what there is', the determinate datum that 'es gibt'. Nietzsche sometimes, especially in *Human, All Too Human*, tries to emulate the art of the *moraliste*, analysing the data of humanity in sentences beginning 'il y a des gens qui', 'es gibt Leute, die'. But the metaphysical prejudice against the 'donnée' is too strong. Neither the masculine 'Erkenntnis' that reveals the nullity of transcendence, nor the hermaphrodite play with self-conscious illusion, nor the eroticisation and subjectivisation of the world of things that he so aptly calls 'idealisation' can ultimately release language from the circle of metaphorical transformation. 'To see *what is*', after the fashion of the Parisian novelists (particularly

Flaubert and the Goncourt brothers) seems to Nietzsche a capitulation, a submission to the alien will of 'petits faits', the very antithesis of an imposition on things of the writer's creative urge, and so essentially 'antiartistic' (II 994–5). Not even the joint abolition of the 'true' world and the 'apparent', not even Zarathustra's dionysiac art, can bring the middle mode of discourse to touch ground. To acknowledge any sort of *datum* would be an intolerable limitation on Zarathustra's will. Were 'Being' a *datum*, it would limit his right to the endless metaphoricisation of endlessly interpretable experience – under the 'régime des guillemets' 'being' is merely that which 'interpretation' and 'evaluation' subsume. Were sexual difference a *datum*, it would limit his urge to the erotic transformation of all objects into his own image – under the 'régime des guillemets' reciprocal sexual difference, the generative process, merely prepares the way for the absolute monarchy of the male principle. It is not, shall we say, the philosophy of a married man. But then, 'which of the great philosophers has been married?' (*On the Genealogy of Morals* II 848). The answer, of course, is Hegel, whom Friedrich Heer one called the philosopher of marriage, and whose understanding of reciprocal determination is the most subtle of any to be found outside the realm of the realistic novel. If we were to turn to Hegel, the peculiarities of Nietzsche's middle mode could doubtless soon be identified for us in philosophical terms.[13] But there may still be something to be gained by considering the problem from the point of view of literature.

4

I'd prefer art to mirror life,
if it's all the same to you.   (Act II)

'My first transvaluation of all values' Nietzsche, in 1888, called *The Birth of Tragedy from the Spirit of Music* (II 1032), and in style as well as content there is surprisingly little difference between Nietzsche's first published non-philological work and his last. The controlling belief that, measured against the wordless world to which it claims to refer, language is a tissue of lies is established from the start. The resultant impossibility of distinguishing literal from metaphorical usage leads on the small scale to the 'neverending interchange in the function of words' that we have already examined, and on the large scale to a general confusion of literary modes. The question 'are Nietzsche's writings works of history, philosophy, or literature?' is as difficult to answer as the question 'is this or that phrase of Nietzsche's – about Russian wickedness, for example – to be understood as literally anthropological, as metaphorically moral-theological, or as hyperbolically journalistic?' and the reason for the difficulty is the same. If in language we can never tell the truth there can be no control exercised over what we say that derives, not from the nature of language, but from the nature of what we think we are talking about – yet our language still has the form of being about *something*. We cannot apply to what we say the realist's sole requirement, that it should be relevant to the situation we have chosen to depict,[14] nor can we apply to how we say what we say the Aristotelian requirement, that it should have the degree of precision appropriate to the subject matter[15] – yet the subject matter still seems to be there. We lose even the ability to order our utterances purely by social convention, since those conventions are themselves formulated and applied in language, the very medium of lies, and are only metaphors for the conformations of the will to power. Yet our thoughts remain couched in the form of communication, in the form of public utterance. Language remains, interminably – Nietzsche does not himself fall into mystical silence – and with it there remains the *appearance* of speaking to someone about things. It is reference that is lost, not referentiality, community, not the form of communication. Though language is all lies, it is not all meaningless, and through it the philosopher, even if in total isolation, glimpses 'reality', unspoken of course, and unspeakable.[16] That *The Birth of Tragedy* is already the first instalment of Nietzsche's 'theory of morals for deaf-mutes and other philosophers' is revealed in that work's refusal (or its inability) to be bound by such conventional and public distinctions as those between scholarship and poetry, history and philosophy, exposition and exhortation, fact and fable – in its being 'a work of mixed mode' (Silk and Stern, *Nietzsche on Tragedy* p. 188).

'The great variety of separate topics that Nietzsche deals with [in *The Birth of Tragedy*] give one a feeling of being related, even though it is not easy to say in what their relatedness consists' (*Nietzsche on Tragedy* p. 196). Silk and Stern materially assist the understanding of Nietzsche's style by identifying what they call 'centripetal' and 'metaleptic' imagery as a principal source of that obscure feeling of cohesiveness. The essence of the centripetal procedure is 'Nietzsche's method of allowing his arguments to be guided and determined by the very metaphors, analogies and myths which are, or are derived from, the material of his inquiry' (*Nietzsche on Tragedy* p. 338). Nietzsche does not say that the religion of 'Apollo,

as the dominant force in the Greece of the Homeric period, nullified
the threat posed to the Greeks by [. . .] Dionysiac worship among their
barbarian neighbours'; he says instead ' "the Greeks were apparently
perfectly insulated [. . .] against the feverish excitements of these
festivals, though knowledge of them came to Greece on all the routes
of land and sea; for the figure of Apollo, rising full of pride, held out
the Gorgon's head to this grotesquely uncouth Dionysiac power." '
Silk and Stern comment: 'It is appropriate that *Apollo* should turn
the uncouth power to *stone*, because the Nietzschean Apollo is associated with stone in his capacity as god of sculpture. And it is of
course especially appropriate that he should be made to do the
turning-to-stone in the terminology of Greek myth ("Gorgon's head")
to which he himself belongs. But there is no logic to this appropriateness, except for the logic of metalepsis [. . .] What is [. . .] enhanced
[. . .] is the homogeneity [. . .] of Nietzsche's work as a whole'.
(*Nietzsche on Tragedy* pp. 197–8). We need to add, however, that the
'logic of metalepsis' is actually a substitute for any other kind of logic
whatever – sociological, theological, historical – and that the 'homogeneity of Nietzsche's work' is here enhanced at the cost of the
homogeneity of the objects with which it purports to deal. While the
mention of 'the Gorgon's head' advances the metaphorical cohesiveness of *The Birth of Tragedy*, the socio-economic account of Greek
religion, begun in the mention of 'all the routes of land and sea', is,
by the very recourse to a metaleptic development of the image of
Apollo, left fractured and incomplete. By the transfer from the
historical to the poetic mode Nietzsche draws our attention to the
language in which he is writing and away from the object he is pur-
portedly writing about. The crucial step is perhaps the preference of
the transhistorical personification 'Apollo' to the historically specific
'the Greek cult of Apollo'. It is made difficult for us to ask *to what*
Nietzsche's primal image of Apollo *refers*, though the assumption of
its referentiality remains.

Indeed, to call Nietzsche's method centripetal is to assume that we
know what is the centre of his enquiry, that despite the mixture of
modes we can determine what is the material from which the
metaleptic elaboration begins. Throughout the treatise it remains
obscure whether Nietzsche is conducting a conceptual argument – an
amendment of Schopenhauer, for example – about the relation
between music and tragedy, or whether he is conducting a historical
argument about the course of Hellenic religion, and then of Occidental culture in general. The retention of apparent historical

referentiality alongside a loss of actual historical reference is nowhere clearer than in the case of the primal images of 'Apollo', 'Dionysus', and 'Socrates' (though the case is not fundamentally different with other major images, notably 'Euripides', 'Italian opera' and 'Wagner'). 'For Nietzsche Dionysus and Apollo are neither logical entities nor Greek gods. They are cast in a middle mode of language' (*Nietzsche on Tragedy* p. 338). In other words Nietzsche never decides whether the terms 'apolline' and 'dionysiac' contain a necessary allusion (one imposed by the facts of the matter, a *datum*) to pre-Christian Greek religion – whether they are terms like 'Marxism' and 'Gaullism' which require, if they are to be applicable, a historical link with Marx or De Gaulle. Or whether any allusion they contain is illustrative, a matter of his heuristic and arbitrary choice, rather like the allusions to Caesar and Machiavelli in the terms 'Caesarism' and 'Machiavellianism', which can be perfectly well defined without any specific historical reference. The position is similar with Socrates, whose historical individuality is dissolved away by making him 'the very type of Theoretical Man' (I 84), while his historical example is the only evidence given us from which we can deduce in what this new 'form of existence', the 'Daseinsform' of Theoretical Man, consists. Nietzsche makes no distinction between those attributes of his primal images which are historically – that is, publicly – acknowledged, those for which he is indebted to some source other than his own interpretative ingenuity, and those for which he is himself more or less wholly responsible. *That* is what is meant by a 'mixed' or 'middle' mode. Nietzsche associates the name of Dionysus not only with the dithyramb (for which there is ample historical support), but also with the doctrine of the ultimate unity of all things (for which the support is more dubious), and with music in general (for which there is no real support at all). Silk and Stern (pp. 204–9) provide us with these and other examples of the spectrum of associationist possibilities, ranging from the 'literal' (or historically authorised) to the extremely 'paraliteral' (at the end of a convoluted metaleptic process), by which Nietzsche builds up his primal images or archetypes. The essential common characteristic of these figures is that while they claim some initial – perhaps single, perhaps purely nominal – relation with the 'literal' – the historical, the conventionally acknowledged, the determinately real – that relation is not capable of expansion, exploration or correction through any established public mode of discourse, whether that of historical or 'scientific' or of personal experience. And it is of the essence of 'the given' – that to which reference is ultimately made, if it is made at all – that 'the given' is not some single, isolated 'Ansatzpunkt', some privileged datum in consciousness, but is a characteristic of a whole given system which, as a system, is capable of discussion, expansion, and development.[17] The apparent referentiality of Nietzsche's writing is illusory precisely because of the isolation – the privacy and the arbitrariness – of the points at which it touches the world of common knowledge. It is not possible to find more evidence for – or for that matter against – the argument of *The Birth of Tragedy*. The only admissible expansion of Nietzsche's mention of Socrates for example – the only one that has authority – is that which takes place within Nietzsche's text itself. About this 'Dionysus', this 'Apollo', this 'Socrates', we have to think what the writer tells us to think, and mentions of 'reality' are present for their shock value only.

Nietzsche's archetypes belong to a species eerily familiar to the traveller across the lunar landscape[18] of twentieth-century thought and literature. They have meaning, but no determinate meaning, no reference to a shared world of specific things, events or people, about which it is possible to speak in different and publicly acknowledged modes without dissolving their identity – Hugo's Waterloo is as much Waterloo as Tolstoy's, and we may legitimately compare them in respect of their truth to the event, but Rilke's Apollo is no more Apollo than Nietzsche's, and we may compare them only as visions in the night. In place of realism, even apparently realistic prose offers us, in Nietzsche's term, 'idealisation' – a transformation into image, reality 'repeated' and suffused with subjectivity. The writers in whom the process is closest to Nietzsche's own are his fellow psychologists. The archetypes that stalk the pages of *Totem and Taboo* or *Moses and Monotheism* have the same hectic, cardboard, Wagnerian quality as the *dramatis personae* of *The Birth of Tragedy*, monsters born of the sleep, not of reason, but of realism. The concept of historicity which underlies the derivation of Christianity from a conspiracy of Jewish priests in *On the Genealogy of Morals* combines the same apparent referentiality with the same absence of assessable reference that we find in Freud's derivation of Christianity from the guilt feelings of 'the' assassins of Moses, not to mention the similar feelings of 'the' parricidal primal horde. Nietzsche could perfectly well have adopted Freud's justification for the acknowledged arbitrariness of his historical procedure : that it would be vindicated by its success in uncovering the 'secret motives' for the 'distortions' of the historical tradition.[19] Freud in turn made an even more successful paraliteral exploitation of his cultural heritage than the inventor of 'Apollo' and 'Dionysus' when he remarked that every one of his neurotics had 'been an Oedipus, or, which comes down to the same thing', 'had become a Hamlet'.[20] It is true that Freud's concern for the 'scientific' status of his conclusions leads him to formulate them in a mode in which clear reference to publicly discussable facts does occur and which to that extent is realistic. When Freud tells us of a patient whose neurosis can be traced back to the traumatic moment when his mother threatened him with castration,[21] we are still in the realistic world of tales from the Vienna nurseries. When by contrast he asserts that the difference in the psychosexual development of men and women 'corresponds to the difference between a castration that has been executed and one that has been merely threatened'[22] we are in the Nietzschean middle mode of rootless metaphor, the 'régime des guillemets', for 'threatened' here means (in the majority of cases) 'thought to have been threatened', and 'executed' means (in all cases) 'thought to have been executed', and furthermore – since we are reconstructing the origins of thought – 'thought' means 'what we may for the sake of our argument call "thought" '. Indeed we may apply to the world of Freudian sex Stern's apt comment about Nietzschean theology : that from Nietzsche's middle mode of language 'springs that entirely modern (and depressingly familiar) habit of talking metaphorically about "God", "saintliness", "divine creation", "sin" and the like without ever quite deciding what non-metaphorical meanings, and what beliefs (if any) go with the talking' (*A Study of Nietzsche* pp. 199–200). If the 'true' world of divine transcendence has been abolished and become a fable, so too has the 'true' world of unconscious sexuality. As a Nietzschean post-Freudian, who accepts that 'la castration n'a pas lieu', Derrida engages in much presumably metaphorical talk about sexual members, castration and a 'style éperonnant' without any decision as to what non-metaphorical statements about events, actions or psychological mechanisms are implied by the talking. *Éperons. Les styles de Nietzsche* is written throughout in the middle mode.

The process of 'idealisation', the translation of reality into image, and the creation among the images of a subjective order (rather than the acceptance of a real order from which the images are abstracted and to which they refer) – that is a literary process that is also 'entirely modern (and depressingly familiar)'. There is in *Ulysses* a mountain of *petits faits*, as there is in *Das steinerne Herz*, but before none of them do Joyce or Arno Schmidt bow in submission; rather the 'facts' are compelled into a literary order (or disorder) in which subjectivity appears to have created them rather than contingency. Subtly deprived of reference, by the implication that they are the products of some refined literary or linguistic causality, some immensely diluted 'logic of metalepsis', the 'facts' in these novels float half an inch above the ground, to which fan-clubs of both authors endeavour to return them by pilgrimages to 'the real thing' in Dublin or Lower Saxony. Even the popular novel of the late twentieth century feels obliged to some exhibitionist play with its own fictionality – witness the work of John Fowles, or even David Lodge's *Changing Places*, of which the appeal lies precisely in what it is about and not in what it is. The effacing of the distinction between literal and metaphorical truth, the levelling down of all literary representations into formally equivalent 'images', is the most prominent feature of the works of Hermann Hesse, from the hallucinations of Harry Haller in *Steppenwolf* to the alternative lives of Knecht in *The Glass Bead Game*. Indeed it would be interesting to trace the rise in modern criticism of the terms 'image' and 'imagery', in substitution for the older terms of rhetoric, for these are words whose *raison d'être* is their indifference to the distinction between metaphorical and non-metaphorical writing.

'Seeing the customers in a café someone said to me : "Look how dull they are; nowadays pictures ['images'] are more alive than people." This inversion is perhaps one of the distinguishing marks of our world : we live in the generalisation of the Imaginary. Look at the USA : everything there is transformed into images – only images exist, only images are produced, only images are consumed [. . .] When generalised, the image derealises the human world of conflicts and desires, under the pretence of illustrating it.'[23] Roland Barthes acknowledges that in reflecting on photography he is reflecting on a nineteenth-century genre, but he does not recognise that photography is therefore a genre coeval with the great masterpieces of the realistic novel. He recognises (*La chambre claire* pp. 146–7) that there is already something archaic about his lament for the passing, in the modern world, of the sense for the 'pure contingency' of photographs (p. 52), for the 'wholly non-metaphorical presence of the thing' in them (p. 123), the passing of the astonishment he feels at the unmediated confrontation in a photograph with past reality, what he calls 'le *"Ça a été"* '. Yet he does not recognise that the proper object of his nostalgia is something more, considerably more, than a particular feature of photographs, or that his own belief that photography differs from a linguistic text through its freedom from 'reflection' (p. 52) or 'interpretation' (p. 165), his belief that language is 'by its nature fictional' (p. 134) 'never credible *to the roots*' (p. 151), is itself a contribution to the 'generalisation of the Imaginary'. In photography he still sees – though he knows he belongs to a passing era in seeing it – that pure 'Reference' (p. 120) which his own emphasis on the distinction between the signifier and signified has helped to banish from the literary text. It is the loss of realism that is properly the object of his lament, in an age of images, for the loss of contingency, life and love (p. 147).

5

. . . Rosencrantz and
Guildenstern are dead.   (*Hamlet* V. 2. 385)

Barthes identifies two elements in the structure of photographs, to which he gives the names *studium* and *punctum*. The *studium* is the 'encoded' – one might say, the literary – element, the respect in which the photograph alludes to and obeys public conventions about how photographs are composed. The *punctum* – unlike Derrida's 'style', which lacerates veils in the impersonal void – is the element that 'comes home to' Barthes himself, an arrow discharged from the picture that pierces his affectivity, a moment of contingency that causes *him* pain – and others only in so far as their personal relationship to the subject of the photograph is not greatly different from his own. The *punctum* turns out to be of two kinds.

First, there is the chance detail, a conjunction of figures, the position of a hand, a woman's necklace, the straps on her Sunday-best shoes, in which the absolute singularity and contingency of the recorded moment leaps from the frame. In virtue of that one detail the otherwise unknown subject acquires 'a whole life outside her portrait' (p. 91), a whole area of hidden ground, 'un champ aveugle', is intimated around the picture. In the same way, we might add, the realistic work of literature, if approached without the distrust which Barthes says he can himself never discard (p. 165), suggests that beyond it, between its chapters and before and after, lies *more* of the world, its world and ours, than happens, contingently, to have been articulated. Dickens might have left out a line of his description of Smallweed reading the newspaper, or he might have put in a line more – but, *ex hypothesi* of the realistic mode, Smallweed would not for that have been another man, Dickens would merely have ventured further, or less far, on to the hidden ground. At the end of *Nostromo* there loom both the communists and the North American imperialists, a theme in themselves, though Conrad's principal story is over. Claudius enters in the middle of his conversation with Rosencrantz and Guildenstern – we do not hear what he says before his entry, but we are invited to think that we might have done. We are glad for what the writer has chosen to articulate, we recognise that any picture has its frame, but our mind is projected beyond this particular frame into the one world which we share with the creatures of the writer's fiction and which we know in many modes and from many pictures and many different stories. 'How many children had Lady Macbeth?' is a trivial question, and we may not be able to answer it, but it is not meaningless.

In the middle mode of writing, by contrast, there is no 'champ aveugle', no 'behind the scenes' where things carry on much as they do on the stage until they reach our own experience – behind the scenes in the middle mode there is only non-entity, the acknowledged fiction of 'the thing-in-itself', in relation to which what appears on stage is acknowledged as an appearance, is a lie. Because Shakespeare is, among other things, a realist, because his minor characters, like Cinna the Poet, or the Third Murderer in *Macbeth*, simply graze the principal action while pursuing their own unchronicled lives in the hidden ground, Charles and Mary Lamb could write their *Tales from Shakespeare* and Tom Stoppard could conceive *Rosencrantz and Guildenstern are Dead*. Since however Stoppard emphatically marks off his words and world from Shakespeare's, he writes in the middle mode, and behind the scenes of *his* play there is only emptiness.

The second type of the *punctum* in a photograph is the generalised form, the pure representation (p. 148), of unmediated past reality – 'ça a été' : this thing, this person, this moment, was, and was real, and is no more. The second form of the *punctum*, then, is the finitude (p. 141) imposed by death, and every photograph bears in itself the sign of my death (p. 151), of the death that puts an end to the love that can only exist between finite and mortal beings (p. 147). It is here that we reach the essential distinction between realistic writing and writing in the middle mode. Realistic literature, literature that has the reference that Barthes attributes exclusively to photography, is alone capable of representing death, and so alone capable of representing love. Nietzsche may deal with 'an almost infinite variety of [...] issues' (Stern, *Nietzsche*, p. 199), but he has practically nothing to say on the subject of death.[24] Nietzsche's use of 'was' never has the ultimacy of Barthes's 'Ça a été'. Discourse in the middle mode is, after all, interminable, it is discourse without determinate reference, and the specificity of a human being (and only a specific, only a photographable, human being can be loved) is determined as much by his or her mortality as by his or her sex. The two types of *punctum* are not so very different : contingency, identity, death, ineluctable determination in time, can all be read, and loved, in a shoe-strap, or a button :

> Thou'lt come no more
> Never, never, never, never, never.
> Pray you undo this button.

Lear's terrible lines are at the boundary of articulate utterance and for Barthes, looking at the photograph of his dead mother, the horrible flatness ('platitude') of death consists in there being nothing to say about it :

The horror is this: nothing to say about the death of her whom I love most, nothing to say about her picture which I look at without ever being able to read more into it ['l'approfondir'], to transform it. (p. 145)

These deaths, unlike the death invoked by Pascal, cannot be swept back into a cycle of intellectual and linguistic metamorphoses. They mark the point beyond which there is no more to say : they show language to have the finitude of real experience, not the endlessness of metaphoricity.

Yet before we reach the point beyond which there is no more to say, there is a *great deal* that can be said – provided that finitude and mortality are not forgotten or denied. Barthes admits that the agony of loss that he feels before a photograph is sterile – as perhaps is the conclusion of *King Lear*. 'If dialectic is that thought which masters the corruptible and converts the negation that is death into the power of work, then the Photograph is undialectical : it is denatured theatre in which death cannot "contemplate" itself, reflect itself or internalise itself; or again, it is the dead theatre of Death, the foreclosure of the tragic; it excludes any purification, any *catharsis*' (p. 141). This is why Barthes's cultivation of the photograph as the last fading refuge of realistic reference cannot ultimately stand. The dialectic, like determination, is inescapable, and if in the photograph the pain of loss is not transformed, then it will be repeated and preserved – and *thereby* transformed. But not into a *resurrection from* the dead, the true culmination of the dialectic : the undialectical photograph, in which the real past is interminably translated into present image, offers only a *return of* the dead, the resuscitation of a painted corpse (pp. 23, 56), 'die Realität noch einmal'. This is the process, obscure to Barthes, as a result of which the photograph, which has its origins in agonising immediacy and particularity, nonetheless contributes to the 'generalisation of the Imaginary', the universal production and consumption of images, and so to the detachment of experience from reference, and from reality itself. Realism, by contrast, is dialectical : it has reference, and it knows death, but it is fixated on neither, it is an art for 'the human world of conflicts and desires', an art of motion, and so of language and (perhaps) of film. Hegel tells us that the death of Nature is the birth of the Spirit.[25] We do not have to follow him into the realm of absolute knowledge to appreciate that having something to say about death is what makes our discourse human. We are not, as Nietzsche thought, gesticulating animals drifting at two removes from reality in a sea of metaphor. We can in language realistically depict and assess our condition in so far as our discourse is determined, demarcated, by the knowledge both of death and of death's transcendence. 'Le soleil ni la mort ne se peuvent regarder fixement.' 'So bleibe mir die Sonne denn im Rücken.'[26] The area illuminated by that dual knowledge is the area in which work is possible and in which realism has something to say.

In the middle mode of discourse, death, quite as much as God or sex, is indeterminately reiterable and reinterpretable (as is shown so well by *Rosencrantz and Guildenstern are Dead*). The fact of death can here contribute nothing to the understanding of life, which thus loses individuality, finitude, and meaning. One of the most ingenious modern attempts to write simultaneously in a realistic and in the middle mode, Nabokov's *Lolita*, cannot maintain the symbiosis once it has to relate its characters to their deaths. Quilty is a hallucinatory construct, and his 'execution', at once burlesque and brutally protracted, could come from the pages of *Steppenwolf*. The mortality that counts (and it does) is that of the characters who count, that is the characters who love – Humbert and Lolita – but this mortality is related only arbitrarily and formally to their lives : through the assertion that our reading the narrative is dependent on their both being dead, and through the details coyly provided in the Foreword 'for the benefit of old-fashioned readers who wish to follow the destinies of the "real" people beyond the "true" story'. Yet in a purely realistic narration we do not have to read about deaths in order to know that the characters are mortal. When Morten Schwarzkopf kisses Tony Buddenbrook, leaning against a sandcastle he has built for her on the beach at Travemünde, love and death conjoin to define her, absolutely, without release. 'Thou'lt come no more.' Tony will be, until a death which Mann will not need to narrate, the woman for whom this possibility, perhaps phantasmal, perhaps juvenile, did not become a reality. The irony in the description of Morten's gesture towards the sea, when he attempts to say what he means by 'Freedom', may seem to confirm the view that social forces leave her no alternative. But that does not affect the point, the realism. The realist is committed only to the absolute, the transcendent, importance of the determinate individuality of human beings, not at all to the view that they are absolutely, or even very much, self-determining. Tony Buddenbrook exists, like her brother, between the possibility, however remote, of a transcendence intimated by Morten's 'Freedom', and the certainty of the finite sequence of irredeemable determinations which is called life and ends in death. Because the story which contains her is poised, however ironically, between death and transcendence it is properly called realistic. *Anna Karenina* occupies a similar area of realism, if the limits are drawn less ambiguously and with greater power. The freedom that Anna and Vronsky enjoy in Italy is incompatible with being human, with being determinate, moral, and mortal. It is the image of transcendence abused, of our immortal and absolute worth set against the determinacy of our existence and itself turning into the most inescapable determination of all : the guilt that flows from a wrong that cannot be undone. Or, as the realist prefers to put it :

For a time after uniting his life with hers and putting on civilian clothes, he felt the delight of freedom in general, which he had not known before, and the freedom of love, and he was content; but not for long. He soon became aware that there arose in his heart the desire for desires – boredom [...] Sixteen hours of the day had to be filled somehow, for they were living abroad in complete freedom, cut off from the round of social life which had occupied most of his time in Petersburg.[27]

For those who seek to live beyond determinacy, beyond the human world of conflicts and desires, the return to determinacy, here foreshadowed, can only take the form of retribution. (Which is why Nietzsche *is* responsible for the posthumous abuse of his thoughts.) Others, like Levin, accept their finitude :

Lying on his back, he was now gazing at the high cloudless sky. 'Don't I know that that is infinite space and not a rounded vault? But however much I may screw up my eyes and strain my sight, I cannot see it except as round and finite, and though I know that space is infinite, I am absolutely right when I see a firm blue vault, far more right than when I strain to see beyond it.' (Book 8, Chapter 13, p. 791)

The reward for this realism (and both the literary and the ethical justifications for that term are here equally compelling) is the constant sustaining miracle of transcendence, 'the life of the spirit, the only life that is worth living and the only life that we prize' (ibid.).

Wallace Stevens, that most Nietzschean of poets writing in English, suggested in a famous early poem that, if only thoughts of death and of transcendence were banished, finite things would become instinct with all the eternity of which the human mind was capable :

> Why should she give her bounty to the dead?
> What is divinity if it can come
> Only in silent shadows and in dreams?
> Shall she not find in comforts of the sun,
> In pungent fruit and bright, green wings, or else
> In any balm or beauty of the earth,
> Things to be cherished like the thought of heaven?
>
> ('Sunday Morning')[28]

After a lifetime lived in the middle mode of discourse, however, this magical fruit turns to ashes :

> Life consists
> Of propositions about life. The human
>
> Revery is a solitude in which
> We compose these propositions [...]
>
> ('Men made out of words', pp. 355–6)

The 'middle mode of discourse' is the mode *par excellence* of subjectivity, liberated from all determination, a mode without reference, without public, institutional or historical sanction, without mortality, and without transcendence; it is a mode of apparent referentiality and indefinitely associable metaphor in which language, the private and solitary medium for the infinitely repeatable shock of confronting death and penetrating differentiation, remains – interminably. The 'middle mode of discourse' is realism's negative image.

NOTES

1. Pascal, *Pensées*, ed. L. Brunschvicg, No. 199.
2. J. P. Stern, *A Study of Nietzsche* (Cambridge, 1979) p. 201.
3. G. C. Lichtenberg, *Aphorismen*, ed. Leitzmann, No. J 340, ed. Promies, No. J 357.
4. J. P. Stern, *Lichtenberg. A Doctrine of Scattered Occasions* (London, 1963) pp. 195–6.

Nicholas Boyle

5. Though see now H. Fricke, *Aphorismus* (Stuttgart, 1984) p. 9.
6. References are to the edition *Friedrich Nietzsche. Werke in drei Bänden*, ed. Karl Schlechta (Munich, 1954–6).
7. See J. P. Stern ' "Reality" in Early Twentieth-century German Literature' in *Philosophy and Literature*. Royal Institute of Philosophy Lecture Series: 16. Supplement to *Philosophy* 1983 (Cambridge, 1984) pp. 41–57.
8. Pascal, *Pensées*, No. 17, cp. Nietzsche *Werke* III, 320.
9. M. S. Silk and J. P. Stern, *Nietzsche on Tragedy* (Cambridge, 1981) p. 340.
10. The sequence, (1) 'evil', (2) 'not evil, because only called evil', (3) 'rightly called evil', is an exampe of the dialectic described by Stern, *A Study of Nietzsche*, pp. 160–1.
11. While the histrionic Zarathustra inclines to concluding his reflections with double dashes and exclamation marks.
12. Jacques Derrida, *Spurs. Nietzsche's Styles. Éperons. Les Styles de Nietzsche* (Chicago, 1979). The translations here given are my own.
13. See S. G. Houlgate's unpublished dissertation, 'Metaphysics and its criticism in the philosophies of Hegel and Nietzsche' (Cambridge, 1984).
14. J. P. Stern, *On Realism* (London, 1973) p. 108.
15. Stern, *On Realism*, p. 117, quoting *Nicomachean Ethics* I, iii, 3–4.
16. 'Why does Nietzsche refuse to distinguish between "fictions" and "lies"? [...] only to one who is prepared to take institutionalized life in the world seriously is this difference of any consequence.' Stern, *A Study of Nietzsche*, p. 188.
17. 'the given in experience is always a world or system [...] The given and the isolated, so far from being synonymous, are contradictory [...] the given is neither a collection, nor a series of ideas, but a complex, significant whole [...] Furthermore, the given in experience is given always in order to be transformed [...] In experience [...] a given world of ideas is transformed into a world of ideas which is more of a world.' M. Oakeshott, *Experience and its Modes* (Cambridge, 1933) pp. 28–30. Oakeshott dismisses what we may regard as the Nietzschean view of language as an 'elementary error' and subverts the Nietzschean primacy of interpretation: 'Interpretation requires something to interpret, but when we speak of *it* our language slips under our feet, for there is never in experience an *it*, an original, distinguishable from the interpretation, and consequently there can be no interpretation' (pp. 31–2).
18. Karl Schlechta applies this comparison to Nietzsche's work. See the 'Nachwort' to his edition, III, 1436.
19. 'Der Mann Moses und die monotheistische Religion' in S. Freud *Gesammelte Werke* 16 (London, 1950) p. 125.
20. 'Vorlesungen zur Einführung in die Psychoanalyse. III. Allgemeine Neurosenlehre', Lecture xxi. Freud, *Gesammelte Werke* 11 (London, 1940) p. 348.
21. 'Der Mann Moses [...]', *Gesammelte Werke* 16, p. 184.
22. Einige psychische Folgen des anatomischen Geschlechtsunterschiedes'. *Gesammelte Werke* 14 (London 1948), p. 28.
23. Roland Barthes, *La chambre claire. Note sur la photographie* (Paris, 1980) pp. 181–2.
24. Karl Schlechta's *Nietzsche-Index* (Munich, 1965) contains only nine references in all to 'Tod', 'der Tod' and 'ein Tod' (pp. 362–3).
25. G. W. F. Hegel, 'Enzyklopädie der philosophischen Wissenschaften im

Grundrisse' (1830) § 376, *Werke in 20 Bänden*, ed. E. Moldenhauer and K. M. Michel (Frankfurt a. M., 1970) 9, p. 537.

26. La Rochefoucauld, *Maximes* (1678), No. 26; Goethe, *Faust*, l. 4715.

27. L. Tolstoy, *Anna Karenina*, tr. D. Magarshack (London, 1961) Book 5, Chapter 8, p. 468.

28. *The Collected Poems of Wallace Stevens* (London, 1955) p. 67.

Fabricating histories

PAUL CONNERTON

Milan Kundera begins his novel *The Book of Laughter and Forgetting* like this :

In February 1948, Communist leader Klement Gottwald stepped out on the balcony of a Baroque palace in Prague to address the hundreds of thousands of his fellow citizens packed into Old Town Square. It was a crucial moment in Czech history – a fateful moment of the kind that occurs once or twice in a millennium.

Gottwald was flanked by his comrades, with Clementis standing next to him. There were snow flurries, it was cold, and Gottwald was bareheaded. The solicitous Clementis took off his own fur cap and set it on Gottwald's head.

The Party propaganda section put out hundreds of thousands of copies of a photograph of that balcony with Gottwald, a fur cap on his head and comrades at his side, speaking to the nation. On that balcony the history of Communist Czechoslovakia was born. Every child knew the photograph from posters, schoolbooks, and museums.

Four years later Clementis was charged with treason and hanged. The propaganda section immediately airbrushed him out of history and, obviously, out of all the photographs as well. Ever since, Gottwald has stood on that balcony alone. Where Clementis once stood, there is only bare palace wall. All that remains of Clementis is the cap on Gottwald's head.[1]

The irony of this fabrication – where fabrication is to be understood in the sense both of 'making' and of 'making false' – leads us back to the origins of photography : the art form that was invented in the same century as that in which the discipline of historical research was most systematically developed. In the radical recomposition of the map of knowledge witnessed by the early nineteenth century a crucial position was occupied by historical consciousness; the epoch was marked by a lively curiosity for the documents of traces which time had left behind. The task of historical representation was conceived as the narrowing of the gap between history as an objective course of events and history as the account of those events, between history as it happened and history as it is written. Ranke's wish to reconstruct the past 'wie es eigentlich gewesen' was the canonic statement of this aspiration. But it has its correlate in the succession of technical developments, beyond the sphere of language, which offered the effect of illusory recreation : from lithography and the diorama to photography. Europe in the 1820s saw a ferment of representation : the decade of Niepce's first photographic image, 1822, and of Daguerre's historical diorama, 1823, was also the decade of Ranke's Preface. Photographic representation, we can now see, was integrally bound up with the new historical sensibility of the nineteenth century, which sought to annihilate the gap between the model and the copy; and so, in responding to that overpowering sense of loss of which Scott and Ruskin were classical exponents, to offer the possibility of a restoration of the past in the context of the present.[2]

If the birth of photographic representation and historical interrogation is not merely coincidental, we nonetheless have to wait for a later date for the testimony of the photograph to vie in perceived significance with the testimony of the written document. If we were asked to nominate an emblem of our present condition the camera would surely compete with the computer. Photography now not only records and recovers what we call history; it collaborates in its creation. It is not perhaps entirely ungracious to suggest that the period we refer to as the Depression is in a way an achievement of photography; it was then that a handful of photographers – Walker Evans, Dorothea Lange, Russell Lee, Arthur Rothstein – documented the camera's incomparable capacity to capture the seamier side of American life; to make the blowing dust and abandoned cars, forsaken homes and pieces of luggage, highways bordered with blown tyres, bent and broken men and women and derelict children, the symbols of a common human plight. Later, for some of the century's great moments of drama – the atomic blasts, the landing on the moon – the telling eyewitness was the camera; without it much that is known to have occurred might still be in the realm of rumour and science fiction. The massive development of photography shares with our taste for historical documentation the prestige attached to the notion that 'it happened' : the distinctive trait of photography, by comparison with drawing, being precisely that it signifies that the event represented has *really* taken place.[3]

For all the great nineteenth-century novelists the credibility of events was always intimately tied to the aim of bringing to light the basic causes of the social – that is the historical – situation in which their characters find themselves. If we were to say of such writers

that the stock exchange and government offices, the Church and the
Army, the law and parliament, figure as the background to individual
action, we would fail to do justice to the place of institutions within
this convention of realism. Concentration on the symbols and image
clusters of Dickens's language has obscured how much of the foreground of his novels is taken up by institutions : by the school,
London business, the industrial north, the workhouses, and above all
the law courts; while Flaubert's *L'Éducation sentimentale* marks one
of the highest points in realism's awareness that no personal relationship, amorous or other, can persist beyond the privileged moment
without a network of interpersonal, public bonds. What is at issue
in realism, J. P. Stern tells us, is 'not Dickens's humanitarianism, or
Tolstoy's sentimental love of the Russian peasantry, or Balzac's conservatism, or Stendhal's or Flaubert's contempt for the church, the
politics of a petty Italian court, life in the French provinces, or the
revolution of 1848'; far 'more fundamental than these conative
attitudes is the creative acknowledgement on which they rest – the
creative acknowledgement of the data of social life at a recognizable
moment in history'.[4]

What among other things characterises the moment of history in
which we live is that we have an overload of information about ourselves. Compared to all previous societies we have experienced a
quantum leap in the amount of data about social life circulated
within our society. Work is now increasingly the manipulation of
information; indeed, the availability of information is becoming a
major criterion of social importance. To be sure, much of this
information load is self-cancelling. A historical event sparkles the
morning after with the dew of novelty but is soon forgotten. Kundera
has put the point forcibly : the bloody massacre in Bangladesh quickly
covered over the memory of the Russian invasion of Czechoslovakia,
the assassination of Allende drowned out the groans of Bangladesh,
the war in the Sinai Desert made people forget Allende, and the
Cambodian Massacre made people forget Sinai. Nonetheless, a flow
of information leaves behind a kind of sediment over and above any
particular items of information it may contain, whether the items
are sparse or abundant and whether those details are well or ill
remembered; and this sediment will take the form of certain habits
of cognition and perception which provide us with a mental set more
attuned to the possible existence of some items and more imperceptive to the others. We might then consider the transmission of
information as the practice of a rhetoric to be characterised by its

modes of speech. For the likelihood is that, if not the details of history, then at least our idea of history, our sense of its repertoire of possible narrative shapes, will be generated by the technology of communication in dominance in any particular society.

My suggestion is that the changing rhetoric of history is to a significant extent a precipitate of the changing technology of communication. Certainly this suggestion receives support from the history of earlier rhetorics. Consider for instance the contrast between oral and written transmission, and the rhetorics of history born of these two different forms.

If we try to picture to ourselves in an image the kind of history which is told in preliterate societies it will normally appear to have the same basic shape – the figure of an hourglass. However he fills in the details of his story, the oral historian will see everywhere a recurrent pattern. Extensive personal recollections will enable him to present a good deal of information about the recent past; the narrative of the previous two generations will sometimes be relatively 'thick' with events. But any change which has taken place before this he can imagine only as total and cataclysmic; and he will group all the events that tell of such change in a single period of universal transformation, thus accentuating the drama of the changes he portrays. These he will push back to a so-called period of origins; and having located certain events at that time he will then pass without comment through the succeeding 'middle period'. He clusters his information at the beginning and at the end of the past. In the intervening space of time there is a virtual void. It is not even an immobile history; in so far as it has any informational content at all it leaves the impression of stability at the narrow waist of the hourglass. To the literate outsider this narrative shape will appear strange and fabricated, and certainly not congruent with what he takes to be the 'real' course of events, whatever those events may have been. But for the oral historian his rhetorical shapes appear to be built into the real nature of things – simply because he lacks the written evidence that might lead him ever to imagine otherwise.[5]

Literate historians instinctively want to highlight the middle period which for the oral historian scarcely even exists. That is because, among other things, the written document makes it possible to pinpoint the gradual changes which cannot be phrased easily in the rhetoric of an oral tradition. Even so, the repertoire of narrative possibilities is still limited if the number and type of available documents are drastically restricted. That was the case with the classical

Greek and Roman historians who were essentially concerned with only two types of change : wars and revolutions.[6] They knew how to tell the development of war and how to describe its consequences; and they showed great skill in narrating the conduct of a revolution. But what they appear to have found difficult to narrate is the slow change in laws and customs in non-revolutionary periods; none of the texts of classical historians available to us gives a satisfactory account of long-term slow changes. For that narrative shape to be envisaged, for them to attend to slow change as well as violent change, they would have needed more extensive documentation and more types of documentation. Only when that becomes available is the threshold of noticeability extended to the point which we now take for granted. So that where the constraints of orality led narrators to perceive and present change in the form of abrupt, dichotomous transformations, the literate historian now characteristically perceives change in refined and lengthy series of gradual modifications. The literate historian has a new rhetoric; he wants to tell the story of steady incremental change, the narrative of intermediate steps.

What I have been suggesting about the role of certain rhetorical figures in the shaping of our sense of history has an analogy in the field of art. We are accustomed to think of certain paintings as triumphs of naturalism, and there is the temptation to feel that in them, as nowhere else, is to be found a true transcription of what the painter saw. But the belief that 'what one sees' is an unambiguous concept rests upon a naive view of perception : as though in the process of seeing there were imprinted upon the passive mind some 'sensation' or 'idea' which can be captured by the innocent eye. Any such conception of 'the given' ignores the fact that in deciphering what we see we come to the act of seeing with our receivers already attuned; we expect to be presented with a certain notation and we make ready to cope with it. When we step in front of a bust we do not, as a rule, take it to be a representation of a cut-off head, but understand what we are expected to look for because we know that what we see belongs to the convention called 'busts'; and when we copy what is called a 'nonsense figure', an inkblot, let us say, or an irregular patch, we try first to classify the blot and fit it into some sort of familiar scheme, so that we will say, for instance, that it is a triangle or that it looks like a fish. Perception is conditioned by the expectations, by the 'mental set', of the observer; and what the observer sees cannot be dissociated from the schemata or patterns which they impose upon experience.

The fact that narrative predominates in both mythic and fictional discourse makes it suspect as a way of speaking about 'real' events. Nonetheless, 'plot' is not a structural component of mythical or fictional stories alone, but is crucial to the historical representation of events. Thus, to be seen as historical, an event must be more than a singular occurrence, a unique happening; it receives its definition in part from its contribution to the development of a plot.

Let us consider, in the light of these claims, two such different results of camerawork as Leni Riefenstahl's film record of the 1934 Nuremberg Rally, *Triumph of the Will*, and the televised documentation of current affairs.

Triumph of the Will was commissioned by Hitler as a record and celebration of the 1934 Party Rally in Nuremberg; it was shot and edited by Leni Riefenstahl and premiered in Berlin on 28 March 1935, and subsequently awarded the National Film Prize by Goebbels during the Festival of the Nation in May 1935. An inauspicious little bundle of facts; and so, after the war, Riefenstahl sought to extricate herself from the suspicion of having produced a work of propaganda by claiming that her true concern had been to make an independent documentary. Her self-justification is set out in some detail in an interview she gave to *Cahiers du Cinéma* in September 1965, where she asserted that 'not a single scene' of *Triumph of the Will* is staged. Everything is genuine. And there is no tendentious commentary for the simple reason that there is no commentary at all. 'It is *history – pure history*'. Susan Sontag has set the record straight in a famous essay.[7] She shows how, thirty years earlier, in 1935, Riefenstahl had published her first report on the making of the film which reveals the stuff of which pure history is made. Page 31 contains a photograph of Riefenstahl with Hitler bending over some plans with the caption: 'The preparations for the Party Congress were made hand in hand with the preparations for the camera work.' In the same text she relates how she began work in May for the film of the rally which was held in early September; how in planning the film sequences she had to supervise the construction of elaborate bridges and towers for the cameras; how Speer, who built the site of the rally, came to be listed in the credits as the architect of the film; how at the suggestion of the Chief of Staff, Lutze, her cameramen were dressed in SA uniform throughout the shooting 'so that no one will distort the solemnity of the image with his civilian clothing'; how, when some of the footage of party leaders at the speakers' rostrum was damaged, Hitler gave orders for the shots to be refilmed; and how Streicher,

Rosenberg, Hess and Frank repledged their oath of loyalty to the Führer several weeks later without either Hitler or an audience, on a studio set built by Speer. The whole operation entailed a complicity among those who staged it : from the very beginning the rally was conceived as the set of a film spectacle.

The formal properties of the film confirm the fact of this complicity. It is not simply that most of the film's sequences are organised as displays : the folk parade, the cavalry parade, the Youth and Labour rallies, the Storm Troopers' rally, the ceremony of the war dead. It is also that the act of looking, which is the behaviour appropriate to our presence at a spectacular display, is installed within the film as the principle of its cohesion. This effect is produced by linking images in an oscillating movement between the act of looking and the object of the look, and back again. Thus for instance: beginning with a close-up of a flag near a hotel window, the camera moves left to frame the window itself, with the sign 'Heil Hitler' clearly visible, displayed beneath it. The gap between the look and its object is signified by the empty window frame. Then, as Hitler comes into view, we cut back to the crowd gazing off-screen right. We then return to Hitler, now framed in the window, marked out by this for the gaze of both crowd and spectator; this framing being reinforced by his own look, first to right and then to left, as he acknowledges the look of the crowd. It is the device of the double frame – the frame of the window and the frame of the film image – together with the scene's theatricality – Hitler in the window elevated above the crowd as if on stage – that establishes spectacle as the organising principle of coherence. Or rather we should say : reaffirms spectacle as that mode of coherence. For we have already been inserted into the figure of the double frame at the outset of the film. The very first scene consists in a view through the cockpit window of an aircraft, followed by a sequence of shots from the plane, each focussed on various aspects of the cloud formation visible from the aircraft window, and each including within the frame visible evidence of the presence of the aircraft itself. So that aircraft and cloud formation have established for us from the film's beginning the movement between the look and its object. Hitler's relationship with the crowd hinges upon looking. He is the privileged object of the gaze, the ultimately significant spectacle both for the crowds in the film and for the spectators of the film : the point of rest to which we are led by a sustained condition of visual expectancy.

Riefenstahl cannot be said to have produced a work of documentation. But could a very different deployment of the camera's resources, the television coverage of a demonstration for instance, be said to be an independent documentary? Probably not, for here too we have a form of complicity, though differently arrived at. It is essential in producing the effects for which the demonstration was organised that it succeed in precipitating extensive reviews in the press, written, spoken, and above all televised : this is the obligatory point of passage if it is to be perceived within the field of acknowledged public occurrences. To create an event like a demonstration is to succeed in making a performance; the cameras present at a march or installed in specially arranged press rooms are not simply giving an account of a demonstration but participating crucially in its realisation. One could even say that the real place where demonstrations take place, whether they are violent and spontaneous or pacific and organised, is not the space of the street but the space of the screen. What is set in motion, then, is a kind of circular causality. The more the media 'speak about it', the more the demonstration seems to grow in force; but the more force the demonstration appears to display, the more the media speak about it. The conviction that the demonstration-event has an objective existence, the feeling that it seems to exist in itself and not to be an 'invention' of journalists, tends to grow to the degree to which the number of daily reports which make it an 'event' grow. Paradoxically, then, the more the media agree about the existence and social definition of an event, the more the event seems to exist independently of the media. The use of such a phrase as 'television coverage of the demonstration' is therefore a misnomer. Television could be said to provide 'coverage of' a demonstration if the demonstration had an existence independent of the presence of television. But it cannot now possess such independence : we do not have television coverage of a demonstration; we have television-demonstrations.

The formal properties of television current affairs confirm the fact of this complicity. It is possible to identify a basic repertoire of elementary televisual forms which are mobilised in the work of narration.[8] A typical sequence will run as follows : live studio 'piece to camera' – live studio report – actuality film sequence – actuality film sequence with commentary over – actuality interview – live studio 'piece to camera'. Notice that the persuasiveness of this organisation depends upon the establishment of a reciprocal relationship between two sets of elements. The first set is the live studio 'piece to camera' and the live studio report. The second set is the actuality film sequence, the actuality film sequence with commentary, and the actuality interview. The statements made in the first set of items appear to highlight and set in place for the audience the 'truth' contained in the actuality shots; while the latter, in turn, appear to ground, to license, and to authenticate the first set of items. The convention of visual composition organises the material in such a way as to imply that the constructed reality is independent of the process of visual construction. Thus newsreaders and correspondents are always to be seen talking direct to camera, seemingly 'to us'; while those placed within the drama of the news as protagonists are always to be seen talking at the angle to the line of vision of the camera, seemingly 'to others'. By composing the protagonists' behaviour in this way a distance is inserted between them and viewers. This produces the dominant sense of witnessing : of being present at, and yet not directly involved in, a 'reality' which is made to seem separate from those positioned as witnesses. In this way the extensive reliance on 'actuality' forms is the principal device for masking the productivity of television's specific practices : its capacity to produce the impression of a reality that is 'transparent' to us, seemingly independent of the organisation of the visual discourse.

In the television presentation of current affairs and in Riefenstahl's *Triumph of the Will* we have two different genres of film which may be called respectively documentary and spectacle.[9] What counts in documentary is the visible as the guarantee of veracity. It therefore makes a fetish of the apparently self-evident and unmediated 'truth' of the visible by disavowing the gap between what is visible and the art of looking. The spectator is an observer, and the signs of the production of meaning are subject to a work of effacement. Spectacle, on the other hand, is content neither with rendering visible what can be observed nor with situating the spectator in the position of an observer. Far from disavowing the gap between the visible and the art of looking, it makes a fetish of that gap as such. For what counts here is the visible as a solicitation and the look as a gaze. It therefore addresses the drive to look itself.

The two cases just examined are divided by more than this distinction in genre between documentary and spectacle. In saying this I do not mean simply that one film narrative has been compared with an almost universally dispersed form of public address used for the most part for recording episodes. Beyond this, and more importantly, in *Triumph of the Will* 'fabrication' is to be understood as indicating both 'making' and 'making false'; whereas in the televised documentation of current affairs 'fabrication' is to be understood as describing only the 'making' of events. My overall claim, therefore, concerns the effect of the technology of communication upon the rhetoric of history, where by the rhetoric of history is meant the fabrication of historical events in this more limited sense.

Nonetheless, whatever the difference in general between spectacle and documentary, and in technical apparatus between film and telesion, the mechanical reproduction of images which is common to both makes possible an awareness of histories as fabricated in a new way. The production of histories as a form of social legitimation, as a retrospective justification for a present organisation of social power, is known in all societies and has its prototype in the genealogical narrative. But here, in Riefenstahl's spectacular commemoration of the 1934 Nuremberg Rally and in the televised documentation of current affairs, there is a type of history produced which could not have existed before the mechanical reproduction of moving pictures. In this form of fabricating histories, the document – that is, the image – is not only the record of reality; it is one reason for which the reality has been constructed. What we might expect to arise from this situation, as far as literature is concerned, is a particular spirit of parody. The object of this parody would not be, as it was for a writer of the last century like Stendhal or Tolstoy, the notion that some intelligible meaning or design was there to be discovered in the randomness and manifest disorder of historical events. Its object, rather, would be the very process whereby people set out to produce historical accounts, and in particular the new rhetoric of complicity between those who organise 'reality' and those who record it. Perhaps what Stendhal and Tolstoy did for Ranke's nineteenth-century 'photographically realist' historiography is being done for the age of the film and television camera by writers like Kurt Vonnegut, Joseph Heller and Thomas Pynchon.

NOTES

1. M. Kundera, *The Book of Laughter and Forgetting*, tr. M. M. Heim (Harmondsworth, 1983).
2. See S. Bann, *The Clothing of Clio. A Study in the representation of history in nineteenth-century Britain and France* (Cambridge, 1984).
3. See R. Barthes, 'The discourse of history', tr. and intro. S. Bann, *Comparative Criticism* 3 (1981) pp. 3–20.
4. J. P. Stern, *On Realism* (London, 1973) p. 94.
5. See J. C. Miller, 'Introduction: Listening for the African Past' in *The African Past Speaks. Essays on Oral Tradition and History*, ed. J. C. Miller (Folkestone, 1980) pp. 1–59.

6. See A. Momigliano, *Studies in Historiography* (London, 1977) *passim*.
7. 'Fascinating Fascism' in S. Sontag, *Under the Sign of Saturn* (New York, 1980) pp. 77ff.
8. See I. Connell, 'Television News and the Social Contract', *Screen* 20 (1979) pp. 87–108.
9. See A. Kuhn, 'The Camera I – Observations on Documentary', *Screen* 19 (1978) pp. 71–84.

Ounces of example: Henry James, philosopher

RENFORD BAMBROUGH

'All my life I have (like M. Jourdain) unconsciously pragmatised.'[1]
Henry James wrote this acknowledgement to his brother William
after reading *Pragmatism*. It is debatable whether he can reasonably
enrol himself in his brother's philosophical school, or in any other.
What is unquestionable is that he consciously and unconsciously and
constantly philosophised. And that is what he thought the novelist
must do :

Mr Dickens is a great observer and a great humorist, but he is nothing
of a philosopher. Some people may hereupon say, so much the better;
we say, so much the worse. For a novelist very soon has need of a little
philosophy. In treating of Micawber, and Boffin, and Pickwick, *et hoc
genus omne*, he can, indeed, dispense with it, for this – we say it with
all deference – is not serious writing. But when he comes to tell the
story of a passion, a story like that of Headstone and Wrayburn, he
becomes a moralist as well as an artist. He must know *man* as well as
men, and to know man is to be a philosopher.[2]

His claim is as emphatic as that of D. H. Lawrence : 'The novel
is a great discovery : far greater than Galileo's telescope or somebody
else's wireless. The novel is the highest form of human expression
so far attained.' It is 'the highest form of subtle interrelatedness that
man has discovered'.[3]

William H. Gass, himself a philosopher–novelist, gives to his essay
on *The Portrait of a Lady* an epigraph to the same effect : 'The great
question as to a poet or a novelist is, how does he feel about life?
What, in the last analysis, is his philosophy?'[4] Rebecca West said
that Henry James wrote fiction as though it were philosophy, and
William James wrote philosophy as though it were fiction.[5]

In 'The Future of the Novel' James speaks of 'a primary need of
the mind' that the novelist fulfils : ultimately and always he falls
back on

his recognition that man's constant demand for what he has to offer is
simply man's general appetite for a *picture*. The novel is of all pictures
the most comprehensive and the most elastic. It will stretch anywhere – it

will take in absolutely anything. All it needs is a subject and a painter. But for its subject, magnificently, it has the whole human consciousness.[6]

What has the whole human consciousness for its subject will also have for its subject the subject of the whole human consciousness: the whole human world. Dorothea Krook widens to James's leading characters in general the author's description of Kate Croy in *The Wings of the Dove* : she was 'made for being and seeing';[7] so were they all, and so was their creator.

In one of the essays in *The Hope of Progress* Sir Peter Medawar, with the air of one making an initial concession before scotching a superstition, acknowledges that some graduates in English might be as clever as the cleverest graduates in the physical and biological sciences. The difference, he says, is that the scientists have something important to be clever about.[8] In *The Art of the Soluble* Medawar speaks of the need to resist 'the tyranny of the particular'.[9]

We shall be resisting the growth of a superstition if we set against this a passage from Henry James's letter declining an invitation to take part in the Deerfield Summer School on the Art of Novel :

an ounce of example is worth a ton of generalities; do something with the great art and the great form; do something with life. Any point of view is interesting that is a direct impression of life. You each have an impression coloured by your individual conditions; make that into a picture, a picture framed by your own personal wisdom, your glimpse of the American world. The field is vast for freedom, for study, for observation, for satire, for truth.[10]

The same consciousness of the primacy of the concrete is displayed in a passage of *Notes of a Son and a Brother* in which James testifies that he had not always been clear on the matter. In his late teens in 1860 he already felt the first stirrings of a desire for the life of literature and criticism, but he had barely escaped from 'the black shadow of the École Préparatoire aux Écoles Spéciales', and was living in 'the house of our good Herr Doctor Humpert, professor at the Bonn Gymnasium'. In these surroundings he could delight in but not confess the prominence in his young life of his *impressions* that had 'begun – that was what was the matter with them – to scratch quite audibly at the door of liberation, of extension, of projection'. That was perhaps what the Herr Doctor would have thought was the matter with them :

Impressions were not merely all right but were the dearest things in the world; only one would have gone to the stake rather than in the first place confessed to some of them, or in the second announced that one really lived by them and built on them. This failure then to take one's stand in the connection could but come from the troubled view that they were naught without a backing, a stout stiff hardgrained underside that would hold them together and of which the terrible name was simply science.[11]

It never occurred to him at that time 'that impressions might themselves *be* science' – something worth being clever about. And this he explained by his being 'under the impression – this in fact the very liveliest of what might have been called the lot – that life and knowledge were simply mutual opposites, one inconsistent with the other; [. . .] to whichever of the opposites one gave oneself it was with a sense of all but basely sacrificing the other'. It was only much later that he achieved complete liberation from this sense of contrariety, and was able to insist to H. G. Wells that 'It is art that *makes* life, makes interest, makes importance, for our consideration and application of these things, and I know of no substitute whatever for the force and beauty of its process.'[12]

Galileo's telescope was both a discovery and a means of making discoveries. James's concern with *seeing* is not a mere instrument for pursuing his concern with *being*. The human world is a world of knowing and understanding, perplexity and oversight, vision and memory and hope, of a hundred species of seeing and failing to see. So the natural historian of our life (Wittgenstein, or William James in *The Principles of Psychology*, or Henry James in *The Ambassadors* or *The Golden Bowl*) must picture the seeing as part of the being.

James is a philosopher not only in the popular sense of a seeker of wisdom and student of life – one with 'a philosophy'. He studies minutely what more formal philosophers call cognitive states, propositional attitudes, cognitive dissonance, intellectual virtues, *akrasia*, self-deception, self-knowledge and intuition. Like the formal philosopher, but more explicitly, he seeks knowledge of good and evil, and understanding of the heart of man. The titles of the novels and tales already advertise this preoccupation. We are invited to learn what Maisie knew, to see what is visible to a prisoner in the cage, to trace the figure in the carpet, seek the Aspern Papers. But in these and other works James is constantly aware that cognitive states and propositional attitudes have *objects*, and some of the titles remind us of them. Ambassadors, Americans, Europeans, Bostonians, the Awkward Age. When the titles are those of the characters – the Princess Casamassima or Daisy Miller or Roderick Hudson – the works are still studies of species or situations or possibilities (the artist, the radical, the American in Europe). The Prefaces and Notebooks are full of evidence of the aspiration of the natural historian. Again and again James records the finding of the 'germ' of a tale in an anecdote or a remark, a newspaper report or a chance meeting. The ounces of example added up to something worth a thousand pounds of principle or general statement.

Henry James is often enough called a realist, but is sometimes thought to have progressed or declined beyond realism in the late great novels. At all periods and in nearly every novel and tale he qualifies as a realist within the meaning of Peter Stern's account :

The riches of the represented world; its weightiness and resistance to ideals; its consequential logic and circumstantiality – these I take to be among the attributes one would expect to find in realistic literature.

What we require for our present undertaking is not a 'definition of reality' at all but a certain kind of description of the world. Such a description, moreover, is not antecedent to or a condition of realism, it is the thing itself. That is what realism is.[13]

The word 'description' comes well from one who has just been endorsing (on pp. 28–9) what Wittgenstein said about family resemblances and definitions – Wittgenstein who also said that the philosopher [not to speak of the novelist] should renounce all attempts at explanation and allow description to take its place.

We may say of James's fiction, as Stern says of realism, that it places its objects in the middle distance, in what Nabokov called the 'delicate meeting place between imagination and knowledge' :

In order to retrace the differences and similarities in the real world, realism must stand back from it at a certain distance – neither too far away nor too close by. In other words, it is neither philosophy nor history, neither naturalism nor *chosisme* : it focuses on the world neither from the far point where only the broad movements and skeleton structures of the world are discernible, nor as through a microscope, where each discrete object looms so large that it assumes a totality and a meaning of its own.[14]

The philosopher's difficulty – including that of the philosopher who philosophises by writing novels – is that he needs to be not just reflective but reflexive. He must set in the middle distance not just the object of his vision (the heart of man, 'the great relation', or aristocracy or radicalism) but his vision itself as the object of a further contemplation. Self-consciousness and self-knowledge are knowledge and consciousness of a self that is knowing and conscious, so that what has to be in the middle distance is also nearer than breathing.

'He must know *man* as well as *men*, and to know man is to be a philosopher.' Yet this generality is achieved by means of particular characters and states and circumstances, by ounces of example. William and Henry James both knew this well in practice, but some of William's comments on Henry's novels suggest that he sometimes forgot that it is also right in theory. If we can understand the source of this occasional lapse we may be better equipped to see how realism and reality and philosophy and literature all stand to each other, and to the things that Sir Peter Medawar and his colleagues are trained to be clever about.

William's objection was to remoteness, refinement, indirectness, and he did not see that these were merits of the method, not deficiencies in the material. His objection was the Medawar objection. He wanted the picture to be a direct representation of an easily identifiable sitter.

William James and Sir Peter Medawar are not alone in their distaste for certain kinds of literary subtlety, and they and their companions are particularly liable to be suspicious of the late novels of Henry James. Their suspicion arises from or involves them in misrepresentations of those novels; in confusions about literature and its tasks and modes of operation; and in serious misunderstandings of the natural sciences and *their* tasks and modes of operation. This last failing often escapes their own notice and even that of their critics because both sides assume that Dr William and Sir Peter surely know at least their own scientific business, and because the critics are often literary people with little or no scientific or philosophical learning. This makes them defensive about literature and nervous about science and philosophy. Such an atmosphere is one in which muddles about the ends and means of all modes of representation and communication increase and multiply.

Peter Stern's *On Realism* provides much of the needful ventilation, and he uproots some troublesome weeds. But we can achieve an even juster view of realism and reality, art and science, men and women and manners and morals, if we apply to himself the manoeuvre that he employs at a turning point in his own book, where he admirably calls it a reversal of emphasis. On p. 121 he declares that 'it is with individuals that the social truth of realism is concerned – not with trends or inchoate masses of humanity, and not with fragments of consciousness either'. The emphasis that this reverses is that given on p. 101 to 'the interconnections between self and social world'. The generalisation is supported by an ounce of weighty example:

'*L'ÉducationSentimentale* marks one of the highest points in realism's creative awareness that no personal relationship, amorous or any other, can subsist beyond the privileged moment without a network of interpersonal, public bonds.'

The realist's seeing of what is in the middle distance, we were assured in an earlier quotation from Stern, is not naturalism or *chosisme* any more than it is philosophy or history : 'Realism is as compatible with selection as is any other mode of experience' (p. 67). If it were not so, the case of Henry James might need to be reconsidered. But the more topical reason for dwelling on the concession is that it focusses for me on the point at which Stern invites the corrective reversal of emphasis that is my tribute to him and to his impressive work on this theme.

On the same page Stern quotes (and slightly misquotes) a sentence of mine that points in the direction in which I now want to move: 'The ideal limiting case of representation is reduplication, and a duplicate is too true to be useful.'[15] His own remarks in the context show an understanding sympathy with what I was doing in the quoted passage. But I am not satisfied that he has looked far enough in the direction in which I was pointing, even if only because of the difficulty, inherent in any literary and any philosophical enterprise, of remembering the merits of an emphasis when one is consciously concerned to display the merits of the reversal of that emphasis.

That this is at least a part of the explanation is shown by some of Peter Stern's own comments. More than once (e.g. on p. 122 and p. 140) he explicitly reminds himself and us that literature is all one field. This reminder offers some counterweight to his prevailing stress on the *contrasts* between realist and other genres of literature, and between individual works representing realist and other genres. To put my complaint generally before I measure out a few ounces of example, it is that we need from Stern, or otherwise from ourselves, just what a philosopher nearly always needs to seek or offer after making or attending to any important distinction or contrast : a re-presentation of the unity and continuity that full attention to diversity and plurality may disguise.

Painting is all one field, too, and drawing is all one field, and painting-and-drawing is all one field. When James speaks of the need of the mind for a *picture* he may not be forgetting, and could easily be reminded, that there are other kinds of picture than the realist portrait and the naturalist landscape and the *chosiste* still life.

Yet the case of James *v.* Dickens shows that a reminder that is easy to give may be harder to take. James does not need to be told – he is telling himself and us – that besides the telling of 'the story of a passion, a story like that of Headstone and Wrayburn' there is such a thing as 'treating of Micawber, and Boffin, and Pickwick, *et hoc genus omne*'. But even if we were all happy to dismiss *Pickwick* and *David Copperfield* and *Our Mutual Friend* as 'not serious writing' there would still be much more to be said. Some of it could be said by again reminding him of his own words : 'The field is vast for freedom, for study, for observation, for satire, for truth.' For *satire.* Are we to say – 'with all deference' – that *A Modest Proposal* and *Gulliver's Travels* are 'not serious writing'? If so, to what depths of deference must we plunge before we deny that Hogarth and Hieronymus Bosch, Kafka and Klee, Borges and Blake, have produced serious writing and drawing and painting?

When Wittgenstein spoke of natural history he added : 'But we can also invent fictitious natural history for our purposes.'[16] When we look at Henry James's aims and methods we see that what he breeds from his 'germs' are descriptions of possibilities as much as descriptions of actualities. In these plain observations lie half hidden two of the features of artistic production that are most likely to alarm or bemuse apostles or exponents of 'the scientific method'. Why should we try to be clever about possibilities when there are so many actualities to be clever about? And why are so many of the possibilities so recondite and remote, so much of the representation distorted and oblique? Yet to put these questions together is to ask an oblique and distorted version of the lunatic question 'Why should we resort to the use of images, imagery and imagination when we write imaginative literature? Why should the imagination of man be allowed or encouraged to dwell upon imaginary people and places, pleasures and pains, births and deaths, voyages, plagues and battles?'

What is striking and useful in this pattern of perversity is that it is the same apostles whose most insistent plea is that natural science is an imaginative enterprise, calling for the exercise of all the powers of the human mind. Here again we may speak of the fulfilling of 'a primary need of the mind', and it is the same mind and the same primary need : man's constant desire for what the physicist or the biologist has to offer is simply man's general appetite for a *picture.* And if you try to drive the wedge in again by saying that this time the demand is for a *true* picture you will have to have your emphasis again reversed. For again what can be said on one side of your supposed divide can also be said on the other side. The scientist too represents what is possible as well as what is actual, and represents what is actual by comparison with what is possible. Neither Rumpelstiltskin, nor Scylla and Charybdis, nor any hobgoblin or foul fiend is more imaginary or more imaginatively conceived than any of the ideal gases or irresistible forces or immovable objects of the natural philosopher, than his absolute zero and his square root of minus one.

Wittgenstein's remark about fictitious natural history is reminiscent of his use of the idea of an *object of comparison*.[17] We often explicitly, and always at least implicitly, say what something is by saying how it is like and how it is unlike what it is not. A comparison of our method of measuring quantities of wood in a timber yard with the practice of an imaginary tribe may illuminate our familiar method, possibly by making it strike us as unfamiliar. One of Wittgenstein's tribes charges for wood not by weight or length or volume but in proportion to the ground area that a particular consignment happens to cover.[18]

Realist literature compares actualities with imaginary possibilities. But it is non-realist literature that most strikingly contributes to our grasp of reality in this way. David Garnett's *Lady into Fox* might have been sub-titled *A Study in Loyalty*, and thus have announced on its title-page that it is designed to throw light on cases where a wife or a husband or an adolescent child or an ageing parent undergoes changes as extensive and alarming as those that happened to Mrs Tebrick and are summarised in the main title. Kafka's *Metamorphosis* represents in the imagined conflict between Gregor's sister and the rest of his family the inner tensions and outer conflicts that can be bred by misfortunes that differ not in degree of severity or monstrosity but only in frequency from transformation into a six-foot insect : Down's syndrome or *dementia praecox*, madness or murder. If time and space allowed we could go on from here to see how literary contributions to the study of the question 'What is man?', ranging from Adam and Oedipus to Orwell's animals and Swift's Houyhnhnms, from the Cyclops Polyphemus to the Midwich Cuckoos, could and do help us to think about problems in public and private life whose solutions, if any, turn or partly turn on what is a human being and what is not a human being : problems about contraception, abortion, infanticide, euthanasia, test-tube babies and surrogate motherhood. 'Non-realist' literature is more realist and realistic than some of Stern's remarks suggest. And well outside the 'one field' that is made up of realist and non-realist literature there is much revelation of reality whose methods are as oblique as those of satire or parody, burlesque or caricature. The natural sciences are not always 'natural' or 'realistic' in the means by which they serve their realist ends. Even Stern needs to benefit from a comparable reversal of emphasis about literature : the novelist or the lyric poet, the tragedian or the satirist, the comedian of manners or the writer of epic verse, may also use non-realist means and still be serving realist ends. The same reminder is needed by those who expect or require literature to be as realistic and scientific as possible, whether they are nineteenth-century French novelists or twentieth-century British scientists – Emile Zola or Peter Medawar : '[...] science, to Zola, is *all* truth, the mention of any other kind being mere imbecility'.[19] Is literature, to Medawar, *no* truth, but only self-indulgence, a servile surrender to the tyranny of the particular?

But particulars are not tyrannical; they are *authoritative*. Like Bishop Butler's conscience, if they had power, as they have manifest authority, they would absolutely govern the world of thought. Henry James knew this, and it was because T. S. Eliot knew it too, but as a Harvard-trained philosopher was ambivalent about it, that he could declare Henry James to have 'a mind so fine that no idea could violate it', and sound to some as if he deplored such refinement.[20] James's freedom from ideas was of the kind that Wittgenstein was fostering when he complained against other philosophers that they imposed *requirements*, were enslaved by pictures, and hence failed to describe the saving details, rejecting *false* accounts of the matter *as* false.[21] Henry James's unconscious pragmatism, like the conscious pragmatism of his brother William, was a devoted loyalty to complexity, particularity, plurality, actuality. Loyalty to such authority is not servitude. It is as perfect a freedom as the mind's appetite for pictures will allow to any inquirer blessed with a merely human understanding.

William's ambivalence is as old as Socrates, who also aspired after tons of generality but hit every general definition amidships with a piercing ounce of example. And even Henry compromised his inviolable mind with a novelist's ambition to know *man* as well as *men*, though he guarded his honour by recognising that only through men can man be known, the species only through the specimens. But in all three – in Socrates, in William, and supremely in Henry – the ambivalence is theoretical and the practice is one that could be articulated into a better theory. Like other philosophers and other poets and dramatists all three want to have it both ways, want to have comprehensiveness of scope and grasp but also the concreteness and complexity that can be achieved only by attending to *differences* (Wittgenstein), by an unservile submission to the untyrannical authority of the particular. The articulation of the practice will make a better theory because it will replace the ambivalence by *oscillation*: we need the large picture *and* the elusive detail, the general definition and the destructive example, the clash of platitude against paradox, the contraries without which there is no progression (Blake) before and after the harmony to which we may hope to progress, a harmony that retains its stability by struggling against itself, like the *harmonie* of the bow and lyre (Heraclitus).

All these means are familiar to us from the pursuit of our present ends. The just and realistic representation of realist and non-realist literature is served by emphasis and reversal of emphasis, by descriptions too true to be useful, by pictures and paradoxes too useful to be true, by ounces but also by tons. Nothing stays fixed in the middle distance : we see what it would look like if it did only by seeing how it looks from afar and how it looks from close by. And the *it* may be anything familiar enough to need to be displaced into the background and/or the foreground before we can see it straight, and anything puzzling enough to need to be moved back and forth and finally restored to the middle distance before we can see it at all in its accustomed place.

It may be science. We do not cease to learn what science is until we have learned what can be learned both from Medawar's amalgam of Popper and positivism and from Feyerabend's *Against Method*,[22] from Pearson's sycophantic *Grammar of Science*[23] but also from Kuhn's less flattering depiction of 'normal science' and his dithyramb on the almighty power of the revolutionary paradigm-shift.[24] We may learn all this without reading these authors, but only if we find or produce a description that balances the creativity and imaginativeness of scientific enquiry with the accuracy and fidelity that show whether this or that imaginative and creative account is veridical or merely chimerical.

It may be the idea of being clever about something. What are pure mathematicians clever about? Not about nothing, like Medawar's graduates in English. But not about something, like Medawar's molecular biologists. Yet how can one be clever at all without being clever about something or at least clever about nothing? When Medawar has told us a good story about the mathematicians he may be readier to listen to the corresponding story about the scholars and the critics and the poets and the novelists.

In literary theory, too, man's appetite is for a picture, and a picture may hold him captive, and he may need a liberating description. But such a description will not liberate one who is not a captive to the power it overcomes. If what we are looking at is already firmly placed in the middle distance we may not seriously be looking at it at all until we are jolted by a comparison that shifts the angle and the distance of our view. Whatever can achieve this shift will also be capable of misleading us; the more useful, the less life-like, and the less life-like the more dangerous to the just apprehension of one who is no longer or not yet suffering from the passive or distorted vision that it is calculated or inspired to rectify.

The vision that we seek in philosophy and in literature is seldom the vision of what is framed and fixed, or, though moving, is moving on a screen that we look at from a fixed angle and a standard distance. It is active – pragmatic – like the vision sought by a sightseer or a naturalist or a space traveller.

Each of these enquirers makes *excursions* to seek what he wants or needs to see. An excursion has two destinations. A trip to Paris or Margate takes us to Paris or Margate but it also brings us home.

We do not always or usually need to go to the lighthouse. That we can see it from here is a great part of its point and its charm, the main source of our interest in it. A visit to it is something special, a departure and arrival after which we return to seeing it on ordinary occasions, and to seeing it differently although it looks the same.

These means serve the ends of life as well as those of literature and of philosophy, and to see this is to administer a mild reversal of emphasis to Henry James's letter to Wells. Just as the seeing is part of the being, so the art is part of the life. He speaks well in speaking of the form and beauty of the *process* – the process that has been mapped here by speaking of oscillations, excursions, of looking far and near and back and forth. But life has made art before art can make life. Remembering and foreseeing, stepping back and peering forward, scaling the tower or probing the undergrowth, clutching and climbing – all this begins when life begins, the life of the individual and the life of the species. The seeing has always been part of the being.

The seeing has always been by means of the pictures that man's appetite craves for, the pictures that hold us captive, that we impose as requirements. James is more conscious of our healthy appetite for such pictures, Wittgenstein more guarded against their power to dominate and enslave. But Wittgenstein is conscious of their value as well as of their dangers, and James is aware of the risks as well as the advantages. When they consciously or unconsciously pragmatise they are recognising the need of our thought for process, dynamic, oscillation. This orderly and purposeful movement belongs to thought about thought, to the inquiries about the representation of modes of representation that we and Peter Stern have been and are here engaged in.

Violation by an idea is ordinarily violation by a *general* idea. There is such a thing as too great an innocence of general ideas. In life as well as in art and in philosophy we need range and grasp as well as vivid particularity. Henry James's beloved impressions may remain authoritative even when we have enough of them in the right relation to each other to amount to a world – a lived world or a created world. It does not much matter in general, though it may matter much in this or that conversation, whether we put this by saying that we need general ideas as well as impressions, or by saying that a purposeful and orderly arrangement of impressions is what we need instead of general ideas. Let us oscillate beteween the two in different conversations, and also when as now we are recollecting such conversations in tranquillity, so long as we are thereby working towards a grasp of the unity of the pluralistic universe as well as a respect for the plurality of what every picture, whether or not it is a picture of a world, is designed to represent. Wittgenstein's overlapping and criss-crossing pattern of particularity shares its structure with Henry James's fine-spun filaments of qualification, reservation, elaboration and complication.

We have been seeing that the representation of modes of representation, which we must be engaged in when we discuss realism in its literary or in any other form, itself proceeds by oscillation between pictures. It consists of portraits and caricatures and maps and diagrams which portray or map or sketch or caricature the ways in which one thing may be represented by another. For the task is a philosophical task, and philosophy is less often naturalistic or realistic than highly coloured and paradoxical, arresting the attention by strong colours and simple lines. Its pictures of literature and science and life are often and ought more often still to be unrecognisable to those who are engaged at first hand in these activities, but the practitioners themselves have the philosophical craving for simplicity and generality, and many of them have been parties to the unconscious frauds of the philosophers. When Wittgenstein or Moore or Butler or Sidgwick recalls philosophers to a sense of reality there ensues one of those dramas of disagreement of which philosophy so often consists. Such drama is the drama of debate, of inquiry, outside philosophy as well as within it. And the drama of the seeing and the being in Henry James has similar scenes and acts and recognitions and crises and reconciliations and *dénouements*.

It is because these same materials occur both in life and in art, and form in both realms the frames within which what is seen and grasped is captured, that James is led to say to Wells that art makes life, forgetting that though life does not exist without them, it does exist outside art, and so is not beholden to art for them. Or here too we can oscillate, and say that they *are* art, and that they *do* make life, provided that we then see and say that we are all our own artists, individually and corporately, and do not need Henry James come from a study in Lamb House to tell us what we must know before we can be told any of the many things that we do need to be told – by Henry or by William or by Peter.

NOTES

1. F. O. Matthiessen, *The James Family* (New York, 1947) p. 343.
2. Henry James, *The House of Fiction*, ed. Leon Edel (London, 1957) p. 257.
3. Quoted by F. R. Leavis, *Anna Karenina and other Essays* (London, 1967) p. 11.
4. William H. Gass, 'The High Brutality of Good Intentions', in *Perspectives on James's The Portrait of a Lady*, ed. William T. Stafford (New York and London, 1967) p. 206. Gass attributes the sentence to James but gives no reference.
5. Rebecca West, *Henry James* (London, 1916) p. 11. I am grateful to Mr Peter Rawlings of Fitzwilliam College, Cambridge for supplying this reference.
6. *The House of Fiction*, pp. 50–1.
7. Dorothea Krook, *The Ordeal of Consciousness in Henry James* (Cambridge, 1962) pp. ix, 16 and 22.
8. P. B. Medawar, *The Hope of Progress* (London, 1974) p. 106.
9. P. B. Medawar, *The Art of the Soluble* (London, 1967) p. 114.
10. *The House of Fiction*, p. 46.
11. Henry James, *Autobiography* (New York, 1956) p. 254.
12. *The Letters of Henry James*, ed. Percy Lubbock, 2 (New York, 1920) p. 503ff.
13. J. P. Stern, *On Realism* (London, 1973) pp. 28, 31–2.
14. *On Realism*, p. 55.
15. Renford Bambrough, 'Principia Metaphysica', *Philosophy*, 39 (1964) p. 98.
16. Ludwig Wittgenstein, *Philosophical Investigations*, tr. G. E. M. Anscombe (Oxford, ²1958) p. 230.
17. *Philosophical Investigations*, § 130.

18. Ludwig Wittgenstein, *Remarks on the Foundations of Mathematics*, tr. G. E. M. Anscombe (Oxford, ³1978) Part I, §§ 143ff.

19. Henry James, *The House of Fiction*, p. 238.

20. T. S. Eliot, 'On Henry James', *The Question of Henry James*, ed. F. W. Dupee (London, 1947) p. 125.

21. *Philosophical Investigations*, p. 200.

22. Paul Feyerabend, *Against Method* (London, 1975).

23. Karl Pearson, *The Grammar of Science* (London, 1937).

24. Thomas S. Kuhn, *The Structure of Scientific Revolutions* (Chicago, ²1970).

Afterthoughts on realism

RICHARD BRINKMANN

J. P. Stern's book *On Realism*, when it first appeared in the early 1970s, represented a new way of approaching a hotly debated problem. The title 'On Realism' – a form which can on occasion bespeak a somewhat grandiloquent understatement – was entirely appropriate : Stern offered us many and various reflections on realism, always deriving from and justified in terms of particular texts – but constantly in the service of systematic conclusions. What might both have struck and delighted those – particularly German – theoreticians and concept-hunters who find it so difficult to displace the merciless 'Totalitätsdenker' from their hearts and minds was the very open and relaxed theoretical impulse which informed Stern's reflections. He seemed not to be after any kind of closed system or definitive statements on the 'essence of realism' which would stand in need of no further modification : rather he offered us, in both senses of the word, an 'essay' (we should not forget that the term 'essay' as a loan word in German denotes a particular literary species in a sense that is marginally different from its normal Anglo-Saxon usage, that is, a tentative form of analysis couched in an equally tentative medium). Of course Stern does frequently break off his 'meditations' and analyses in order to draw conclusions and to formulate definitions. Which phenomena permit the term 'realism' to be employed, which demand it, and which forbid it? Which phenomena may be combined in the service of realism, which prove to be mutually exclusive? With which historical circumstances is the emergence of that literature associated which invites, indeed demands, that we employ the term 'realism'? Stern gives answers to such questions. But his answers are not developed discursively from a sustained conceptual framework, they are not deduced one from the other. Rather, they arise from new and various approaches, from sometimes unexpected logical contexts. The subdivision into numbered paragraphs, which could seem arch, in fact corresponds to the intellectual sequence of moving from one suggestive insight to the next. The chapter titles in the table of contents are there to inform the reader where each particular aspect is discussed – and not to schematise and summarise a logical structure. Those who, when Stern's book appeared, had had enough of the tormenting mass of abstraction, of epistemological huffing and puffing, of the 'endless refrain of objective and subjective' (Demetz), of ideological strait-jackets, in the discussion of literary realism, greeted the intelligent compendium of thoughts 'On Realism' as a welcome discussion of both texts and 'philosophy'. Clearly the writer of this present paper was not the only one to react in this way, for its critical reception was generally very positive. And that Stern was able recently (ten years after the original publication) to bring out a German version[1] bears witness to the need in German literary criticism for this kind of essayistic scholarly enterprise. Admittedly, there are certain reservations which must be mentioned – no one who proceeds as Stern does would expect or want the difficulties to go unnoticed. The engaging refusal to ride systematic hobby-horses, the retreat from anguished conceptual to-do does bring certain kinds of imprecision in its train. It means that argumentative sequences are not rigorously pursued to their logical conclusion but are left hanging as assertions or hypotheses to which one is expected to assent without any logical proof or argument – which most probably one is happy to do. But that some questions are left open is shown by the contributions to this volume – although the fundamental agreement with Stern's position is often greater when the contributors superficially appear to contradict him. Of course time has not stood still since Stern's study was written, and 'realism' has continued to exercise critics even when they were heartily sick of both the topic and the term. The notion of realism as a 'perennial mode' caused much unease – particularly with those scholars who are unwilling to use 'Romanticism' or 'Baroque' as anything more than period terms. But Stern was categorical in the distinction he drew between such historical and stylistic terms and the notion of 'realism' which, he argued, leads an 'amphibian existence in literature and in "life" '. But that did not cope with the problem as to which reality is meant by the term 'realistic' – as to how we are supposed to know what kind of strategy represents a particularly appropriate access to 'reality' and a particularly appropriate expression of this 'reality'. Admittedly Stern did diagnose certain symptoms and made a plausible case that they were specific to realism. But there was the problem of the nineteenth century with that rich literature to which the diagnosis of 'realism' was peculiarly and obviously apposite. Why should this be? Critics were not slow to ask this question soon after Stern's book had appeared. In the German version Stern gives a hint of a possible explanation : 'the age offers a greater variety of human possibilities, offers *more and more various areas of social interaction and friction* than ever before existed' (p. 196). Whoever accepts Stern's general symptomatology of realism and his definitions (if one may call them such) will not be entirely happy with this causative explanation of the special richness of 'realistic' literature – nor with Stern's account of the disappearance of realism from representative literature of the twentieth century. A number of the critical essays in this volume take issue with this point and seek to disagree with Stern, in part at least, and to extend and modify his position and conclusion. In the process, many of these essays, in both approach and terminology, argue in methodological terms which bear the imprint of the development in the scholarly discussion of realism since the early 1970s.

There would hardly be any point in my giving a detailed paraphrase and critical commentary for all the essays in this volume. They must be allowed to speak for themselves and they stand in no need of a pat on the shoulder – whether approving or reproving – from some kind of headmasterly higher authority. My purpose involves no such pretentious claim. Rather, I want to offer some comments on the state of the realism debate, in the context of which the individual essays are to be understood. That in the process I will not be able entirely to avoid summary and criticism is, I trust, obvious.

In the various skirmishes of recent years, the discussion of the 'realism' of the so-called 'age of realism', of nineteenth-century 'bourgeois' realism (or whatever one may choose to call it) has seemed to be running out of steam. After the appearance of the various studies and collections of material which I discussed in the introduction to the third edition of my realism book[2] – I hope I may be allowed to mention this, for the sake of convenience – the historical and systematic concern with literary realism has changed in direction and emphasis. Perhaps one might say that two different and to a certain extent opposite tendencies have emerged. Some scholars and critics have moved towards a form of abstract 'semantics' – if I may be allowed a somewhat dilettantish use of the label. They are concerned to ask how it is that in poetic and 'semi-poetic' texts meaning and reference come about – and how these can be precisely defined. On the one hand, that can sound like pure – poetic – semiotics, on the

other it can suggest the kind of epistemological inquiry which has
fallen into much disfavour with a number of literary critics. Sometimes it seems to be a mixture of both. Is there something behind the
signs and images of literature to which reference is made and which,
by whatever means, so determines the textual sequence, constellation,
and configuration, that conclusions can be drawn from the signifier
to the signified – or are we thereby instantly succumbing to a naive
deception, indeed self-deception? Can one assume that there is a
'grammar' of 'reality' which finds a corresponding form in the
language and imagery of fiction? Because such a case cannot be
proved, the representatives of the, as it were, 'abstract' tendency tend
to reject as illegitimate any attempt to reduce the literary work to
anything more or other than its own functioning structure : thereby
they reject 'interpretation' in the traditional sense. Stern chose as the
cover illustration for the German edition of his book a lithograph by
M. C. Escher entitled 'Drawing Hands'. The subject of this, as it
were, 'transcendental drawing' is one hand which draws the hand
which draws the hand which draws the hand (it would not,
incidentally, be correct to speak of the hand as drawing itself – the
plural is all-important). This theme which, incidentally, we find in
modified form with other artists (e.g. Steinberg) is somewhat misleading as a summary of Stern's own view of 'realistic' literature, its
origins and interpretability. Because, if we are to take him at his
word, his notion of realism is by no means so 'functional'. Rather he
occupies the middle ground between the, to employ again my
schematic simplification, 'abstract' tendency and the position of
those who in some way or other wish to understand 'reality' and
'realism' in terms of a signified which does not exist simply by the
grace and favour of a subject – even a 'transcendental' one. Such
critics cannot bring themselves to view that table on which, even
when it occurs within the confines of a poetic reality, a character can
strike his head really quite painfully, as the pure product of language
or as a 'deconstructible' piece of reality. At any rate, Stern is miles
away from the position that would locate the reality of 'realism'
exclusively within the operations of language itself, although he never
for a moment forgets that the 'modality' of linguistic organisation
plays a considerable part in the constitution of reality itself. But it
then follows that there must be a something that is already constituted
before its linguistic-cum-poetic fashioning, a something towards
which the linguistic making with all its specific and historically conditioned modes is intentionally directed. In many and various ways

Stern speaks of things that have actually happened somewhere, or could have happened, and of the various carefully considered methods or processes ('strategies' is the favoured term nowadays of the more conciliatory critics) – such as the 'middle distance' – which can offer the most appropriate, analogically most 'correct' presentation of these actual events and their proportions – they include, for example, the actual freedoms and constraints of the individual in society which are simply there, independent of any act of linguistic creation. Why such an appropriate presentation should also be beautiful, why it should appeal to our aesthetic responses, is not dealt with at any great length by Stern. But it is an old question with centuries of discussion behind it. Even so it would be welcome if the professionals would help in explaining why we gladly read so-called 'realistic' literature, when it is good – and clearly for different reasons from those we invoke when we are not prepared to call the literature 'realistic'. But I leave that as a footnote.

The distinctions which I have made above are, of course, like all such schematisations, greatly simplified and, it need hardly be added, they would strike philosophers, hermeneutic theoreticians, structuralists as very naive. Moreover, no one critic is to be located firmly and pinned down within one or other tendency – nor, indeed, in the middle ground between the two. Rather, scholars and critics betray collectively and individually certain tendencies, directions, accents. But even so, the thrust of the argument goes – perhaps decisively – in certain directions, and, equally decisively, not in others. And sometimes the motive for the choice can be an unashamedly emotional aversion to some methodological one-sidedness and obstinacy which seeks to claim that it alone sails under the flag of true scholarship. An example of this is the paper by Erich Heller in this volume. With the authority of his respected name he insists that linguistic and literary statements are by nature referential and attacks with decisive common sense the paradoxes of the deconstructionists and similar 'modernists' and 'postmodernists' in literary scholarship whose more or less absurd theories, so his argument runs, are furthermore by no means as new or original as is claimed.

I will recall that it is not my intention here to comment only on the articles in this volume. Another study, in book form, deserves mention in this context. It too derives its energy in large measure from a scepticism about the excessively sophisticated kind of theory of fiction in which, so it seems, nothing can be taken at its face – its 'realistic' – value at all. *Die leidigen Tatsachen* (Tiresome Facts) is the title. And the author is Bernd W. Seiler.[3] Why should the normal, yet well educated, reader of poetic – and particularly narrative – texts, the 'practical man' (p. 33) not be allowed to look in them for the depiction of experienceable and experienced factual reality? That is Seiler's initial question. The goal of the scholarly argument in this book is to demonstrate the relevance of facts for literature in defiance of the dogma which asserts the necessarily fictional character of literature, its aesthetic and linguistic autonomy. Current theories of fiction are logically false according to Seiler. And historical analysis can demonstrate that 'there have been, and are, demands placed on literature in respect of factual accuracy which have in all probability had an impact on the actual development of literature' (p. 43). By means of the thorough study of notions of the 'vraisemblable' in the seventeenth and eighteenth centuries and by tracing the role of factuality for important thematic areas of literary concern, Seiler comes to a conclusion which, at one level anyway, is perhaps not all that removed from the results of my own analyses and reflections in *Wirklichkeit und Illusion*. Seiler suggests that with the 'degree of *describedness*', that is, with the – literally – scientific and thorough identifiability of facts in the widest sense, with the ever-increasing '*analytical penetration* of present and past circumstances', the 'scope for a literature of verisimilitude declines within certain dimensions' (p. 90). Now this is a paradoxical but very convincing conclusion. The more the author and his readers are able to know about all manner of real facts and circumstances, the more difficult does it become for literature to offer a factually faithful narrative that can be precisely verified as 'probable'. Moreover, there is the further difficulty that the category of probability cannot be clearly distinguished from that of 'truth'. The force of Seiler's argument is clear. And he is far from that rage for simplification which can on occasion overcome the literary scholar when he asks himself what his highly theoretical reflections are supposed to mean to the vast majority of people for whom almost all literature is written. For even pretty esoteric texts are printed in their thousands : so presumably somebody is supposed to consume and understand them – even somebody who is not 'in the trade'. Although Seiler's attack may implicitly be sustained by the unease that occasionally befalls sophisticated literary critics who make great intellectual efforts to disavow the 'realistic' innocence of the reader – yet he does not fall below the current level of method-ological and theoretical discussion, but is fully a match for it. But even though Seiler does show that logical mistakes have been made in the theoretical analysis and definition of fictional texts, yet a number of questions remain as thorns in our flesh : how fictional texts are different from non-fictional ones; how 'reality' is represented, how it comes about, in the former; is reality perhaps constituted *only in them*, and is it thereby restricted in its realisation to them, to their functioning as texts – or, to put it negatively and critically – are those texts but a cage and prison house? Even if all those critics – for example in this present volume – who are clearly concerned with theories of the nature, and not just the history, of literature had taken note of Seiler's refreshing and learned challenge, they would probably not have been converted and could probably not have brought themselves to regard certain problems as over and done with – as the misshapen products of overheated professorial minds.

Now it is of course possible that without being either excessively or explicitly self-conscious in theoretical terms a critic can reach conclusions which are new and productive for the interpretation of the individual text and can contribute to the historical and systematic understanding of 'realism' by means of the exemplary test-case. At least three of the contributions to this volume confirm this : Graham Hough, in his discussion of Dickens's *Bleak House*, draws in part on Stern, and distances himself from French Structuralism. He steers a middle course between the extremes of a naive 'positivism' with its optimistic belief that language mirrors reality simply and faithfully, and the view that reality only exists once it has been constituted by language. He shows by close discussion of the text how the perspectives of the narrator, that is of Dickens the author, and of the central figure and her first-person narration complement, confirm, and modify one another. That for some critics the Balzacian form of narrative has had the monopoly on 'realistic' writing produces one-sided definitions of the ways in which reality can be represented and confirmed in fictional portrayal. With Dickens it is clearer than with Balzac that, as Stern had observed, the psychology of the characters can underscore both the constitutive role of language and its relationship to extra-linguistic reality, and thereby also the very nature of reality itself in the novel. The complexity of this reality does not admit of notions of the deterministic power of society. But 'reality' in Dickens and in *Bleak House* exhibits specific features which cannot be reduced to an all-purpose realism formula, but which at the same time do allow certain generalisations to be made in respect of the constitution of reality in the nineteenth-century novel.

Martin Swales's essay also makes no special methodological claims; in it he attempts to offer a historical re-evaluation of nineteenth-century German realism. Many critics, among them Preisendanz, who forms the starting point of Swales's investigation (as does Stern, albeit in a different sense), see the German novel of the nineteenth century as being excluded from the 'realistic' norm of European literature. The reproach that it displays aesthetic-cum-transcendental inwardness rather than commitment to sociopolitical reality is well known and widespread. Stern had differentiated what was on occasion an all too simple and trivial judgment by arguing that German prose of the nineteenth century displayed a concern not for some 'objective' reality but for reality understood as the product of collective agreements and interpretations. In so far as German prose is to be taken seriously, Swales argues, one has to ask where and how it makes the emergence of such agreements and modes of consensus the object of its narrative interest. Precisely this would, under particular political, social, and intellectual conditions, which in themselves must be accepted as facts, qualify for the term 'realistic'. The different development of Germany did not mark the cultural consciousness with a gulf between private and public experience to anything like the same degree as in the European nation states. In this sense German literature of the nineteenth century is in its way as true to its age as other European literatures, 'contemporaneous' in so far as it manages, by means of its 'literary', that is aesthetic and symbolic, forms, to represent the correspondence between public and private realms and the social constraints operative on the individual's structure of thought and experience. Swales gives several persuasive examples of his thesis. Under its auspices the history of German literature – or, more accurately, of literature written in German – could be re-written. That would amount not to a renewed defence of German inwardness, but to a historical inquiry which would not allow critical evaluation to take precedence over historical comprehension. Admittedly one may not overlook the danger that such a degree of historical generosity extends the notion of realism unacceptably far – not, admittedly, to the point where it becomes 'bad aesthetics' as Wellek once suggested, but at least to the point where realism is the name for any and every form of artistic representation that is appropriate to its age. In other words, there is the danger of one's developing an extreme position which is the opposite of Wellek's : realism is good aesthetics or good aesthetics is realism, and this will apply whenever literature offers, in terms of both form and content, an adequate representation of the reality of its age, whatever that reality may look like. This would entail the sanctioning of ideologies transposed into aesthetic form on the one hand : and on the other it would mean applying the term 'realistic' to kinds of linguistic representation such as have emerged, for example, in the twentieth century which, even allowing for a generous interpretation of the term, scarcely anybody would want so to describe. Perhaps it is after all the case that German 'realism' of the nineteenth century, compared with other European national literatures, is indeed characterised by a tentative relationship to reality which is made no less problematic by the fact that, in the *extra-literary* world as well, the inhabitants of nineteenth-century Germany stood in a tentative relationship to reality.

How productive and unconventional the discussion of 'influences' can be is shown by a third essay which does not put theory at the centre of attention : 'Proust's Balzac' by Sheila Stern. Traces of Balzac in Proust are identified. And with no great terminological fuss Sheila Stern shows the kind of metamorphosis 'realistic' elements deriving from a paradigmatic name and exemplum of nineteenth-century fiction can and must undergo in order to function productively as a kind of integral and effective 'vocabulary', if one may put it that way, within a quite different 'realistic' text which works within a different historical dimension, with different forms of utterance, while all the time acknowledging the provenance of these elements, indeed demonstrating and confirming continuities. Perhaps this is a true example of what is meant by 'intertextuality', which after all is supposed to involve more than the one-way traffic of linear 'influence'.

Of course many literary scholars, when they speak of realism, cannot make do with so modest an amount of theoretical and philosophical questioning, with such suppression of epistemological scruple. And this is true not only of the Germans to whom the label of abstraction and profundity, even in their commerce with literary texts, is most readily affixed. At least in recent decades that would not be wholly just. But who is going to exhort those who have strayed into the labyrinth of theoretical reflection, who have eaten of the fruit of the tree of hermeneutic or structuralist or post-structuralist knowledge, to break out of this web of rumination and throw every 'epistemological' (this is the catch-all term) scruple to the winds? Even Marxist scholarship concerned with realism has – admittedly with much delay – invested its old conception of the dialectic with a new dynamic – that of reception theory. The old model of infrastructure and superstructure has in the process gained in differentiation, although it has by no means abandoned the quasi 'metaphysical' options. There is no need to discuss this in detail here.[4] Moreover it would in this context be equally supererogatory to offer a detailed analysis of the ways in which the fossilised subject/object opposition in Western scholarship – that is in 'bourgeois' literary criticism – has been freed from its immobility by the notion that, put simply, a text does not exist as an objective entity but only comes into being and 'meaning' within particular, historically determined, horizons of interpretative expectation and continues to function as the interaction of textual openness with the modes of its specific 'treatment' and processing, according to individual and collective – but always essentially historical – conditions. The whole complex of problems to do with reception theory and its relevance to the concept of realism may be left at this point – although it would belong in any review of the current debate on realism. It is sufficient if one simply draws attention to the prolonged debate about reception theory with which everybody is by now familiar. Moreover, the essential and systematic contribution that it has made under the aspect of literary realism belongs to that area of discussion of and from first principles which one, with a pinch of salt, might call 'epistemological'.

Admittedly, nobody who is concerned with the theoretical and historical discussion of realism has remained unaffected by the insights of reception theory – even if this fact is neither noticed nor admitted. The whole question of the 'mediation' whereby literary reality comes into being has shifted its ground as the result of the changed 'paradigm'. This has been particularly noteworthy in Marxist literary criticism from the GDR – although, as has already been noted, the delay was considerable. But the debate has proceeded not only there. It is legitimate to understand the term 'mediation' relatively simply to mean that 'facts' are present in texts, and in fictional texts they are present as formal properties, figures which at first sight would seem rather to conceal these 'facts' than to demonstrate or reveal them : at the very least, these 'facts' are presented in an indirect, modified, transposed way. It is true that one does not necessarily have to situate 'mediation' in the system of a dialectical model – but this is to touch on another, larger complex of questions which I do not wish to consider here.

With greater or lesser precision the concept of 'factuality' has long been associated with that of 'realism', though in the process it has already suffered a considerable loss of the prestige and relevance it used to have, assuming we disregard Seiler's attempt at a rehabilitation : it is now problematic in a new and more serious sense. In Swales's article we could see the conviction that it is a misunderstanding of the 'facts' to take them too straightforwardly. There is here no strict limit on what the 'facts' may be. In Swales's paper the danger of an indefinite extension of the concept 'realism' could not be ignored. In his thoughts on 'Realism, modernism and "language-consciousness" ' Stephen Heath faces these consequences even more fearlessly. He cannot agree with Stern's thesis that modern literature, in so far as it is a literature of language-consciousness, is incompatible with a concept of realism that has any degree of specificity. Even when authors such as Proust, Woolf or Joyce give up that 'middle distance' which Stern identified as constitutive of realism, they are nonetheless giving artistic form to 'reality', even though, indeed precisely because, they are representing that change in the interconnection of world, self, meaning and language which results in the dissolution of the opposition between subject and object. Such procedures of modern literature are a logical continuation of tendencies in realistic literature of the nineteenth century. For Heath always sees the political contexts of realism, in that realistic literature incorporates within the horizon of the work's awareness the historically concrete, and not least the economic and political, determinants of individual perspectives in the experience of the world, of reality. Even in the so-called 'realism' of the nineteenth century, reality cannot be represented by abstraction from the subjective codes of experience and perception. Heath asserts, in opposition to Roland Barthes's distinction of 'signifié' and 'signifiant', that the real problem of 'language-conscious' literature is not so much the formalistic separation of language and reality but rather the insight into the productive power of language, in virtue of which it determines reality, both in the subjective realm and in the social dimension. In this medium reality appears as something that can be changed. In principle this applies as much to the significant literature of bourgeois realism in the nineteenth century as to the representative works of 'language-consciousness' in the twentieth century : no less than their predecessors these latter deserve the predicate 'realistic' (in both senses that the word 'predicate' has in German – attribute and accolade). It is reassuring for me that this analysis of the subsequent development of realism since the nineteenth century corresponds to my own conclusions in *Wirklichkeit und Illusion*. Moreover, certain of Heath's systematic propositions confirm Swales's discoveries in his consideration of the nineteenth century, with his enlargement of the concept of realism. But with Heath too there is still the problem that his argument makes *any* literature 'realistic' that does justice to its time and is appropriate to its period, and can in that sense be called 'good'. Anything in any period that is not realistic in the sense indicated cannot – we are compelled to conclude – be serious art. So constituted, the term 'realism' is hardly tenable as a stylistic concept specific to a particular era (or even as a stylistic concept applicable to a 'perennial mode'). But of course there is still the question whether, or at any rate in what sense, we need such a tenable concept at all. Such thoughts always impose themselves unbidden on the literary historian (or indeed the art historian) when he deals with unitary stylistic concepts that are also supposed at the same time to apply to periods or subdivisions of periods. But experience confirms that established concepts, like realism, for example, however contradictory and elusive their application, cannot be abolished and always demand to be reidentified and redefined as precisely as possible.[5] But it is practically a law of poetic and hermeneutic nature that the potential applications of such concepts are always being tried out on various materials and objects to which they *might* be made to refer and about which they may – perhaps – make relevant discourse possible.

It is not exactly normal practice to include reference to the genre of aphorisms when discussing or describing realism. No one has yet discovered realism, *qua* image of a reality one might experience, in these well-formed abbreviations of chains of thought – at most there is a realistic attitude or way of thinking, a generally realistic response to the world, and so on, though not as something specifically aesthetic and literary. However, we seem to be prepared to ascribe realism to the 'literature of language-consciousness', which is manifestly more or less remote from that imaging of a reality which could be experienced through the senses. So why not also, by way of experiment, investigate those types of text that lie between fictionality and expository utterance to see if they contain something like a construction of reality through the medium of language – and not simply a rhetorically interesting presentation of constellations of discursive thoughts? Such an attempt has been made in this volume by Nicholas Boyle. Nietzsche is his subject and is the occasion, along with various other authors on the way (we start with a telling analysis of the mode of utterance of an aphorism by Pascal), for dealing with the fundamental problem of that 'middle mode of discourse' and its relation to reality, its potential 'realism'. This species of text is characterised by the intermediate position meaning holds in it between the concrete and the abstract, the literal and the metaphorical; within this relationship, reference remains indeterminate. In the context of a discussion of Nietzsche's criticism of the theory of language in occidental metaphysics, Boyle shows the precariousness of the distinction he draws between literal and metaphorical discourse. What are the criteria for choosing an appropriate metaphor for what is real and true? Nietzsche offers particularly dramatic opportunities for exemplifying how easily metaphors can be misunderstood when they are seen against the historical background of their times, and how misunderstanding can be furthered by existing linguistic conventions. And the pose of Zarathustra, as Boyle represents it, is almost evidence that Nietzsche was at least not concerned to *reduce* the ambiguity of metaphorical meaning. As with Pascal and others, Nietzsche's aphorisms integrate the confrontation with reality into their own intellectual system. They do not attempt to make an extrasubjective reality present to the reader's mind. They do not aim at a referential relation to a meaning, so to speak, beyond the business of making metaphors. Derrida's sexually oriented interpretation of Nietzsche, reviewed by Boyle with critical dissent, makes it clear what motivational mechanisms may then play the substantial role in the selection of metaphors and the association of meanings : the conclusion is that Nietzsche's aphorisms never emerge from the hermeticism of metaphor. This is – if I have correctly understood it – the essence of Boyle's theses on the potential for realism of the 'middle mode of discourse', though these are further enriched with interesting individual reflections on the Nietzsche case (and others of exemplary status) and at the end with thoughts about some ideas of Roland Barthes, which perhaps remain too general and oracular. They are far from inapposite, but probably not particularly helpful to anyone struggling to emerge from our contemporary dog's dinner of concepts of realism, and of efforts to clarify them, into cleaner, and necessarily simpler, lines of approach. Nonetheless the 'text-logical' analysis of the difference between realistic writing and writing in 'the middle mode' must be regarded as an advance in the study of realism, for some definition is here achieved in the grey area between fictional texts and aesthetically, rhetorically and metaphorically elaborated propositional prose. The 'metaphysics' of the 'realist' in the last section are unlikely to be able to play any further productive role in the discussion of realism, for the assertions are stimulating but not

Richard Brinkmann

easy to verify. The 'ounces of example' – as another essay, written for J. P. Stern by Renford Bambrough, is called (the title is a quotation from Henry James) – do not weigh in the balance against the 'ton of generalities' (Henry James again) that Boyle attaches to them.

Bambrough, then, taking the James brothers as his point of departure, discusses the tension, the equilibrium, of the pictorial and the 'philosophical' as a presupposition of 'realistic' literature. This too of course is an old rather than a new problem in attempts to define realism: fundamentally it is the simple but frequently reiterated question about the relation in literature of the concrete particular and the universal. Any sensitive observation of lived reality can become the starting point of a novel. But a good novel, by its selection from the material of experience, is at once also a reflection on the whole, on the universal. Imaginary people and situations are compatible with the notion of realistic literature: even the natural sciences do not concern themselves only with what is real, but also with what is possible. So Bambrough makes his own enlargement of the idea of realistic literature: it puts reality and possibility in a relation of comparison. To that extent non-realistic literature, such as Kafka's *Metamorphosis*, also contributes to reflecting on reality, and thus to understanding it. Realistic literature, worthy of the name, in any rigorous sense, is characterised by an oscillation (rather than ambiguity) between the 'large picture *and* the elusive detail, the general definition and the destructive example [. . .]'. Only thus can the knowledge of men lead to the knowledge of man. To say this may seem rather superfluous. But however familiar this tension may be, it is certainly easy to overlook the obvious.

If one reviews what the last few years – say since the appearance of Stephan Kohl's shrewd survey from an international perspective[6] – have yielded for the debate on realism, whether in systematic studies or in the context of monographs on periods or individual authors, one notes that the variations that can currently be regarded as possible, and as probably meaningful, in the treatment of the old question about reality in literature, and the reality of literature, are more or less fully present among the essays collected here. The principal tendencies in the past, at any rate, are represented and there are case studies to indicate what can and cannot be achieved by the combination of new ideas and traditional models of interpretation or by experiments that seek to diverge from the established paths of research. To say this much may perhaps be permitted one who has the task of stocktaking in 'Afterthoughts' without – bearing in mind what was said earlier – his anticipating, as it were, a review of the volume or for that matter surreptitiously dissociating himself from one.

'The state of the discussion' – despite not a few calls to do so, the subject–object relationship has not been abolished in the study of realism. We will continue to wrestle with it – or, as people like to say nowadays, to work ('abarbeiten') at it. We have seen that under the impress of philosophical ideas from the orbit of structuralism and post-structuralism subject and object have, at some points in the study of realism, moved so close together that a distinction seems scarcely possible any longer. According to this view not only is the text so shaped by the subject by which it is written or spoken that there can be no question of recovering from it a 'thing in itself', but, in addition, there is no longer any referential relation at all other than that to itself and thereby – through an extreme of mediation or with simple immediacy, depending on how one looks at it – to the subject which, in the text, realises itself, establishes its own meaning or indeed deconstructs meaning : literature thus becomes the *realisation* of the subject, realism equals the realisation of the subject and of its reality in the text – far surpassing the role of the transcendental ego in any variant whatever of the Kantian tradition. To be sure, so extreme a position is comparatively rarely to be met with in the ordinary business of exegesis. It is moreover easy to see that the concrete interpretation of literary texts becomes extremely difficult unless one is prepared either to proceed 'deconstructively' – and then practically one single exemplary case, or at any rate a very few such cases, will suffice to verify the theory – or to extrapolate a constellation of meaning by – in some variant or other of the notion – psychoanalytic methods. Few attempts at a theoretical orientation go so far. And Barthes, Foucault, Derrida, and Lacan as an 'assimilated cultural heritage' and manipulated by fascinated adepts who are certainly learned by usually less original, are not much (scholarly or other) fun. The most useful things are happening in the intermediate zone between advanced theoretical reflection and solid interpretation, the possibility of which can always be recovered by swallowing a little intellectual pride, by so to speak a pragmatic, ad hoc restriction of the theoretical energies for the sake of a belief, *quia absurdum*, and in the light of experience, in the ability of literary language after all to depict reality as it is or could be, or can be taken as being, or as being capable of being. This procedure is not contradictory of the rigorous claims of systematic and fundamental reflections and caveats, but it does create breathing-spaces between our sojournings in the thinner air of high abstractions, spaces in which for a time at least the interpreter can live and work and at the last even enjoy a text. And then the dichotomy of subject and object will always, if not always overtly, be presupposed and used as an epistemological model. Is that merely a regression to an obsolete level of reflection, a comfortable evasion of the intellectual exertions of the scientifically hermeneutic and post-structuralist avant-garde? Their challenge remains. But in dealing with literary and poetic texts we are always having to make bricks with the straw of creative simplification – and that for perfectly legitimate and compelling reasons and not at all as a concession *ad misericordiam* to the vulgar masses of simple souls. That may appear inconsistent, unrigorous, even trivial. But it is 'realistic'; for it is obviously the critical 'condition humaine', and not only on the lowest level of taste and intellect.

How do things look in the other disciplines that have an interest in the question of realism? Art historians have been plagued by the problem in their own way, which I cannot elaborate here. The study of literature has of course repeatedly allowed itself to be influenced by proposed definitions in the field of the fine arts. First of all there was the temptation to see in the plastic arts the capacity for an apparently less complicated process of depiction, an altogether less problematic notion of image, where there was 'realistic' reproduction of an observed reality. Art specialists themselves knew perfectly well, as also did literary historians who involved themselves with more or less dilettantism in the neighbouring discipline – and this of course has a very long history in the aesthetic debate – that things were not that simple for art either, or for art historians. It was not merely that even for that kind of art which sought to make an artistic picture out of a piece of sensuously observable reality theoretical reflection was necessitated by the function of the signs and their arrangement, and by the manner of the mediation of reality in different materials and dimensions. It was also – as in literature – not all that certain which reality had to be depicted, or represented, or in which forms, if the use – still – of the term 'realism' were to be permitted or not. The decisive questions in the discussion of realism within art-history, at any rate from the point when it becomes theoretical, have a certain resemblance to those in the literary discussion. For from that point on the art-historians suffer the same epistemological ills. And the investigation of the elements of which pictures are composed and by which they create 'meaning' has proved attractive to semiotics in the art world as well. Semiotics, or semiology, as a professionally acceptable method of understanding signs, their arrangement, function and reception, is well known to be booming in the description of poetic texts. How the illusion of reality, 'the illusion of reference' (Barthes) is generated in so-called realistic literature has been shown by Rosmarie Zeller in a discussion of the relevant theoretical literature.[7] It is interesting to see how certain mechanisms (at least, probably) function. But for dealing productively with individual texts, for specifically defining realism – which has semiotic mechanisms in common with texts that are not usually or cannot be called realistic – semiotic analysis would not seem to be a useful instrument. The same is true, *mutatis mutandis*, for art criticism. So when it comes to the specific question of realism, literature can expect to find in art a fellow-sufferer rather than a source of assistance. All the same, new impulses might emerge from the conclusions and methodological refinements of iconological investigations, which have not by any means stood still since the days of Panofsky's insights and procedures and those of the earlier iconologists. But that, however, attractive, is too broad a field to be ventured on now in our 'Afterthoughts'.

Musicology has long seen the problem of realism in exceedingly simple terms. It seemed an obvious step in the first instance to regard as 'realism' every incursion into its 'abstract' medium of non-abstract elements, of elements that were not merely *attached* to the music through belonging to that different genus, the *text*, but were *integrated* into the music itself. Carl Dahlhaus has contributed some clarifications as to what in music can and cannot meaningfully be called realism.[8] It is true that his interest is directed towards the history of music in the nineteenth century, but his fundamental discussion of musical realism does not apply only to the one epoch but has a manifestly general significance. With its well-pondered distinctions it could be stimulating for the debate about literary realism as well. And it is undoubtedly refreshing that Dahlhaus, who is very well acquainted with aesthetic theory, particularly but not exclusively as it applies to music, from Hegel to the present, and including literary theory,[9] seeks to suppress 'epistemological scruples' (p. 22). By a series of concrete approaches he comes to conclusions that can sensibly and plausibly be employed both for historical and for systematic purposes. Among the 'traps which a theory of musical realism should avoid' he includes the 'fallacious argument that great art, simply because it is great, is also realistic' (p. 23). Here we may note that in the literary theory of realism also, as we have already

seen, one can easily and unintentionally argue towards similar conclusions through having an insufficiently specific definition of realism
and through an over-generous enlargement of the concept. The
phasal displacement in the history of music in the nineteenth century
by comparison with the history of literature, given music's delayed
and protracted period of Romanticism, is of course well known. But
Dahlhaus is able to make the reasons for this clearer than hitherto.
And that is helpful in further discussion of literary realism in the
nineteenth century. The reflections, which might be called 'historico-
logical', about the presence of realistic characteristics in major works
of nineteenth-century music, are also significant for literary theory
even though no conclusion is reached which might justify the identification of a new period. It is certainly nothing new to point to the
anti-establishment element in realistic trends, but it is revealing to see
the observation made in respect of the different medium of music.
Overall, at any rate, a question mark is put against any oversimplify-
ing notions of periodisation in the history of music, art or literature,
in the German as in the European context. Both these historical considerations and systematic ones make it worthwhile for the literary
historian to read Dahlhaus's individual studies of Berlioz, Verdi,
Mussorgsky, Janáček and Mahler. What Dahlhaus offers is in a sense
a beginning. The dialogue with the musicologist could be no less
useful for the literary critic, in the matter of realism, than that with
the art historian.

So there we are. The trends and positions indicated here give an
admittedly rough outline of what is noteworthy in current realism
studies, including the numerous larger and smaller investigations,
often intelligent and illuminating, of specific problems and individual
authors and texts. No new concept of realism has been vouchsafed
us by work since Stern's *On Realism*, not even by the present scholarly
bouquet. Nor could one say that the tangled debate has grown
notably simpler. But there are certain intellectual impulses which
promise to lead the debate out of the stagnation in which it had, or
could have, landed. If, for example, we leave on one side sophisticated versions of sociological, psychological or purely aesthetic
analyses, the factor common to these burgeoning new approaches is
an enlargement of the concept that may endanger its distinctness.
Stern – to return to our starting point – had combined conceptual
abstractions with a typology of the aesthetic qualities of realism
derived from the concrete reading of texts. Ultimately it is only by
means of such a procedure that we shall be able to make any future

progress either, in the matter of realism. The 'ounces of example' continue to be essential even when the attempt is being made to develop theory out of its own inner logic – e.g. in respect of the by now highly developed notion of the place of reflexive subjectivity within the definition of textuality. In future too we could do with a somewhat more distinct presence of 'ounces of example' when their role in underpinning the 'generality' and in relating the individual observation to 'philosophy' is under discussion. We should take care that the analysis of the subject's self-realisation in the text does not end up in tautology simply because we have lost the courage to believe in referential 'meanings', referential relations to 'facts' (in whatever sense of the word), to verify them, to treat them as 'credible', even if only for one particular, historically conditioned, moment of reception. And however hopelessly antiquated it may sound : unless realism studies can make persuasive and accessible the specific aesthetic attraction, and thereby the specific truth-value, of texts that can specifically be called realistic, they, together with all the resounding *haute école* of hermeneutics and *theoria*, with all the attempts at critical demystification of ideology, will become tedious, esoteric and pseudo-elitist, only accessible to a tiny group whose members keep each other amused – or just keep each other – by taking in each other's washing. And this is as true of the business of socialist criticism as it is of the so-called 'bourgeois' version. This observation is a summons not to reaction but to a bit of common sense, which realism studies should not sacrifice to a timorous feeling that they should nowadays speak of their texts only at the cost of extreme theoretical exertion, and of the aesthetic qualities of those texts only as of something unmentionable in polite company. And *there*, precisely at the level where the freedom of theoretical reflection has been attained, there is still a certain amount to be done.[10]

NOTES

1. Joseph Peter Stern, *Über literarischen Realismus* (Munich, 1983).
2. Richard Brinkmann, *Wirklichkeit und Illusion. Studien über Gehalt und Grenzen des Begriffs Realismus für die erzählende Dichtung des neunzehnten Jahrhunderts* (Tübingen, [3]1977), pp. ix–xxx.
3. Bernd W. Seiler, *Die leidigen Tatsachen. Von den Grenzen der Wahrscheinlichkeit in der deutschen Literatur seit dem 18. Jahrhundert*, Sprache und Geschichte, 6 (Stuttgart, 1983).
4. As examples of the elaboration of ideas drawn from the history and theory of *Rezeption* within Marxist literary criticism I here mention only the articles of Rita Schober, 'Immer noch: Realismus', *Weimarer Beiträge*

XXVI, 7 (1980) 5–21, and: 'Rezeption und Realismus', *Weimarer Beiträge* XXVIII, 1 (1982) 5–48; also Robert Weimann's 'Zu Genesis und Struktur realistischer Weltaneignung. Grundzüge eines historisch-funktionalen Realismusbegriffs', *Jahrbuch für Internationale Germanistik* XI, 2 (1979) 12–41.

5. On this cp. Richard Brinkmann, 'Gedanken über einige Kategorien der Literaturgeschichtsschreibung. Anlässlich der ersten beiden Bände von Friedrich Sengles "Biedermeierzeit"', *Euphorion* 69 (1975) 41–68.

6. Stephan Kohl, *Realismus: Theorie und Geschichte* (Munich, 1977), in which there will be found a bibliography which is fairly complete up to the date of publication. Cp. also Hugo Aust, *Literatur des Realismus* (Stuttgart, 2 1981), and the same author's 'Bürgerlicher Realismus. Forschungsbericht', *Wirkendes Wort* XXX, 6 (1980) 427–47. Further: Fritz Martini, 'Neue Realismusforschungen. Eine Übersicht', *Zeitschrift für deutsche Philologie*, CI, 2 (1982) 262–85. Klaus-Detlef Müller, 'Wirklichkeitsverständnis und Kunst. Zur Realismus-Diskussion in der Literaturwissenschaft', *Universitas* 37 (1982) 269–78. I mention also the following titles from the English-speaking world which appeared after Kohl's survey, i.e. after 1977: George J. Becker, *Master European Realists of the 19th Century* (New York, 1982), and *Realism in Modern Literature* (New York, 1980), Michael Bell, *The Sentiment of Reality. Truth of Feeling in the European Novel* (London/Boston, 1983), Gregory L. Lucente, *The Narrative of Realism and Myth: Verga, Lawrence, Faulkner, and Pavese* (Baltimore, 1981), *The Monster in the Mirror: Studies in 19th-Century Realism*, ed. D. A. Williams (Oxford, 1978). There is little that is new here in respect of the fundamental questions, but these works do illuminate individual aspects with which I cannot concern myself here. There is not the least intention that this essay should furnish a statistically complete survey of the literature with bibliography to match!

7. Rosmarie Zeller, 'Realismusprobleme in semiotischer Sicht', *Jahrbuch für Internationale Germanistik* XII, 1 (1980) 84–101.

8. Carl Dahlhaus, *Musikalischer Realismus. Zur Musikgeschichte des 19. Jahrhunderts* (Munich, 1982).

9. Though where Dahlhaus thinks he read my 'assertion' that 'impressionism is the true realism' (p. 22) I have been unable to discover.

10. As always I have to thank my younger colleagues in Tübingen for their critical assistance and their friendly collaboration in reading, and in discussing and formulating these thoughts.

Index

Index